KING

A PLEASURE IN WORDS

A PLEASURE IN WORDS

by

Eugene T. Maleska

Edited by
Hugh Young

HAMISH HAMILTON · LONDON

Grateful acknowledgement is hereby made to:

George Braziller, Inc., Publishers, for permission to quote passages from *A Dictionary of Colorful Italian Idioms* copyright © 1965 by Carla Pekelis.

Cut and edited for the British edition by Hugh Young

First published in this edition in Great Britain in 1983 by
Hamish Hamilton Ltd.,
Garden House, 57-59 Long Acre, London WC2E 9JZ

British Library Cataloguing in Publication Data

Maleska, Eugene T.
  A pleasure in words.
  1. Semantics
  I. Title
  422   P325

ISBN 0-241-10999-X

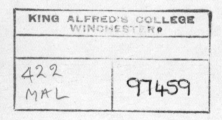
Typeset by Pioneer, East Sussex
Printed in Great Britain by Richard Clay Ltd.,
The Chaucer Press, Bungay, Suffolk.

Outline of Chapters

Foreword

Those of us who toil in the vineyards of English linguistics and lexicography approach our tasks in a general spirit of sobriety, but we know very well that language does not serve humankind only for communication any more than food serves only for nourishment. Aeons ago, people huddling around a fire in a cave somewhere must have learned that language is, *inter alia*, for playing with. And so arose puns and comic verse and charades and anagrams and crossword puzzles.

Eugene Maleska, a former teacher, a writer, and one of the great crossword-puzzle constructors, has spent a lifetime compiling oddments about the lexis that makes up the vocabulary of English. And in this lively work he shares with us his exhilaration at discovering the relationship between words that on the surface appear to have no connection whatsoever (as between *apothecary* and *boutique* or between *pawn* and *pioneer*) and the strange and varied routes by which the words we use have found their way into our language.

This rich olio (a word well-known to American crossword-puzzle fans) of little etymologies, interspersed with literary allusions, pungent puns and what Maleska calls his 'cursed tercets', offers a painless method for learning about the ways of language and for expanding one's vocabulary.

Start at the beginning of this book and follow the author's logical connections, or dip at random in the treasures that abound. Either way, if you have any interest at all in the luxuriant and eclectic vocabulary that has made the English language one of humankind's most effective and flexible tools for transmitting knowledge and feelings, you will be enriched. This is a particularly lovely book to browse in, in the etymological sense of that term, for it does offer nourishment as well as pleasure.

DAVID B. GURALNIK
Editor in Chief
Webster's New World Dictionaries

To The Reader

This book has been simmering on the back burner for decades. It probably stems from my ancestral genes, because words have fascinated me ever since I can remember. But the impetus was first provided on a New York City subway when I was a teenager travelling from New Jersey to Regis High School, in Manhattan. One day I picked up a discarded newspaper on the seat next to me and happened upon the crossword puzzle. Since English was my favourite subject, I figured I could easily solve the puzzle.

What a surprise awaited me! One four-letter word was defined as 'Very long time'. It seemed to begin with AE. *The answer to the puzzle was on another page. Impatient, I peeked.* AEON! *I had never come across that word before. In the same puzzle a feudal serf turned out to be* ESNE, *a trout worked out as* CHARR *and a card game evolved as* SKAT.

When I got home I checked my dictionary just to see whether the creator of the puzzle hadn't made up those strange words. They were all listed. My ego had been deflated but I had learned four new words. I was hooked! I began to keep a notebook — a kind of personal thesaurus — and during my years in college I became an expert solver.

But the hobby, as well as the notebook, expanded as the years flew by. Simultaneously I had developed a profound interest in the derivations of English words. It fascinated me to learn that the scallion *is probably a corruption of 'Ascalon', a seaport in southern Palestine. I chuckled when I learned that William de la Pole, Duke of Suffolk, was nicknamed Jac Napes and willy-nilly handed down the word jackanapes. And I felt sorry for the people of Wales when I discovered that the verb* welsh *is an opprobrious reference to their alleged propensities for swindling or failing to pay their debts.*

A second notebook labelled 'Etymology' emerged. Others followed: 'Words from Mythology', 'Spelling Demons', 'Nice but Naughty Words', 'Eponyms' and so on.

Such was the genesis of A PLEASURE IN WORDS. *The book evolved gradually and naturally from years of scanning dictionaries,* mainly in connexion with my work as a crossword puzzle constructor and editor. It is an attempt to share the results of somewhat haphazard and perhaps dilettantish research in the wonderful world of words.

Let me emphasize that I am not a lexicographer and that I have tremendous respect and admiration for the experts who put together excellent dictionaries. But I do claim to be a philologer in the literal sense of that noun — 'lover of words' — and I hope that I shall manage to transmit to the reader the feeling of personal joy that I experience each time I make a new linguistic discovery in a lexicon or elsewhere.

Another point to be stressed is that I have not attempted to be all-encompassing. The book provides eclectic samplings in etymology and related fields that I hope will whet the reader's appetite for further explorations on his own. Incidentally, such areas as grammar and diction are deliberately omitted, and the general history of our language is discussed only in brief terms.

Finally, I wish to thank Peter Cancro and Lois and Robert Hughes for typing and proofreading the manuscript. Last, and certainly not least, I am indebted to the lovely coed whom I married. Without her patience, encouragement and help with research I never could have produced this book.

Pax, amor et felicitas,
Eugene T. Maleska

For Cisatlantic Readers

An American philologer naturally writes about words as his countrymen use them and spells them as they spell them. To make Dr Maleska's attractive book more readily acceptable to British readers I have kept an eye open for words and locutions that are altogether too foreign — for, as H. L. Mencken wrote and Dr Maleska reminds us, there is an English language and an American language, and they are often quite different. Sometimes, rather than leave the Americanisms out, I have looked for equivalents: 'M.P.' for 'congressman', 'grasshoppers' for 'katydids', 'Ian Botham' for 'Mickey Mantle'. I have also preferred cisatlantic spelling. But I haven't tried to turn Dr Maleska into an Englishman. He remains an American, of Polish-Lithuanian-Irish descent, with an Italian wife. No wonder he has an eye for 'words from everywhere'.

Hugh Young
1983

1 Our Hellenic Heritage

Are you a *misocapnist*? Have you recently written to a *thesmothete* or a *diaskeuast*? At dinner are you a *deipnosophist*? Do you enjoy gazing on *callipygian* beauties?

All of the foregoing esoteric words can be found in unabridged dictionaries. Like many others that are unfamiliar to most people, they have come down to us from the ancient Greeks.

About 15 per cent of our words have a Hellenic origin. They have been transliterated into English largely because of the influence of the Romans and the scholars. When the Roman legions conquered Greece, they enslaved the Athenians and brought back the bright oldsters to teach their children.

Let's return to the words in the first paragraph. One of my fantasies is to own a bus line. In each vehicle a prominent sign would read: 'NO SMOKING. HAVE REGARD FOR THE MISOCAPNISTS.' Yes, a *misocapnist* is one who has a hatred of tobacco smoke. *Miso*, as you can readily ascertain, is a Greek form meaning 'hatred'. Another example is *misanthrope*, a person who hates mankind. Note that *miso* has been shortened to *mis*. It should not be confused with the prefix *mis*, which means 'wrong' or 'incorrect'.

Thesmothete literally means 'a person who lays down the law'. Your M.P. is one, because today the word is defined as 'a legislator'.

Diaskeuast was a word I discovered when I began to construct crossword puzzles. In search of a new definition for *editor*, I leaped with joy when I came across this gift from the Greeks. You can imagine my excitement when I first used my new word as a clue!

A *deipnosophist* to the Greeks meant 'a wise man at a meal'. By the way, it's interesting to observe that the classical words often seem to read backwards. *Deipnon* is the 'meal' part. The same is true of *hippopotamus*; if you translate sequentially, it's a 'horse river' rather than a 'river horse'. At any rate, a *deipnosophist* is a person skilled in the art of table talk.

Callipygian, or *callipygous*, means 'having shapely buttocks'. A lovely ancient statue, now located in a museum in Naples, is called the Callipygian Venus. It is rumoured that the guards have a difficult time preventing Neapolitan males from pinching the sculpture.

Let's take our minds off Venus for a while and consider *calli*. It translates into 'beautiful'. *Callisthenics* is another example. To Athenians it meant 'beautiful strength' — an instance of a nonbackward word. But *calli* and its opposite, *caco* (meaning 'bad, unpleasant'), tell us something fascinating about ourselves. For some reason we humans tend to dwell more on what is evil than on what is good. Take *smell*, for instance. To most people the word has an offensive connotation. They immediately think *stink*! Of course it can mean 'perfume', 'fragrance', 'bouquet' or any other delightful olfactory synonym. But the word has decayed into rottenness through the years. *Aroma* and *scent* have taken its place in positive thinking.

Let us get back to the *calli-caco* contrast. On the one hand we find *calligraphy* as one of the few remaining vestiges of the bright side. It means, of course, 'elegant penmanship'. A *calligrapher's* handwriting is beautiful. However, in this age of the typewriter even *calligraphy* seems to be doomed to extinction.

But the *caco* words retain their vigour and grow more popular with every new generation.

cacophony	harsh or discordant sound; dissonance. (Incidentally, why isn't there a *calliphony*, meaning 'sweet harmony'?)
cacodemon	an evil spirit
cacodemonia	insanity in which the patient has the delusion of being possessed by an evil spirit.
cacodoxy	perverse teachings. (What, no *callidoxy*?)
cacoepy	bad pronunciation. (Here the opposite is *orthoepy*.)
cacoëthes	a habitual and uncontrollable desire; a mania or itch. (What an interesting word!)
cacoëthes scribendi	an uncontrollable urge to write. (Dickens' problem?)
cacography	bad handwriting. (My problem.)
cacology	bad diction or pronunciation

Two more words that can be traced back to the Greeks are *rhyme* and its cousin *rhythm*. Their word was *rhythmos* ('measure, measured motion') and was related to the verb *rhein* ('to flow').

The rhythm of Homer's Iliad flows along smoothly in *dactylic hexameter*. Now let's pause for a while and examine those two words.

Dactyl was the Athenians' word for finger. Looking down at their hands, they noticed that, starting at the knuckles, the first joints of the fingers are much longer than the other two. Hence, to a poet, a *dactyl* became a metrical unit beginning with a 'long' (or stressed) sound and ending with two 'short' sounds. The symbol for the dactyl is $- \cup \cup$.

But the original nonpoetic meaning of *dactyl* has been preserved in several interesting English words:

dactyliomancy	divination by means of finger rings
dactylion	the tip of the middle finger
dactyliotheca	a. a case for a collection of such items as rings and gems
	b. an illustrated catalogue of rings and gems
dactylogram or *dactylograph*	fingerprint
dactylography	scientific study of fingerprints. (Note that a *dactylographer* becomes a *dactyloscopist* when he classifies or compares fingerprints!)

Finally, let us not forget the *pterodactyl*, that grotesque flying reptile of yore. The creature's name actually means 'wing finger' — and the appellation is apt. The wings were attached to greatly enlarged fourth digits at the ends of two skinny arms.

All the cousins of *dactyl* come from the Greek too. It's somewhat ironic that it should be defined as a 'metrical foot' rather than 'hand' or 'finger'.

iamb	$\cup -$
trochee	$- \cup$ This metrical foot comes from *trochos*, Greek for 'a wheel'.
spondee	$- -$ What an interesting history this word has! It's derived from the Greeks' term for 'libation', because it was the form used in the solemn music accompanying sacrificial rites, when it was the custom to pour wine either on the ground or on the victim.
anapaest	$\cup \cup -$ This direct opposite of the dactyl is derived from *anapaistos* — struck back. Byron 'struck back' perfectly in such a line as: 'And his cohorts were gleaming in purple and gold.'

Hexameter is derived from *hexa* ('six') and *metron* ('metre, measure'). We're all familiar with *hexagons*, but did you know that ants, bees and flies are *hexapods*? And, of course, *hexapody* is a poetic line or group of verses containing six feet.

Drop down one notch and we find *penta* — a source of words that deserve attention. Here are some of them.

pentacle	a. a five-pointed star
	b. an occult symbol (For some strange reason the occult symbol is really a six-pointed star, equivalent to a hexagram.)
pentacular	the adjective for the above
pentact	having five rays
pentadactyl	having five digits on hand or foot; or five fingerlike parts.
pentaglot	a. using five different languages
	b. a *pentaglot* work
pentagon	a polygon having five angles and therefore five sides
pentalogy	a. fivefoldness
	b. a series of five closely related works
pentameter	a line of five metrical feet. (Iambic pentameter is a form favoured by many English poets.)
pentarchy	government by five persons
Pentateuch	the first five books of the Old Testament. (*Teuchas* is the Greek word for 'tool' and, in a scholarly sense, 'book'. The *Pentateuch* is also called the Five Books of Moses.)
pentathlete	an athlete in a pentathlon
pentathlon	athletic contest involving participation by each contestant in five different events. (Today the most gruelling of all Olympic events is the *decathlon*. This doubles the number for a *pentathlon*. Here are the contests: 100 metres, 400 metres and 1,500 metres; 110 metres high hurdles; the javelin and discus throws; the shot put, pole vault, high jump and long jump.)
Pentecost	a. a solemn Hebrew festival, so called because it is celebrated on the fiftieth day after the second day of Passover.
	b. Whit Sunday, a Christian festival. (Note the ecumenical flavour of the word. Why fifty? The reason is that the second part of *Pentecost* originally meant 'ten times'.)

Before leaving *penta* let me point out the *pentagamists*. They are people who have been married (sometimes bigamously) five times.

I wonder if Mickey Rooney, Zsa Zsa Gabor, Elizabeth Taylor et al have ever heard of 'pentagamy'.

In that connection, I recently learned the difference between *bigamy* and *digamy*. The former is illegal, but the latter is licit. In other words, if one's spouse has died or if there is a divorce followed by a remarriage, it's a case of *digamy*.

Yes, Virginia, there is a *trigamy* and a *tetragamy*, but no lexicon at my command lists *hexagamy*. From there on up, *polygamy* seems to be the proper terminology.

Tetra (meaning 'four') has given us its own legacy. Any reader who has hung in there up to this point can easily evolve the meanings of *tetrad, tetraglot, tetragon, tetralogy, tetrapod* and *tetrarchy*.

But pornographers may be surprised to learn that a *tetragram* is a four-letter word. And urban dwellers may be interested to hear that a *tetrapolis* is a group or confederation of four cities. *Tetraphony* is not the art practised by fourflushers but a term equivalent to dissonance in Greek music.

Poly (meaning 'many, much, diverse') is a combining form coming from the Greek *polys*. It has supplied us with a Golconda of interesting entries in our dictionaries. Here is only a sampling:

polyandry	a marriage form in which one woman has more than one husband at the same time. (This is a counterpart of *polygyny*, in which the male has several wives. Both are forms of *polygamy*. Incidentally, *monandry* is the commonly accepted practice today.)
polyacoustics	the art of magnifying sounds. (Rock'n'roll groups today seem to have perfected this skill almost beyond human endurance!)
polyarticular	affecting many joints. (This adjective is often applied to polyarthritis.)
polychord	having many strings.
polychrest	a drug or medicine of value as a remedy for several diseases.
polychresty	a. a thing that has several uses b. same as *polychrest*
polychromatist	one who advocates the use of many colours, as in painting.
polydactyl	having more than the normal number of toes or fingers. (Note how *dactyl* is here extended to pedal digits.)

5

polydipsia	excessive or abnormal thirst. (In this connection, a *dipsomaniac* is, literally, a madman with a certain form of *polydipsia*.)
polydomous	inhabiting several nests. (Zoologists use the adjective for a group of ants that spread their colony in several directions. Their opposites are *monodomous*.)
polyethnic	formed or inhabited by people of many races.
polygraph	a. a voluminous or versatile writer b. an apparatus for producing copies of a drawing or writing. c. an instrument for receiving and recording simultaneously variations in pulse, blood pressure and other pulsations d. a lie detector
polyhistor	person of encyclopaedic learning. (*Histor* means 'judge' or 'learned man' in Greek. From this root we also get such words as *history, historian, historic*.)
polylemma	an argument in which there are usually at least three alternatives. (*Lemma* is the Greek word for 'proposition'. In logic today a lemma is a preliminary proposition or a premise. *Dilemma* of course is the most commonly used descendant of the root. When you're on the horns of a *dilemma*, you have a choice between two alternatives.)
Polynesia	large number of islands in the central Pacific Ocean (*nesos* — island)
polyonymous	having many names; known by many names.
polyonymy	plurality of names; the use of various names for one thing. The root word, *onyma*, means 'name'. From it we have also inherited *anonymous* — without a name. Other cousins in the family are *synonym, antonym, homonym, pseudonym* and *eponym*. My own favourite is *cryptonym* — a secret name. *Heteronyms* are also fascinating. They are words spelled the same but having two meanings. The noun 'sow' (pig) and the verb 'sow' are examples. *Paronymous* words contain the same root or stem. 'Wise' and 'wisdom' fit into this category. *Polynym* and *mononym*, two opposites, seem to be dropping out of our language. *Autonym*, too, appears to be obsolescent, but I hate to see it go. In contrast with *pseudonym*, it literally means 'one's own name', but it can also be defined as 'a book published under the author's real name'.

polyphagia	excessive desire to eat. (This Greek root for 'eating' has given us several other intriguing words. For example, if your diet is oysters, then you're *ostreophagous*. The starfish, by the way, is a voracious *ostreophage*. And then there are those *xylophagous* little creatures that feed on wood.)
polyphony	a. in music, counterpoint b. a multiplicity of sounds; reverberations caused by an echo.
polyphyodont	having several or many sets of teeth in succession. (Sharks are *polyphyodonts*. The *odont* root obviously means 'tooth'. Related words are *polyodontia* and *odontologist*. And when Socrates had a toothache, he suffered — as we sometimes do — from *odontalgia*.)
polypragmatist	busybody or fussy person. (*Pragma* means 'deed' or 'affair'. Hence it's easy to see how this word came into existence.)
polytheism	belief in a plurality of gods.
polytropic	visiting many kinds of flower for nectar. (*Tropos* means 'turning' or 'changing'. Another marvellous word from this root is *heliotrope,* a garden plant that turns towards the sun, *helios*.)

Most readers will be familiar with *polyclinic, polyglot, polygon* and *polytechnic*. And it's relatively simple to educe the definition for *polydaemonism*. But it's also easy to confuse that word with *polydemic*.

Demos was the ancient Greek word for 'the populace'. From it we get such words as *democracy, demography* and *demagogue*. Literally, *polydemic* means 'of many peoples'. As its usage has evolved through the centuries, the present definition is 'native to or occurring in several regions or countries'.

Endemic is a close relative. It means 'restricted or native to a particular area or people'. Medical men breathe a sigh of relief when a disease is *endemic* rather than *epidemic* (spreading widely). And when the disease is of foreign origin it is said to be *ecdemic*.

But the most all-embracing member of this family is *pandemic* — affecting all the people. Actually *pan* is another borrowing from those remarkable old Greeks. It means 'all', and it has nothing to do with a kitchen utensil or — to the best of my knowledge — with a certain playful Greek god of the forests and pastures who gave us the term 'panic'. But it has bequeathed us a cluster of charming words. Before presenting some selected examples, let me point out that the greatest number of our words from Greece are scientific in nature. Botanists, biologists, chemists, physicists, zoologists et al seem to be confirmed graecophiles. This is only natural because of the historical fact that Greek became the language of the learned in ancient times and its study was intensified during the Renaissance. However, since most readers would rightfully find technical terms boring, I am deliberately omitting most of them from this chapter.

panacea	a cure-all. (The last part of this word comes from *akeisthai* — to heal.)
panchromatic	sensitive to the light of all colours in the visible spectrum.
pancratic	giving mastery of all subjects
pancyclopaedic	pertaining to the whole range of knowledge
pandect	a. any complete code of laws
	b. a treatise covering an entire subject; a complete digest
Pandora	a. first woman of Greek mythology. A creation of Hephaestus, she was beautiful and gifted.
	b. a mollusc or its genus
	(*Dora*, the plural of *doron*, is the Greeks' word for 'gifts'. Thus Pandora was well named, for she had 'all gifts' — beauty, intelligence, charm. Theodore, Dorothy and Dorothea come from the same root. Such people are 'gifts of the gods'.)
panegyric	a eulogy or laudatory discourse. (The word can be traced back to *agora*, the Greek marketplace. It originally embodied the idea of a festival where all the people were assembled — a natural place for orators to deliver commendations to V.I.P.s whose favour they wished to curry.)
panentheism	the doctrine that God includes the world as only a part of his being. (How many 'theisms' can there be?)
Panesthia	a genius of subsocial burrowing cockroaches. (I couldn't resist this one! If we break down the word, it means that these insects 'eat all'. Actually, their habit is to eat each other's wings.
panoply	a full suit of armour. (*Hopla* was the Greek word for 'armour'. The initial letter got lost somewhere between now and then — an elision that occurs often. A related word is *hoplite* — a heavily armed infantryman of ancient Greece.

panoptic or *panoptical*	all-seeing. (It also means 'letting everything be seen', tempting us irresistibly to think of *ecdysiasts* — strip-teasers, from Greek *ecdysis* — act of getting out.)
panorama	comprehensive view. (The *orama* root leads us to *cyclorama*, a large pictorial representation encircling the spectator. *Dioramas* are often three-dimensional spectacular and translucent.)
Pan-Satanism	doctrine that the world is an expression of the personality of the Devil.
pansexualism	the view that all desire and interest are derived from the sex instinct.
pansophy	universal wisdom or encyclopaedic knowledge. Hence *pansophist*, one claiming pansophy.
pantarchic	cosmopolitan
pantheon	a. a temple devoted to all the gods b. a treatise on pagan gods c. the gods of a people d. a building serving as a burial place for national heroes or containing memorials to them. e. the person most highly esteemed by an individual or a group (Take a second look at the above definitions and you'll receive a lesson in the evolution of the meanings of a word.)
pantocrator	the omnipotent lord of the universe (epithet applied to Christ)
pantology	a systematic view of all knowledge

The words *pansophy* and *pansophist* remind me of another interesting noun from the same root — *sophos* ('wise'). The word is *sophomore*. The last four letters of that word come from *moros* ('stupid'). Thus a second-year student in an American university is wise, yet stupid.

Sophistry has a fascinating history. It means 'reasoning that is superficially plausible but is really fallacious or deceptive'. *Sophists* were a group of teachers of philosophy and rhetoric in ancient Greece. Actually, they were learned men, and that definition for *Sophists* still applies. But their unorthodox ideas and the fact that they accepted money for their instruction caused them to fall into disrepute. Their detractors labelled their arguments as specious, and this connotation persists today. *Sophistic* means 'fallacious'.

The Romans took it up from there, and as a result we have been given the adjective *sophisticated*. The most common definition is 'worldly-wise', but the word also means 'adulterated; not in a natural state; many-sided; complex'.

Let's return to *sophomore*. The second root in the word is the basis for *moron*. In some unabridged dictionaries you can also find *moronity* and *moronism* as synonyms for stupidity or feeble-mindedness.

Erudite psychologists use a different term — *oligophrenia*. This word combines two Greek roots, *olig* or *oligo* ('little' or 'few') and *phren* ('mind'). Literally, an *oligophrenic* has a little mind.

Many people are familiar with *oligarchy* ('rule by the few'), but *oligopoly* is not so well known. It's a sort of standoff in industry. Specifically, it's a situation in which each of a few producers is strong enough to influence the market but cannot disregard the reaction of his competitors. The word is related to *monopoly* and is next of kin to *duopoly*. Another sibling, by the way, is *oligopsony* ('purchase by the few').

If you started at the beginning of this chapter, you will surely be able to evolve the meaning of *oligodactylism* (and don't forget that toes must be included). And it's not difficult to define an *oligochronometer*. Well, to save you precious seconds, it's an instrument for measuring very small intervals of time. It's certainly not an *oligosyllabic* word.

Have you ever seen a *chronogram*? Literally, it means 'time writing', but it's also a kind of numerical stunt or puzzle. *Chronogrammatists* concoct inscriptions, phrases or sentences in which the Roman numerals form a certain date when put together. King Gustavus Adolphus of Sweden had a medal struck in 1632 with the following *chronogrammatic* motto: ChrIstVs DVX; ergo trIVMphVs. Now, if you take each capital letter separately and translate it into a number, you will come out with 1632 when you add up all the numbers. Don't forget the first capital letter, C, equal to 100!

Most of us are familiar with *chronic, chronicle, chronological* and *chronometer*. A polysyllabic modern offshoot is *chrono-cinematography,* in which measurements of intervals of time are made via motion pictures.

Cinema may sound like a Spanish or Italian derivative, but it has a Greek ancestry. It's a shortening of the invention called a *cinematograph* or *kinematograph* (a motion-picture projector). In Athens *kinema* meant 'movement'.

10

Let us not forget that the old Greek root was *kinema*, not *cinema*. When the original letter is retained, we are greeted by a cluster of beauties, especially if we are aware that *kinema* itself is an offshoot of the verb *kinein* ('to move').

kinematics	the branch of mechanics or dynamics that deals with pure motion
kinesalgia	pain occurring in conjunction with muscular action. (Beware, you joggers, wrestlers and other athletes!)
kinescope	the recording of a TV programme on motion pictures for subsequent use; also a tube used in television receivers and monitors.
kinesimeter	an instrument for measuring bodily movements.
kinesiology	the study of the anatomy with respect to movement.
kinesthesia	the sensation of movement or strain in muscles, joints or tendons; 'muscle sense'
kinesthetic	of bodily reaction or motor memory. (We get a *kinesthetic* feeling watching an Astaire movie.)
kinetic	active or lively; dynamic
kinetosis	motion sickness, seasickness, *mal de mer*

To return to the *cine* alteration, a brand-new word for a movie buff is *cineast*. The last part of that word eventually comes from the Greek *astes*, an equivalent of our suffix *ist*. Now let's take a look at some of the engrossing offshoots:

chiliast	one who believes in the millennium. (This word deserves careful consideration. It stems from *chilloi*, the Greeks' equivalent of the Romans' *mille*, meaning 'thousand'. *Chiliasm* is the doctrine that Christ will come to earth and usher in the millennium. Those familiar with the Bible know that in Revelations 20:1-7 the millennium is the period of a thousand years during which Christ will reign on earth.
	The French changed *chilloi* to *kilo*. Thus a *kilowatt* is equal to one thousand watts, a kilometre is a thousand metres, and so on.
	(*Chiliad* and *millennium*, by the way, are synonyms.)
dynast	a. hereditary ruler
	b. one of a line of kings or princes
	c. member of a family powerful in a particular field.
	The noun, known to most as the title of Thomas Hardy's epic drama, is only one of a whole host of words

that can eventually be traced back to a Greek verb, *dynasthai* or *dunasthai* — to be able. The concept of ability soon came to mean 'power'. Today most of us never think of the Greeks when we use such words as *dynasty, dynamic, dynamite* and *dynamo*. For the benefit of physicists and crossword puzzle fans, let me not forget *dyne* — a unit of force.)

encomiast one who praises; a panegyrist. (An *encomium*, of course, is an expression of praise. It has a fascinating background, similar to that of *panegyric*. Literally, it means 'in a revel or celebration'. *Comus* was the god of festive joy and mirth in late Greek and in Roman mythology. Milton wrote a poetic masque about that Olympian.)

enthusiast a fanatic or zealot. (*Theos* meant 'god' in Athens. Enthusiasm once meant 'inspiration by a god'. I wonder how many people are aware than *fan* is a shortened form of fanatic.)

fantast a visionary or dreamer. (This word is related to *phantasy, phantom, fantasia, fancy* and others of that type. All of these come from a Greek root meaning 'idea'. Most delightful to contemplate is *phantasmagoria* — a constantly changing succession of scenes or things observed or imagined, as in a dream.)

gymnast an expert in callisthenics and bodily exercises. (Here is another word with an exciting history. It stems from *gymnastes* — a trainer of athletes. Obviously it's an offshoot of *gymnasium* — a school where Greek youths were given athletic training when naked. Yes, the root *gymnos* meant 'naked'. Now you should be able to identify the Hindu sect called *gymnosophists*. But you may have trouble with *gymnogyps*. They are not chisellers in the buff or nude gypsies but a genus of very large carrion-eating birds. *Gyps* meant 'vulture' in Greece.)

scholiast an annotator or commentator on the classics. (Sad to say, the *scholiasts* are a dead or dying breed. But the word itself has some very familiar relatives: *scholastic, scholar* and *school*. The Romans borrowed the Greek word *scholē* or *skholē* and changed it to *schola*.)

In connection with the foregoing statement, let us take a look at *pedagogue*. The Greek root *paed* (for 'child') became shortened into *ped* as the centuries flowed on, and got confused with a

Roman root with the same spelling. The Roman *ped*, however, meant 'foot'. It will be dealt with in a later chapter.

Pedagogue is a combination of *paed* and *agogos* ('leader' or 'escort'). Literally, this person is a leader of children. Pedagogy, of course, is instruction or teaching. Since schoolmasters tended to be pompous, the word *pedant* soon took on a pejorative* connotation. A fault that I'm trying to avoid in this book is *pedantry*, but when you try to share something you've learned, there's a temptation to become pedantic.

Returning to *pedagogue*, we find that the second part of the word is rooted in the Greek verb *agein* ('to lead or drive'). It has also given us *synagogue*, originally a place where Athenians were brought together — an assembly, if you will. Perhaps some erudite reader can inform me why this word has come to mean only a Jewish house of worship.

A *galactogogue* is the answer to every dairyman's prayer; it's an agency for increasing the flow of milk. A related word from the Greeks is *galaxy*. Hence, the Milky Way.

Finally, let me lay this one on you: *mystagogue*. This is an expert in religious mysteries who instructs neophytes in the sacraments.

Neophyte itself is a word with two ubiquitous† Hellenic progenitors combined — *neos* ('new') and *phytas*, from the infinitive *phyein* ('to grow or bring forth').

Phytos provides us with a cluster of botanical words. The *epiphytes* and *aerophytes* are plants that grow chiefly in the air. The *lithophytes* are corals (growing on stone) and the *thallophytes* or *protophytes* are algae and fungi. A hydrophyte, naturally, flourishes in water, but a *saprophyte* lives on dead or decaying organic matter. Ugh! A *zoophyte* is easy to define, even if you never saw one. Yes, it's an animal resembling a plant.

Stay away from *dermophytes*. They're fungi parasitic on the skin. *Microphytes*, as you can guess, are minute plants or bacteria.

---

* *Pejorative* — depreciatory or disparaging. For a change, here's a word that doesn't come from the Greeks. Its origin lies in *pejor*, the Latin adjective for 'worse'. But *pejor* itself is related to *ped* ('foot'). Apparently when a Roman made things worse, he put his foot in it.

† *Ubiquitous* — existing everywhere; omnipresent. Again, this is a Latin inheritance. *Ubique* is the Latin for 'everywhere'. Those who seem to be everywhere at once are *ubiquitous*.

13

A *pteridophyte* (another spelling demon!) is a flowerless plant, such as a fern.

But enough of the flora! Although I had firmly intended to eschew these horticultural terms, they were just too enticing. Turning our attention to the first part of *neophyte*, we are rewarded with a dazzling array of arresting words. Let's skip such obvious ones as *neoclassic*, *Neo-Impressionism* and *Neoplatonism*.

neolalia	speech, as of a psychotic, that includes strange words
Neolithic	a. of the latest period of the Stone Age
	b. of an earlier, outmoded age
	(*Lithos* meant 'stone'. When Zeus turned Niobe into stone because she had taunted Leto about her children, he *lithified* her!)
neologism	a new word or expression; a new usage of an established word or expression.
neomenia	the time of the new moon
neomycin	an antibiotic. (Here's another surprise. *Mycin* is a combining form meaning 'substance derived from fungus'. The Greek word *mykes* meant 'fungus'. *Mycosis* is a disease caused by fungus, and a *mycologist* studies fungi.)
neon	inert gaseous element. (This gas was discovered in 1898 by Ramsay and Travers. Their reason for giving it that title is obvious.)
neophilism	morbid or excessive desire for novelty. (To coin a word, or use a neologism, people afflicted with this craving are *neophilistic*. They're faddists. And do you know what a fad is? It's something that goes in one era and out the other.)
neoteric	modern; new.

In the past, neologists were careful not to create hybrids lest they be scoffed at by scholars. When Edison invented the *phonograph* in 1877, he used two Greek roots *phone* ('sound') and *graphein* ('to write'). His device actually wrote the sounds. And when Emile Berliner came up with his Gramophone ten years later, he just reversed the roots. In ancient Greece *gramma* was a letter or piece of writing and was closely related to *graphein*.

Morse had no trouble with terminology when he devised the electric *telegraph* (*tele* means 'far' or 'afar'). As early as 300 B.C. those amazing Greeks had already developed the first systematic system of telegraphy!

Bell's *telephone* (exhibited in 1876) and his *photophone* did not violate any nonhybrid rules. Nor did Edison's *mimeograph*. In Athens a *mimos* was an imitator. From the same root we are given such words as *mime, pantomime* and *mimesis* ('imitation, mimicry'), among others. The sage of Menlo Park also adhered to tradition when he brought forth his *cinematograph*.

Even the *typewriter* can be claimed to be all Greek in origin as far as roots are concerned. *Typos* was an Athenian word for 'blow, impression, image or model'. *Writer* can be traced back to a Greek word, although it gets all mixed up with German and Icelandic heritages.

The *telescope* adheres to the conventional rules for neologists' nomenclature. *Skopein* was the Greek infinitive for 'to view'.

When the Wright brothers astounded the world with their *aeroplane* or *airplane*, they were right on the mark. The first Greek root is easy to ascertain; the other is *planos,* meaning 'wandering'. Think of that word for a moment. An aeroplane wanders in the air! So does a planet — from the same root.

The *locomotive,* on the other hand, is a 'pure' neologism from the Romans. It combines two Latin words, *locus* and *motus* ('place' and 'movement').

But tradition and meticulous concern for details have been put aside in our free-and-easy twentieth century. Let's start with the automobile. *Auto* is a Greek root meaning 'self'. But the last half of the word is from the Romans. *Mobilis* is a form of *movere* ('to move'). Thus an automobile moves by itself, but it will always carry the stigma of having parents from two different word groups.

The same goes for *television.* The pioneers in that field probably avoided *telescopy* because it was already a word meaning 'the art or practice of using or making telescopes'. *Tele,* as we have already noted, was the Greek form for 'far'. But *vision* comes directly from the last principal part of *videre* (the Romans' infinitive for 'to see'). In fact, *video* is a synonym for television. As most people know, that word means 'I see' in Latin.

Readers can probably dredge up many more examples of modern hybrids, but I don't wish to labour the point. Really, I am not against this neoteric trend; it's interesting to see it happening and to be aware that the times are a-changing.

2   Latin — Living and Surviving

The only living language is the language of now. And Latin is alive and well in all English-speaking countries. It also breathes vitally in Italy, France, Portugal, Spain and Romania — the lands of the Romance languages.

Most scholars conclude that at least 60 per cent of our words come directly or indirectly from the ancient Romans. It's also been estimated that a person combing an unabridged English dictionary and copying every word of Latin origin would take more than forty years to complete the task if he jotted down forty words each day.

In daily speech we depend more on our Anglo-Saxon heritage than on words of Latin ancestry. But most writers lean towards the classical and Romance languages. Essayists are especially prone to follow this course. One of the great ones was Sir Francis Bacon, a contemporary of Shakespeare's. Here's an example from 'Of Youth and Age':

> 'Young men are fitter to *invent* than to *judge*, fitter for *execution* than for *counsel*, and fitter for *new projects* than for *settled business.*'

The words in italics are of Latin origin, although it must be added that 'new' and 'settled' are a mixed breed.

Lawyers and physicians use Latin every day. When the Spiro Agnew case hit the headlines in America, Agnew's attorneys pleaded *nolo contendere* (literally, 'I am unwilling to contend'). In other words, Agnew did not admit guilt but subjected himself to punishment as though he had pleaded guilty. And all those lawyer-senators on Capitol Hill agree to adjourn *sine die***** ('without a future day being designated for resumption'). These are just a couple of the many uses of the so-called dead language in the legal profession.

---

* *Sine die* is a perfect example of how some Latin expressions become Anglicized in pronunciation. In ancient Rome the phrase sounded like this: 'see-nay dee-ay'. Today it is pronounced 'sigh-nee die-ee'!

As for the medical men, their prescriptions are sometimes scrawled in Latin abbreviations. In their anatomy courses they learn that a vein is a *vena* and the *venae cavae* are the large veins that discharge blood into the right atrium of the heart. *Atrium* itself is a word they borrowed from Caesar's compatriots. It was originally the central hall of a Roman house. Examples could be cited *ad infinitum* regarding the usage of Latin in the medical profession, but it behoves me not to elaborate on the argument *ad nauseam*.

Actually, Latin phrases flourish abundantly in our language and have many applications. Consider our abbreviations alone:

A.D.	(Anno Domini)	in the year of our Lord
A.M.	(ante meridiem)	before noon
P.M.	(post meridiem)	after noon
e.g.	(exempli gratia)	for the sake of the example; for example
Q.E.D.	(quod erat demonstrandum)	which was to be demonstrated
i.e.	(id est)	that is
M.O.	(modus operandi)	manner of operating or working. This abbreviation has been popularized by mystery books and TV programmes. Its sister is *modus vivendi* ('manner of living or getting along'). A compromise between disputants is called a *modus vivendi*.
N.B.	(nota bene)	Note well
D.T.s	(delirium tremens)	violent state caused by prolonged alcoholism. Victims may be said to be *non compos mentis* ('not of sound mind').
R.I.P.	(requiescat in pace)	May he or she rest in peace. Associated phrases are *in memoriam* and *hic jacet*.

And, of course, many who graduate from their *alma mater* (fostering mother) receive a B.A. (Baccalaureus Artium) degree. The M in M.A. stands for *magister*. From this Latin noun for 'master' we have inherited *magistrate*.

Those same graduates may be given such honours as: *cum laude* — with praise; *magna cum laude* — with great praise; *summa cum laude* — with the highest praise.

Latin phrases are often used in mottoes. Try and match the mottoes on the left with the places or groups on the right. The answers appear on p. 220, in the Appendix.

1. E pluribus unum (One out of many)   a. Queen Elizabeth
2. Deo juvante (With God's help)   b. Virginia
3. Semper eadem (Always the same)   c. Monaco
4. Crescit eundo (It grows as it goes)   d. Yale
5. Per ardua ad astra (Through   e. U.S.A.
   difficulties to the stars)
6. Sic semper tyrannis (Thus ever   f. R.A.F.
   to tyrants)
7. Lux et veritas (Light and truth)   g. Constantine the Great
8. In hoc signo vinces (In this sign   h. New Mexico
   thou shalt conquer)

It is amazing how many Latin words have come down to us *in toto*, or completely unchanged. Since so many of them end in *um, us, a* and *or,* let us concentrate on those words.

Let's start with words ending in *um*, because there are so many of them that we have inherited either from the early Romans or from Medieval Latin.

Herewith begins a partial list:

addendum	atrium	curriculum	encomium
album	auditorium	datum	erratum
alluvium	bacterium	decorum	exordium
aluminium	candelabrum	delirium	factotum
antrum	cerebrum	desideratum	forum
aquarium	chrysanthemum	dictum	fulcrum
arboretum	colosseum	effluvium	
asylum	consortium	emporium	

Let us examine a few of the above words.

Album is the neuter form of *albus*, the Latin adjective for 'white'. Since the tablet on which Roman edicts were written was white, it was called an *album*. Fittingly enough, today most photographic albums for weddings have white covers.

Consortium means 'association; fellowship'. From this same root we get *consort*, which can be a verb or a noun. As the former it means 'to associate'. The noun carries the idea of 'mate or spouse'.

Curriculum is 'a body of courses offered by an educational institution'. Once more we encounter a noun taken bodily from Latin but changed in meaning through the years. The early Romans called a racecourse a *curriculum*. Later it became the running itself, and finally a career. This word, by the way, has a slew of relatives — all coming from *currere* ('to run'). Consider *current, currency, concur, occur, recur,* and even *course, discourse* and *recourse*.

Exordium today means 'the introduction to a speech or composition'. The Latin noun is an offshoot of *exordiri* ('to begin a web'). Thus when an orator or writer starts off, he is beginning to spin a web of words in the hope that his *exordium* will catch the interest of the listener or reader.

Factotum literally means 'do everything'. An employee who has a variety of tasks and responsibilities is called a *factotum*.

Fulcrum in Latin came to mean 'bedpost'. The noun was derived from *fulcire* ('to support or prop up'). Today it is defined as 'the support on which a lever turns'.

As we continue with the *um* category, it should be noted that the Romans borrowed some of these words from the Greeks and usually changed an *on* ending to *um*. Also it's interesting to observe how many of these words retain the Latin plural in *-a* instead of adding an *s*. For example, misprints are called *errata*, not *erratums*.

geranium	labium	memorandum	museum
gymnasium	lustrum	millennium	nostrum
helium	magnum	minimum	odium
herbarium	mausoleum	modicum	opprobrium
honorarium	maximum	momentum	
interregnum	medium	moratorium	

A second look at some of the words in the above columns will be rewarding.

Geranium is one of the Latin words borrowed from the Greeks. To the Athenians a *geranion* was a small crane. Its resemblance to a crane's bill gave the flower its name. In fact, a modern synonym for geranium is cranesbill.

Helium is a New Latin word. The gas was named for *helios*, the Greek noun for 'sun'. The reason is that the element was discovered during an examination of the solar spectrum.

19

Lustrum has a fascinating history. Today it means a period of five years, or a *quinquennium*. It's related to *lucere* ('to shine'). The Romans' lustrum was a ceremonious purification of the populace. It was conducted after the census, which was taken every five years. Thus the Romans were forced to 'rise and shine' twice each decade!

Magnum is a wine bottle holding twice as much as the usual vessel does. It contains about two-fifths of a gallon. In other words, it's large. The noun comes from the neuter form of *magnus,* the Latin adjective for 'great'. *Maximum* is the superlative form.

Mausoleum is also a derivative of a Greek word. The original mausoleion was the tomb of King Mausolus at Halicarnassus.

Medium meant 'middle' to Cicero. One use of the word today applies to a person through whom communications are supposedly sent to the living from the spirits of the dead. A *medium*, then, in that sense, is a middleman — or should I say middleperson?

Moratorium today means an 'authorized delay'. To the Romans a *mora* was a delay. In legal terminology it retains that sense.

Museum once was *mouseion* in Athens. It meant 'a place for the Muses to study'. The Romans altered the spelling, and soon the Muses were left out. It became a place for any would-be scholar to study or learn. The word is a first cousin of *music.*

Now let's conclude our list of those intriguing *um* words.

pabulum	quorum	simulacrum	sudarium
pendulum	referendum	solarium	trivium
petroleum	residuum	spectrum	tympanum
podium	rostrum	stadium	ultimatum
proscenium	scriptorium	stratum	vacuum
quantum			

Most of these nouns deserve our close attention. In my opinion, some of the most exciting words in this book are contained in the above grouping.

Pabulum was the Romans' word for 'food or fodder', and it still retains the same meaning.

Pendulum is the neuter form of *pendulus* ('hanging'). The eventual source is the verb *pendere* ('to hang'). From this root, and its sister verb ('to weigh'), we also obtain such words as *pendant, pendent, dependent, impend, compendium, compensate, pension, pensive, propensity, expend, expensive, dispense, dispensation, perpendicular* and a host of others.

20

Petroleum is one of the most vital sources of energy in this modern era. The word was not known to the ancient Romans, but comes to us via Medieval Latin. Actually, it's a sort of hybrid. The Romans acquired *petra* ('rock') from the Greeks. *Oleum* was the Latin word meaning 'oil'. Sometimes, by the way, it meant 'olive oil'. At any rate, *petroleum* literally means 'rock oil'.

Podium is another Latin borrowing. The Greek word was *podion*, and it meant 'a small foot'. Even today zoologists retain some of the original import. To them, a *podium* is 'a foot or hand, or footlike structure'. The noun can also mean 'a low wall or bench projecting from a wall'. But most of us think of it as a synonym for dais.

Kinship of words always intrigues me. It's somewhat exciting to discover that podium is related to *podiatrist* ('foot specialist') and *chiropodist.* It's even a cousin of *pew.* That word was altered in Medieval French and English.

Proscenium literally means 'the place before the scene'. If you substitute 'set' for 'scene', you'll see how today it is the apron of a stage, or the area in front of the curtain. But the most delightful aspect of the noun is that its mainroot can be traced back to skēnē, the Greek word for 'tent'. Such words as *scene, scenery, scenario* and *scenic*, for example, are in the same tent, so to speak. But not *obscene.* Appropriately, that adjective eventually stems from *caenum*, the Latin word for 'filth'.

But you may ask what connection 'tent' has with 'stage'. Well, the ancient actors used the skēnē as a dressing room.

Quantum is the neuter form of *quantus*, a Latin adjective meaning 'how great or how much'. It is related to *quantity* and means exactly that. But physicists have taken over the word. Their *quantum theory* is based on Max Planck's concepts concerning radiant energy. To them a *quantum jump* or *leap* is an abrupt transition of an atom or other particle from one energy state to another.

Rostrum has an intricate history. In ancient Latin it took on many meanings:

1. the accomplisher of gnawing; hence the bill, beak, snout, mouth or muzzle of an animal
2. the curved end of a ship's prow; a ship's beak
3. structure for speakers in the Forum (usually *rostra*, plural form)

The third definition is one we recognize today. After a war the victorious Romans would decorate the Forum platforms with the beaks of captured ships.

But it should be noted that modern biologists still consider *rostrum* to mean 'a beak or beaklike process or part'.

Simulacrum has a nice ring to it. Today, as in ancient Rome, it means 'an image or likeness'. A second definition is 'mere pretence; sham'. *Simulate* and *dissimulate* ('to hide one's feelings') are members of the same family. The mother root is *simulare* ('to imitate or feign').

Solarium originally meant 'a sundial or a water clock'. In Cicero's day it came to mean 'a flat housetop, a terrace or balcony exposed to the sun'. *Sol*, as you may know, was the Latin word for 'sun'. Today a *solarium* is a sun parlour.

Spectrum and *spectre* are sisters! Both can mean 'an apparition'. In fact, that was the definition given to *spectrum* by the Romans. In 1671, Sir Isaac Newton's special use of the word caught on. Now we consider it as a series of coloured bands diffracted by the passage of white light through a prism.

Today the meaning of *spectrum* has been considerably broadened, probably as a result of that wide array of coloured bands. We use the word to indicate a continuous range or entire extent or broad sequence of ideas.

The word has its origin in *specere* ('to look at'). What a large clan has developed from that verb and its cousin *spectare*! Here are only a few examples: *specimen, spy, spectacles, spectator, respect, inspect, conspectus, prospector* and *expectation*.

Two that appeal to me are *suspect* and *suspicion*. When you *suspect* something or someone, you literally look underneath! But my favourite is *circumspect* ('careful or cautious'). A *circumspect* person will look about before he leaps.

Stadium is another of those words that the Romans took over from the Greeks. In Athens a *stadion* was a measure equalling 600 feet. But the Greeks had enlarged the meaning of the word. Since their courses for footraces were 600 feet long, they called the grounds for such races *stadia*. The Romans followed suit. As time went by, seats for spectators were installed and walls were erected around each *stadium*, or athletic event. Thus today when we speak of Wembley Stadium, we think of the entire structure.

Tympanum was a drum to Caesar. Originally it was a Greek word, *tympanon*, with the same meaning. In modern usage it means the 'eardrum or middle ear'.

From that same Greek root we get *tympany* ('resonance obtained by percussion') and *tympanist* ('kettle-drummer').

But the most thrilling discovery I have recently made is the fact that *tympanum* can be finally traced back to *typtein,* a Greek verb meaning 'to strike or beat'. From that source we derive such words as 'typography', 'prototype', 'archetype', 'typical' and others — even 'typist'.

Ultimatum in Latin means 'the last part'. We use the word to signify a final offer or demand. In plural form both *ultimata* and *ultimatums* are acceptable.

Vacuum, to the best of my knowledge, is one of ten bona fide English nouns that contain successive *u*'s; the others are *continuum, duumvir, duumvirate, individuum, lituus, menstruum, mutuum, muumuu* and *residuum.*

Vacuum is the neuter form of the Latin adjective *vacuus* ('empty, void'). Our own adjective is vacuous, from the same root. Like the Romans, we have extended the scope of the word to mean 'vain or inane'. But *vacuum* itself means 'the absence of matter' or 'empty space'. A device creating or utilizing partially empty space is, naturally, a *vacuum cleaner.*

The parental verb is *vacare* ('to be empty'). Thus when a position is *vacated,* it is emptied, and when people are *evacuated* from a house, they are literally emptied out. The Romans also defined *vacare* as 'to be free from labour or unoccupied'. And so *vacationers* truly live in a *vacuum!*

When scientists coin words, they sometimes use what we call Modern Latin. Some examples are: *planetarium, platinum, radium, sodium* and *uranium. Linoleum* is a word coined in 1863 by an English manufacturer named Walton. He combined *linum* ('flax') with *oleum* ('oil'). Linseed oil (used in the product) does come from flax, so I suppose his neologism was not amiss.

Tedium, premium and *equilibrium* can be linked for one special reason. They are typical of Latin words that have come down to us with one slight change: the *a* in front of the *e* has been dropped. For instance, when Vergil was weary, he suffered from *taedium.* Ovid talked of *praemium* when he was referring to profit taken from booty, and Seneca's *aequilibrium* was a level or horizontal position. The poor fellow found it when Nero ordered him to commit suicide!

Sanatorium and *sanitarium* are New Latin words. Both are descendants of *sanitas* ('health'). Some other members of the family are *sanitary, sane, insane* and *sanity.*

23

What about *bunkum, hokum, hoodlum, tantrum* and *wampum*? Well, it's obvious that those words never reached the ears of Caesar.

Bunkum has made Buncombe County, North Carolina, famous — or infamous, if you will — ever since 1820. Felix Walker, a congressman from that county, took the floor and prattled on and on about matters that had no relation to the question being discussed. When asked to yield, he refused and said that the people of his district expected him to 'make a speech for Buncombe'. Soon the word *buncombe* became a synonym for nonsense or humbug. Later it was shortened to *bunkum*, and finally it became just plain *bunk*.

Does *bunco* or *bunko* (meaning 'a swindle or con game') come from the same source? Some philologers think it does. Others surmise that it's a variation of *banca*, the Italian or Spanish word for 'bank'.

Hokum is thought to be an abridged combination of *hocus-pocus* and *bunkum*. As for *hocus-pocus* itself, it's believed that the term was invented by jugglers in imitation of Latin.

Hoodlum may have come from a Swiss word *hudilump* ('wretch, miserable fellow'). The slang word *hood* is a curtailment of *hoodlum*.

Nobody knows the origin of *tantrum*, but *wampum* comes from a compound Algonquian noun *wampumeage* ('white string of beads'). Since the Indians sometimes used beads for money, *wampum* has become one of the slangy synonyms for currency.

But it's time to return to those Latin words that have come down to us unchanged in spelling, and often in meaning too. Next on our list is the category that ends in *us*, such as *afflatus, arbutus, citrus* and others below.

abacus	angelus	bacillus
acanthus	animus	bolus
alumnus	apparatus	bonus
cactus	colossus	fetus
caduceus	consensus	focus
calculus	conspectus	fungus
callus	corpus	genius
campus	crepitus	genus
census	crus	gladius
cestus	cumulus	Hesperus

chorus	discus	hiatus
circus	emeritus	humerus
cirrus	exodus	humus

Now let's take a hard look at some of the words in the above list before we go on to another group of *us* inheritances.

Acanthus was described by Vergil as a thorny Egyptian evergreen tree. This is one of the many words that the Romans borrowed from the Greeks and transliterated. To the Athenians it meant 'a thorny plant', and that's what it means today. Have you ever noticed the ornamentation atop a Corinthian architectural column? It represents the leaves of the acanthus.

Alumnus meant 'pupil or foster son' in Horace's heyday, and an *alumna* was a foster daughter. Both words stemmed from *alere* ('to nourish'). The British still retain the original idea, but Americans have altered it to mean a 'graduate' or one who has been intellectually nourished by his alma mater.

Angelus is a form of devotion for Roman Catholics. It has the same roots as *angel*.

Animus fascinates me. It originally meant 'soul, aim, mind, will, desire, passion'. Plautus used it to signify affection; but Tacitus described it as 'haughtiness or arrogance', and to Terence it was a synonym for anxiety. As so often happens in linguistic history, evil triumphed. Today most people think of *animus* as ill will or hatred. *Animosity* ('enmity') and *animadversion* ('censure') come from this same root. However, there is still some hope left. In many dictionaries the first meaning of *animus* is 'intention or objective', and another definition is 'inspiration'.

Apparatus literally means 'a making preparation'. If you have the right tools, you are prepared.

Bacillus is one of the rod-shaped bacteria. In Low Latin (of medieval origin) it meant 'little rod'. The parental word is *baculus* ('stick').

Bonus has an obvious history. If your boss gives you a *bonus*, that's good.

Caduceus lives today because it is one of the symbols of physicians. This staff with two snakes wound around it is also the emblem of the Royal Army Medical Corps. To the ancients a snake was a sort of token of reincarnation, because the reptile could slough off its old skin periodically and produce a new covering.

The *caduceus* was also the staff toted by Mercury (or Hermes), the wing-footed messenger of the gods.

Calculus to a Roman meant 'a pebble'. The ancients used little stones when they *calculated.* Q.E.D.

Campus originally meant 'plain or field'. The *Campus Martius* (Field of Mars) was a grassy area in which the Romans held contests, military exercises and assemblies.

Census comes directly to us from Caesar's time. In those days it was a registering and rating of Roman citizens and their property. The parent verb was *censare* ('to assess'). From it we also derive *censor, censorious* and even *censure* — another example of how evil connotations seem to thrive.

Chorus is another word lent by the Greeks to the Romans. The Athenian word was *choros.* In ancient days it meant 'a dance in a ring' and later 'a band of people singing and dancing'. Thus we can see that this word has retained its pristine denotations. Incidentally, *choir* is from the same root.

Circus meant 'ring' to ancient Romans. Their *Circus Maximus* was literally the largest ring. You can still see it today if you visit Rome.

Cirrus in modern times is associated with cloud. A *cirrus* cloud is wispy. In Latin the word means 'tuft of hair'. Enough said!

Colossus still means 'a gigantic statue', but it also carries the idea of any huge or important person or thing. Again, the Greeks were originally responsible for this word. Around 280 B.C., Charles of Lindus designed and built the *Colossus of Rhodes*, one of the Seven Wonders of the World.

The Roman Colosseum and the Coliseum in St. Martin's Lane owe their titles to the same Latin word. And, of course, *colossal* is a derivative.

Consensus literally means 'feeling together'. Hence its present usage as a synonym for unanimity or accord is certainly appropriate. Many people spell this word incorrectly by substituting a *c* for the first *s*.

Conspectus is defined as 'a survey, outline or synopsis'. To the Romans it meant 'a view or range of sight'.

Corpus in Latin means 'body'. Today the *corpus delicti* ('body of the crime') is what the detectives look for in homicide cases. *Habeas corpus* is a legal writ ordering a person to be brought to court. It translates verbatim into 'You should have the body.'

Most interesting is the fact that this word gives us *corps* ('body of troops'), *corporation, corpse, incorporeal* ('having no material body') and *corpulent.* When a person has lost of body, he's *corpulent.* And when a teacher administers *corporal* punishment, he or she hurts the body.

Does the non-commissioned officer come from this same root? Probably not. His ancestry is usually traced back to *caput* ('head').

Crocus is a word you should really look up if etymology excites you. The Romans took it from the Greeks, but that lovely spring bloomer also has a Semitic and Assyrian history.

Discus is a circular object thrown in Olympic games. From that word we have obtained *disc* and *disk.* Did you ever wonder why there is a difference in spelling? Well, the Greek word was *diskos*; hence the confusion. *Disc* is more usual, because of our attachment to the Romans.

From the same root we get *dish.* Actually, this word goes back to *dikein* ('to throw'). Can you picture Xanthippe throwing plates at Socrates?

Exodus is a Medieval Latin extraction from *exodos,* the Greek word for 'a going out'. As you probably know, the *Exodus* is the departure of the Israelites, under Moses, from Egypt.

Focus in old Roman days meant 'fireplace or hearth'. Since it was the spot where the family gathered, it took on the idea of the centre of activity. Somewhere along the line other meanings were attached to it, and the noun even acquired a verbal sense. When you *focus* on a problem, you concentrate on it.

Fungus originally meant 'mushroom' and was probably a Latin modification of *spongos* (the Greek word for 'sponge'). Such writers as Plautus added another dimension to the noun. Because of the texture of the top of a mushroom, *fungus* also came to mean 'a soft-headed fellow; a dolt'. That connotation has not survived. But here's a new word for your list: *fungistatic.* It means 'preventing the growth of fungi without killing them'.

Genius started out as a Roman's tutelary spirit. Just as many people today believe that they are watched over and protected by guardian angels, the ancients felt that a particular spirit was assigned to each person at birth. Soon, by metonymy (the practice of using one word for another with which it is associated), the sense of the word was extended to mean 'wit or talent'. Finally, as time went on, the noun was applied to any person with great mental capacity. Incidentally, through the French, we have also received *genie.* To the Arabs that beneficent or malevolent spirit is

27

a *jinn* or *jinni* or *jinnee*.

Someone may ask if *genial* is a member of this family. The answer is yes if you mean 'amiable; friendly'. But there is another adjective with the same spelling. It means 'relating to the chin' and is derived from Greek. So if you said, 'That *genial* gentleman has a prominent *genial* feature,' your statement would not be tautological.

Genus originally meant 'birth, origin, race, species, kind'. The Romans took it from the Greeks' *genos*. The *gen, gene* root has given us a host of words, among them: *gender, gene, genealogy, general, generation, generic, generosity, genesis, genetics, genocide, genre, genteel, Gentile, gentle, gentleman* and *gentry*.

Also there are *congenital, degenerate, ingenious, ingenuous, progenitor* and so on.

A favourite of mine is *genethliac* ('relating to birthdays'). And naturally I'm pleased to report that *Eugene* means 'well born'.

Hesperus was *Hesperos* to the Greeks. This son of Eos and brother of Atlas became identified with the West. In fact, his name meant 'west' to ancient Athenians. Their appellation for Italy was Hesperia ('the western land'). More specifically the god's name was applied to the evening star, because it sets in the west. Hesperus therefore is a synonym for Venus.

The Romans developed still another synonym as an offshoot of Hesperus. They called the evening star *Vesper* and also applied the word to the evening itself. The transition might be called 'the wreck of the *Hesperus*'. Seriously, *vespers* are now church songs for the late afternoon or evening.

Hiatus is the past participle of *hiare* ('to gape or yawn'). Today a *hiatus* is a break in a manuscript where a part is missing or lost. It is also any gap or opening and is often used to mean an interruption or lapse in a time period.

Humerus today is just what it was in Cicero's era — the bone of the upper arm. When this bone is bumped, the nerve often tingles in a strange or funny sort of way. Thus it's appropriate that some humorous person dubbed it 'the funny bone', and the name has stuck.

Humus almost means the same to us as it did to the Romans. They used the term for 'soil or ground'. We regard it as the organic part of soil.

And now to continue our list

| iambus | lotus | nidus | plus |
| ictus | magus | nimbus | prospectus |

ignoramus	mandamus	nucleus	radius
impetus	minus	octopus	ramulus
incubus	mittimus	omnibus	rebus
incus	naevus	onus	
locus	nexus	plexus	

Iambus (or *iamb*) is just a Latin variation of the Athenians' *iambos* — a metrical foot.

Ictus, according to Cicero and Livy, meant 'a blow, stroke, stab or thrust'. Horace used it to mean 'a beat' in his verses. Today it has that same import. To physicians it's a stroke.

Ignoramus literally means 'We take notice.' It's a former legal term. Circa 1615-22, George Ruggle wrote a play called *Ignoramus*. The stupid lawyer in the drama bore that name. The production was soon forgotten and so was Ruggle, but his character's cognomen became a byword. Today an *ignoramus* is a dunce or know-nothing.

Lotus is a borrowing from *lotos*. In fact, the Romans often spelled the word with an *os* ending. To them it meant 'the water lily of the Nile'. In Greek legend it was a fruit supposed to induce dreamy languor and forgetfulness. Have you ever read Tennyson's 'The Lotos Eaters'? They're the *Lotophagi* in Homer's ODYSSEY. After eating of the *lotus-tree* they lost all desire to return to their homeland. In current usage a lotus-eater is a person who gives himself up to indolence and daydreams. He lives in *lotus land*, and he really ought to see a psychiatrist.

Magus, now and in ancient Rome, is synonymous with the terms 'magician' and 'wise man' — the singular of *magi*, the title given to the three kings who came to do homage to the infant Jesus. Caspar was a *magus*; so were Melchior and Balthasar.

Minus is the neuter singular form of *minor*, the Latin adjective for 'less'. In this case the less said the better.

Naevus was the Romans' word for 'a mole'. It means the same today. It also means 'a birthmark or tumour'.

Nexus comes down to us unchanged. As of yore, it means 'a tie, link, binding'. It should be noted that *annex* is a relative. It's something tied on.

Nimbus originally meant 'a violent rainstorm'. Later the Romans associated it with the cloud that brought such a downpour. But Vergil used *nimbus* to mean 'a bright cloud or cloud-shaped splendour' (which enveloped the gods when they appeared on earth). Hence the noun has become a synonym for halo or a

29

splendid aura. But the adjective *nimbose* still has only one connotation — cloudy or stormy.

Nucleus in ancient Roman times meant 'a small nut'; later it stood for the nut itself, and finally its meaning became 'the kernel or most solid part'. That last definition led to our modern conception for the word. To us the *nucleus* means 'the core'.

Today we talk of *nuclear energy* (a derivative, of course).

Octopus is one of those New Latin words. It doesn't really belong here, because the ancient Romans did not call the creature by that name. The Greeks, however, had the word *oktopous* ('eight-footed'), and that designation suggested the modern name. The octopus does have eight limbs, but they are arms, not feet. To be precise, the mollusc should have been called an *octobrach*. This scary predator has almost half as many plural forms as it has arms: *octopuses, octopi* and *octopodes*.

Omnibus literally means 'for all'. The French had a *voiture omnibus*; the English shortened it to *omnibus* and then settled for *bus*. The plural is *buses* or *busses* — take your choice.

In the U.S. Congress an *omnibus bill* includes a number of miscellaneous provisions or appropriations. In a way it's something for all.

Onus is a Latin noun meaning 'burden', and to us it carries the same import. It's akin to a Sanskrit word *ánas* ('cart or freight'). The Romans' plural was *onera*. They would be horrified to hear us say *onuses*, but they would applaud our adjective *onerous* ('burdensome').

In law *onus probandi* means 'burden of proof'.

Plexus is a New Latin word taken from the past participle of *plectere* ('to braid'). It means 'a network'. Some of its relatives are *complex, duplex, complexion* and *perplexed*.

Plus literally means 'more'. *Surplus* is a derivative. And from a form of *plus* we also obtain *plural, plurality* and others.

Prospectus to Livy and Cicero meant 'a look-out or distant view'. The noun was derived from *prospicere* ('to look forward'). Today a *prospectus* is a statement outlining the main features of a new enterprise. The distant view is a *prospect*.

Radius in Latin means 'a ray, rod or spoke'. Cicero referred to it as a semidiameter. We have extended the scope of the word to mean 'a range of operation, activity, influence, concern or knowledge'.

30

Our word *ray* comes from *radius*. And, through the French, so does *rayon*.

Now let's conclude the list of words ending in *us* that we have taken bodily from Latin:

sinus	strabismus	terminus	versus
solus	stratus	tetanus	virus
status	stylus	tragus	
stimulus	talus	umbilicus	

Sinus in Latin means 'a bent surface or curve'. Today it is that cavity in our skulls that gives many of us trouble where it connects with the nasal passages. The word can also be used for other bodily cavities. And it still means 'a bend or curve'.

Solus means 'alone', as it once did in Rome. Now its usage is largely confined to a stage direction. The Italians changed it to *solo* — an alteration that we eagerly accepted, first in its musical sense and then for other purposes. Lindbergh's solo flight across the Atlantic in 1927 popularized the use of the word in aviation.

Status is the past participle of *stare* (Latin for 'to stand'). But the Romans also used *status* as a noun having the sense of 'position, posture, condition or situation'. We have accepted most of these definitions for the word, but in recent years we have added a new dimension. It now also means 'high prestige or recognition'.

That verb *stare* has sired a legion of words. Among them are *statue, obstacle, stance, distant, constant, constancy, instant, instantaneous, stanza, substance, substantiate, static, statistics, state, reinstate, outstanding, stanchion, stature, extant, circumstance, oust* and many more. Even *rest*, when it means 'remainder', is a member of the family, and so is *arrest*.

Printers and crossword puzzle fans will recognize *stet*. Literally, it means 'Let it stand!' It is the opposite of *dele* ('Take it out!').

Stimulus means the same today as it did in Caesar's time — a goad or spur. *Stimulate* is obviously from the same root.

Strabismus is one of those Modern Latin coinages, with a Greek parentage. To the Athenians, *strabizein* meant 'to squint'. Cross-eyed people have *strabismus*.

Stratus in Latin means 'a strewing'. Stratus clouds do tend to strew themselves in the skies.

Stylus was usually spelled *stilus* by the Romans. At first it meant 'a stake'. Then it took on the meaning of 'a pointed instrument for writing on wax tablets'. In modern times *styluses*, or *styli*, are employed for marking mimeographed stencils or for Braille embossing or for cutting the grooves in gramophone records; also for transmitting the vibrations from the record to the pick-up.

The word *style* comes directly from this source. In its original sense it is a synonym for *stylus*. It's not difficult to see how it developed a new meaning — 'manner or mode of expression'. That connotation was first applied to writing, but eventually it was extended to other areas, such as the world of fashion. How fascinating it is to follow the vagarious extension of words! Does a couturier designing a new *style* for women's dresses realize that his or her art dates back to a pointed stick?

It should also be noted that *stiletto* has the same root. This Italian word for 'a small dagger' has been adopted by us, and it makes sense when we consider the source.

Terminus in Latin means 'limit, boundary or end'. I would guess that few readers are aware that Terminus was the ancient Roman god presiding over boundaries and landmarks. Places like New York City really ought to have such a spirit today to protect those landmarks that are constantly being torn down and replaced. Such a practice needs to be *terminated*, and I use the *term* advisedly. (Yes, *term* does stem from the same root, as does *terminology*.)

Tetanus is a Latin borrowing from the Greeks' *tetanos* ('spasm of the muscles'). Our synonym is the word 'lockjaw'.

Tragus has a complex history. In modern usage, especially among otologists, it means 'the fleshy protrusion of the front of the external ear'. To the Greeks it literally meant 'a goat', and eventually, 'the hairy part of the ear'. Their spelling, transliterated, was *tragos*. To Ovid it was a species of fish, probably with a goatlike appearance.

It may be hard to believe that *tragedy* is linguistically related to a part of the ear, but philologists surmise that it really is. In ancient Greece some performers represented satyrs and were dressed in goatskins.

Umbilicus to a Roman meant 'the navel'. Modern doctors still use the same word for what is vulgarly called 'the belly button'. Most of us know about the *umbilical cord,* the structure that connects the foetus to the mother's placenta and must be severed at birth. Here again we discover new uses for an old phrase. Psychiatrists refer to the *umbilical cord* as an inordinate attachment of the child to the mother. Astronauts use the phrase for a cable that connects a missile with the launching equipment. This is just one of the many instances of the verbal creativity of mankind.

Versus in Latin means 'toward or turned in the direction of'. Today we define it as 'in contest against'. The abbreviation is *v* or (in the U.S.A.) *vs*: 'Arsenal *v* Manchester United'.

Virus meant 'a slimy liquid' to Vergil, and to Lucretius it meant 'an offensive odour; a stench'. In English its meaning was originally 'venom', as of a snake. Today it's an infective agent that causes various diseases. A modern derivative is the adjective *virulent* ('extremely poisonous or harmful').

Some readers may chide me for having omitted a few of their favourite words with *us* endings. But let no one take up the cudgels for *bogus, caucus, ruckus, rumpus* and *syllabus.* Those words do not fit into the category that has been discussed. Let us take a look at them.

Bogus is a slang word meaning 'false or spurious'. It was originally a machine for making counterfeit money. Lexicographers aren't sure, but they surmise that it might come from *bogle, bogy* or *bogie* ('hobgoblin; bugbear; scary thing').

Caucus does sound like a Latin word, but it's probably of Algonquian origin. The Indians had a similar noun, meaning 'adviser'. But there is also a Medieval Greek word that must be considered: *kaukos* ('drinking cup').

Ruckus is probably a combination of *ruction* ('riotous outbreak') and *rumpus*. Nobody knows whence we obtained *rumpus*, but in Ireland (1798) a revolt was called the 'Ruction'. The name, begorra, is a corruption of *insurrection.*

Syllabus does have a Latin background, but the spelling has been changed. In Cicero's time a *sillybus* was not a wayward jitney à la Steinbeck; it meant 'a strip of parchment attached to a book-roll, on which was written the title of the work and the author's name'. The Romans had borrowed the word from the Greek *sillybos.* Today a *syllabus* means 'a summary or outline containing the main points' and is usually applied to a course of study.

Now let's consider some of the many words that end in *a* and have moved over without change from Latin to English. Again we will break them into groups so that we can take a pause now and then.

agenda	caesura	corolla	femora
alga	camera	corona	fibula
angina	catena	costa	flora
antenna	cicada	coxa	formula
arena	circa	dogma	fossa
aura	cithara	et cetera	galena
aurora	cloaca	farina	gemma
bacchanalia	cornea	fascia	

Agenda is the plural of *agendum*, which is also a word in our language but is rarely used. Agenda literally means 'things to be done'. The word is a form of *agere* ('to do'), which has provided us with a lode or load of inheritances. From one principal part or another we have obtained *act, agent, agile, agitate, ambiguous, cogent, exact, exigent, exiguous, fumigate, intransigent, litigate, navigate, prodigal, purge, retroactive, squat, transaction* and numerous others.

Angina was used by Plautus as a synonym for quinsy (abscess of the tonsils). *Angina* comes from a Latin verb *angere* ('to strangle or distress'), and both *anger* and *angry* are closely related to it. Today the word still means 'an inflammatory disease of the throat'. But more and more we have come to associate it with *angina pectoris* ('quinsy of the chest' in ancient days) — a condition caused by a sudden decrease in blood supply to the heart.

Antenna in Roman days meant 'an extended thing'. Ovid used it to mean 'a sail'. It no longer has anything to do with ships. Today *antennae* are the sense organs on the heads of insects, crabs, lobsters and other arthropods. Sometimes they are called feelers. But it pleases me to note that a TV *antenna* is still an extended thing.

Arena has been transformed through the ages. Originally it meant 'the dried thing' and then it was employed to mean 'sand'. Since the centres of the Roman amphitheatres were strewn with sand, that place of combat for gladiators soon became known as the *arena*. Today an *arena* is an enclosed space for a boxing match, basketball game or some other sport.

We still use *arena* in another way that fits its ancestry. It means 'the place where the action is'. An example is the *arena* of politics.

Aura had a dozen meanings in ancient Rome, ranging from 'air or gentle breeze' to 'sound, tone, echo or odour'. In modern times we associate the word largely with atmosphere or aroma. Incidentally, the Romans adapted the word from the Greeks.

Aurora meant 'dawn' to Vergil, and it retains that meaning today, mainly because of the poets. Most people connect it with *aurora borealis* ('northern aurora'), the luminous phenomenon supposed to be of electrical origin and commonly called the 'northern lights'.

Bacchanalia is the neuter plural of *bacchanalis.* Currently it means 'an orgy or drunken party'. The Romans not only stole hundreds of words from the Greeks, they also took over their gods. Bacchus (Roman god of wine) and Dionysus (Greek deity) are one and the same. The *Bacchanalia* was a Roman festival in honour of that god. A shortened form is *bacchanal.* Today a *bacchant* is a drunken reveller.

One might suspect that *bachelor* is a related word, but it isn't. It comes from Medieval Latin *baccalarius* ('dependent farmer, tenant, young clerk or advanced student'). The last of these definitions indicates why some college graduates are granted Bachelor of Arts degrees. Incidentally, *bachelor* is related to *bacterium* because both words can be traced back to *baculum,* the ancient Romans' noun for 'a stick or staff'.

Camera to the Romans meant 'a vault'. That connotation exists today. The word can be defined as 'a chamber, or judge's private office'. But the invention of the *camera obscura* (literally, 'dark chamber') led to our most common use of the word. We dropped the adjective. Incidentally, there is also a *camera lucida* ('light chamber'). It's an apparatus using a prism or mirrors to reflect an object so that its outline can be traced.

Catena is the Latin word for 'chain'. In modern usage it means 'a connected series of related things'. To *catenate* is to link, and a *concatenation* is 'a union in a linked series or chain'. Where did 'chain' come from? It's a derivation of *catena* via the Medieval French.

Cithara was a Roman instrument resembling a lyre. The word was borrowed from the Greeks'*kithara.* From the same root came another instrument, the *cither.* Nor should we omit the *cittern*, which is a blend of *cither* and *gittern.* The latter was a stringed instrument of the Middle Ages. *Zither*, of course, is a member of this family. But the most interesting is the fact that the *guitar* can be traced back linguistically to the *cithara.*

Cloaca in ancient Rome originally meant 'the cleanser'. Then it came to signify 'a sewer or drain' — the definition that applies today. Tarquinius Priscus built an artificial canal to carry the filth from the streets of Rome and it was called the *Cloaca Maxima*.

To modern herpetologists, ornithologists, ichthyologists and amphibiologists the *cloaca* is a chamber inside reptiles, birds, fish and amphibia through which waste matter is excreted.

Cornea is the feminine form of an old Latin adjective meaning 'horny'. The noun arose in medieval times, and denotes the outer coating of the eyeball, probably so named because of its texture. The parent word is *cornu* ('horn'). From it we have inherited *corner, cornet, Capricorn, tricorn, unicorn* and even *horn* itself. You may wish to add *corneous* to your vocabulary. It means 'horny'.

Corolla is a part of a flower. To the Romans it meant 'a garland or small wreath'. It was a diminutive of *corona*, which in Latin means 'crown or garland' and today carries several meanings — crown; halo around the sun or moon; long cigar. The last definition is derived from a trademark, 'La Corona'.

Fascia was the Romans' word for 'a band or bandage'. Today it is used in architecture to mean a kind of moulding or flat strip. The dashboard of an Englishman's car is sometimes called the *fascia board* or *facia board*.

But a relative word from Rome, *fasces*, is even more interesting, because it has given us such words as *fascism* and *fascist*. It means 'a bundle of sticks or rods'. The Roman magistrates carried this bundle, with an axe in the middle, its head projecting at the top. It was the symbol of authority. When Benito Mussolini came into power in Italy he was head of the *Fascisti*, a group that took over the ancient *fasces* as their symbol.

If a plant grows in bundles or clusters, it is said to be *fasciculate*. And a section of a book that appears prior to the publication of the entire work is called a *fascicle*. Isn't that fascinating?

Does *fascinate* have the same source? No, indeed! It's from *fascinare* ('to bewitch or enchant').

Flora was the Roman goddess of flowers. In the 1700s Linnaeus popularized the word in his systematic classification of plants. *Flora* are now the plants of a region, and *fauna* are the animals.

Formula is the Latin diminutive for *forma*. Originally it meant 'a little shape or figure'. So when a modern chemist develops a new *formula* in his laboratory, he can rightfully claim that he's come up with a beauty.

Fossa was a Roman ditch or moat. It came from a participal form of *fodere* ('to dig'). Today doctors partly retain the original idea. To them a *fossa* is pit or cavity in the human anatomy. But we do have another, very similar word, *fosse*, which means 'ditch or moat'. It has come to us via old French and Medieval English.

As you might expect, *fossil* is a relative. It means 'something dug up'. Now if you call someone *an old fossil*, you may feel a bit ghoulish.

There is another *fossa*, of entirely different origin. It's a lithe and slender mammal of Madagascar.

Galena originally was the dross that remained after melting lead. Today it's the principal ore of lead.

Gemma in Latin is the bud of a plant. Botanists have kept that designation. But *gem* is the more popular word from that root. Like a bud, it's lovely to look at.

Now let us continue with our list of Latin words ending in *a*, keeping in mind that their spellings are the same today as they were years ago.

hernia	lamina	notabilia	quota
idea	macula	opera	regalia
impedimenta	marginalia	orchestra	remora
incunabula	memorabilia	patella	reseda
inertia	militia	pica	rota
insignia	miscellanea	piscina	rotunda
insomnia	nebula	pupa	
lacuna			

Some of the above lend themselves to grouping. *Memorabilia* are things worth remembering or recording. Things worthy of notice are called *notabilia*, and marginal notes or extrinsic matters are *marginalia*. Varied collections, especially if works of literature, are *miscellanea*. All these words are neuter plurals of Latin words.

Impedimenta is another neuter plural — and what a delightful word it is! This synonym for encumbrances or things that hinder progress has its roots in *pes, pedis* ('foot, of the foot'). The Latin word *impedire* means 'to entangle or get the feet in something'. Thus an *impediment* really trips you up!

Still another enchanting neuter plural is *incunabula* (literally, 'in the cradle'). Your *incunabula* are your very first stages of infancy. The noun is also used for books published before 1501.

Insignia is also a neuter plural in Latin. The original connotation still remains — namely, 'badges or emblems or distinctive marks'.

Opera naturally comes to us from Italy. But the word in Latin is another neuter plural and literally means 'works'. The Italians changed it to a singular noun.

The last of those neuter plurals from Latin is *regalia*, from *regalis*, meaning 'kingly'. In our day that idea remains. *Regalia* are the rights or privileges of kings, hence the ensigns or emblems of royalty. But the more common definition is 'splendid clothes; finery'.

Now let's return, alphabetically, to the latest line of words ending in *a*.

Hernia and *yarn* have the same roots! The reasons are too complicated to relate, but any reader can look this up in an unabridged dictionary. In Latin, as in English, *hernia* is a rupture.

The Romans borrowed *idea* from the Greeks. In Athens, *idein* meant 'to see'. If you look up *wit* in a good lexicon, you will discover that it too can finally be traced back to the same root as *idea*.

Inertia originally came from another Latin word, *iners*. That adjective meant 'without *ars*' or 'lacking skill'. Eventually Cicero and others used *inertia* in the sense of inactivity or idleness. That concept continues in our language. Aside from the definition given to the word by physicists, it means 'sluggishness' to most *hoi polloi*, including me.

Insomnia in Latin or English means 'the state of sleeplessness'. The victim of this condition is an *insomniac*. Some very expressive words have come from this *somn* root. A sleepwalker is a *somnambulist*. A *somnifacient* is a sleep-producing drug, and *somniloquy* is the practice of talking in one's sleep. If you're *somnolent*, you are sleepy, and if you're *somnolescent*, you are beginning to grow drowsy.

Somnipathy is the state into which a hypnotist puts his patients. His art is *somniferous* ('sleep-producing').

The Romans, like the rest of us, had so much interest in sleep that they developed several other synonyms:

sopor	heavy sleep. From this word we get *soporific* — sleep-inducing drug; *soporose* — morbidly sleepy; and *soporiferous* — inducing sleep.
quies	rest. Some members of the family are *quiet, quiescent, quietude, quietus* and even *quit*.
dormire	to sleep. Descendants are *dormant, dormitory* and *dormer* (window originally in bedrooms only). The *dormouse* is nocturnal and becomes torpid in winter, so the roots for his name can also be traced to *dormire*.

Lacuna in Latin means 'cavity, cavern, pool or pond'. The poet Ovid used it to signify a dimple. Today the word means 'a blank space, gap, hole, missing part, defect or flaw'. It is the parent of *lake* and *lagoon*.

Lamina hasn't changed much in meaning since Caesar's day. It is still defined as 'a layer'. When rock, wood, a fabric or a plastic is *laminated*, it is composed of thin layers. A *lamina* is also a thin layer of tissue on a horse's hoof. Inflammation of this area is called *laminitis*.

Macula was and is a spot or stain. Our most common derivative is *immaculate* (literally, 'not stained'). In a way, an *immaculate* dresser is wearing clean, unspotted clothes. Less familiar descendants are *maculate* and *maculose* ('spotted'), *maculacy* ('smirched, unclean, spotted state') and *macular* ('spotty').

Militia in early Rome meant 'the serving as a soldier'. Finally it denotes 'troops', and that definition has survived. The word is derived from *miles* ('a soldier'). A verb from the same root is *militate* ('to have weight or effect'). When a situation *militates* against you, it causes an army of problems to attack you. Note that some people confuse *militate* with *mitigate*. The latter is derived from our old friend *agere* ('to drive'). *Mitis* is a Latin word for 'soft or gentle'. To *mitigate* means 'to make less severe'. What a difference from *militate*!

Nebula means 'mist, vapour or cloud' in Latin. Today the *nebulae* are immense bodies of highly rarefied gas or dust in the Milky Way and other galaxies. If we say that prospects for success are nebulous, we mean that they are not clear. In other words, they are cloudy or misty. *Nebular* is a synonym for cloudy.

Orchestra was originally a Greek word derived from *orcheisthai* ('to dance'). In ancient theatres the *orchestra* was the semicircular space in front of the stage. Anyone who has ever attended an opera or other kinds of musical performances can see why the word has

39

been applied to the groups of musicians themselves.

The verb *orchestrate* is gradually taking on a non-musical import. Recently I read this sentence by a well known columnist: 'The leaders of the oil powers are *orchestrating* our future.'

Patella, as any crossword puzzle fan knows, is the kneecap or kneepan. In ancient Rome it was a small pan or dish.

Pica in Latin first meant 'the painted one', then 'the variegated one' and finally 'the magpie'. Today *pica* means 'the genus of magpies'. And probably because those birds are omnivorous, the word also means 'a craving to eat substances like chalk, ashes or bones'.

Most people know *pica* as a size of type. In earlier days it was a collection of church rules which, when printed, resembled the colours of a magpie.

Piscina, once a fish pond or swimming pool, is now a basin for the disposal of holy water. It is also called a *sacrarium*. The original meaning of *piscina* has been retained in Italian and Spanish.

Pupa was the Romans' word for 'doll or puppet' — and sometimes for 'girl'. It's easy to see why an insect in its post-larval stage is called *pupa*. Close cousins are *pupil, puppet, pup* and *puppy*.

Quota is the feminine singular of *quotus* ('How many?'). The Latin phrase *quota pars* ('How great a part?') is said to be the reason for our present definition — a proportional share.

An interesting aside: when a Roman asked another about the time of day, he would say, 'Quota?' It was a shortening of 'Quota hora?'

It's also fascinating to discover that *quote* and *quotation* are derived from the same root as *quota*. This came about because of the Latin verb *quotare*, used in medieval days to mean 'to divide into chapters by numbers; to mark references by numbers'.

Remora is a little fish that takes a free ride on a shark or turtle or even under a passing ship. It can do this because it has an oval sucking disc on its head. The word is made up of the prefix *re* and *mora* ('delay'). Sailors believed that the *remoras* hindered ships when they clung to them.

To lawyers *mora* is a familiar word. It still means 'delay'. From the same root we have obtained *moratorium, demur* and *demurrage*. Some lexicographers claim that *memory* is also a relative.

A word about *demurrage*. If you have never been in the shipping business, you might assume that the word meant 'the act of having scruples or objections'. It certainly looks like a synonym for *demurrer*, but it isn't. Its definition is: 'the delaying of a ship, railway wagon, etc. by the freighter's failure to load, unload or sail within the time allowed'. It also means 'the compensation paid for the delay'.

Reseda, according to Pliny, was originally the imperative of *resedare* ('to allay'). The plant was used as a kind of amulet to reduce tumours. In modern times the word is a synonym for the garden mignonette.

Rota in early Rome was 'a wheel'. Later, by metonymy, it came to mean 'a vehicle with wheels; a chariot'. It also came to signify 'the disc of the sun' and Ovid even called it 'the wheel or rack of love'.

The *Sacred Roman Rota* is a tribunal of prelates serving as an appeals court. But in a non-ecclesiastical sense a *rota* is a roster or list of names. It's also a round of golf tournaments.

Some descendants of that Roman wheel are *rotate*, *rotameter*, *rotund*, *rotunds*, *round*, *rote*, *roll*, *roulette*, *rowel*, *rotogravure*, *control*, *rotiform*, *rotor* and *rotary*. It's easy to see why *rodeo* comes from this same source. In Spanish (and also in one of its English uses) it means 'round-up'.

And now it behoves us to finish our list of Latin-English words ending in *a*.

Sagitta	simia	tibia	umbra
salina	spatula	tinea	ungula
saliva	spica	toga	vertebra
saturnalia	stamina	transenna	via
scintilla	stria	trivia	villa
sedilia	tela	tuba	viola
sepia	tessera	ulna	viscera
serra	testa	ultra	
seta	tiara		

Sagitta literally means 'arrow'. It is a small northern constellation and also a sign of the zodiac.

Some leaves are said to be *sagittate* because they are shaped like arrowheads. *Sagittal* is another adjective in this family.

Scintilla meant 'a spark' to Vergil. We use it figuratively today to mean 'the slightest particle or trace'. For example, we might say,

41

'The prosecutor doesn't have a *scintilla* of evidence.'

But the verb *scintillate* really keeps the spark alive. It means 'to emit sparks; to twinkle or sparkle'. Here again we have extended the scope. Sports writers often report that a certain player *scintillated* in the game.

Sedilia is the plural of *sedile*, the Latin word for 'seat'. Like many other words from ancient Rome, it has been preserved by the church. It is defined as 'a set of seats, near the altar, for the officiating clergy'.

More interesting is the amazing number of descendants of *sedere* ('to sit'). Here are some of them: *seance, sedentary, sediment, session, siege, assess, assiduous, dissident, obsess, preside, reside, subsidy, saddle* and *supersede*.

By the way, if you remember that *supersede* literally means 'sit above', you will never misspell the verb.

Simia means 'ape' in Latin. Today it is a Linnaean genus, restricted to the Barbary ape. Its oft-used offshoot is *simian*. Any ape or monkey is a *simian*.

Spatula is a Low Latin diminutive of *spatha* ('blade or broad sword'). The Romans borrowed *spatha* from the Greeks. Bakers, plasterers and nurses use *spatulas* today in different ways. They might be surprised to know that the word is related to *spade, spay* and even *epaulette*.

Stamina has a fascinating history. In Greek mythology, the Fates spun the thread of human life. This thread, or warp, was called *stēmōn*. The Romans latched on to the three goddesses and changed their names from Clotho, Lachesis and Atropos to Nona, Decuma and Morta. They also transliterated *stēmōn* into *stamen*, and the plural became *stamina*.

Today a stamen is a vital, pollen-bearing organ of a flower. *Stamina* means 'endurance'. If your corporeal threads are strong and resistant to tugging and pulling, you've got *stamina*!

Tiara is thought to be of Oriental origin. It was the headdress of the ancient Persians. The Greeks assimilated the word, and the Romans borrowed it from them. Today it has many meanings. It can be a coronet, or a woman's crownlike headdress, or the Pope's triple crown.

Toga came from *tegere* ('to cover'). The *toga virilis* was a robe symbolizing manhood and was draped on Roman boys when they reached the age of fourteen. From then on they wore their *togae* in public. Today the word is used to mean 'a professional, official or academic gown'. An American judge wears a *toga* when he presides at court.

Through its parent verb, *toga* has a fascinating variety of siblings. *Tile, detect, integument, thatch, protect* and *tegular* are some members of the family. A *detective,* by the way, takes away your cover, but a *protector* provides cover for you.

Tuba in ancient Rome was a straight war trumpet. Figuratively, it meant 'an exciter or instigator'. You can see why. Today the *tuba* is a conical brass instrument with an oompah-oompah sound. *Tube* is a close relative.

Umbra has many meanings in Latin ('shade, shadow, ghost, faint trace'). It still means a 'shade or shadow' and is used by astronomers to mean 'the dark cone of shadow projecting from a planet or satellite on the side opposite the sun'. It also means 'the dark central part of a sunspot'.

Obviously, *umbrella* is a derivative through Italian, and lexicographers assume that the pigment *umber* and the fish of the same name owe their heritage to *umbra.* Certainly *umbrage* does. That word has two completely different connotations: (1) 'shade giving foliage' and (2) 'offence or resentment'.

Ungula was 'a hoof' in Cicero's day. To Plautus it meant 'the claw of a hen, vulture or eagle' — in other words, 'a talon'. The poet Horace extended the scope of the noun and used it as a synonym for horse.

Zoologists still use *ungula* to mean 'a hood or claw'. They also use *unguis* in the same sense. An *ungulate* is a hoofed animal, such as a horse.

A delightful cousin is *unguiculate* — a mammal having claws or nails.

Does *unguent* come from the same source? No, it's from *unguere* ('to anoint').

Villa is one of those rare words that have lived through the centuries with little or no change in meaning. In Caesar's time it was a country house. In Italy, France and all English-speaking countries that definition still exists, although the British have extended it to mean 'a suburban, middle-class house'. *Ville* as an offshoot is reflected in the names of many towns.

It's obvious that *villa* has sired our word *village.* But did you know that *villain* comes from the same source? In Medieval England he was a *villein,* a serf working for a lord who owned a grand estate. The rich looked down on this poor fellow and felt they couldn't trust him. Hence he devolved into a scoundrel.

Viscera is the plural of *viscus*, a Latin noun for 'inner part of the body'. Today we speak of having a 'gut feeling' about someone or something. We also talk about '*visceral*' sensations, as when we are zoomed down a roller coaster or subjected to a horror film. The adjective *visceral* has come to mean 'unreasoning'. It also has the connotation of 'earthy or raw' and even 'intensely emotional'.

The exceptional reader who is eager to learn more about words that I don't discuss here is invited to consult his dictionary concerning the following:

azalea	Gloria	propaganda	uvea
cornucopia	intelligentsia	Quadragesima	uvula
diploma	peninsula	tantara	visa

Let us get on to words that ended in *or* in ancient Rome and still do — in America anyway — today. In Britain some of them end in *our* and I have inserted those forms in brackets. I have selected a group of fifty-two, most of which I discuss below. Here is the first half:

agitator	creator	error	junior
anterior	curator	excelsior	lector
arbor (arbour)	dictator	exterior	liberator
censor	doctor	fulgor	major
clamor (clamour)	dolor (dolour)	imperator	mediator
clangor (clangour)	donator	inferior	
color (colour)	emptor	interior	

Agitator in Vergil's time meant 'a driver of cattle'. To Cicero he signified 'a charioteer or competitor in the games at the Circus Maximus'. The noun stems from *agitare* ('to put in motion'). In our century an *agitator* is considered to be a sort of radical. He tries to stir up people concerning social or political causes.

Anterior and its kin are a very interesting family. The word is the comparative form of *ante* ('before'). It can be interpreted to mean 'a little before'. Today it is defined as 'situated toward the front', and it's the opposite of *posterior.*

The basic word *ante* is used in card games. Players must *ante up* before they receive their cards. Today we employ *ante* as a prefix, just as the Romans did; examples are *antecedent, antedate, antemeridian* (a.m.) and *antenatal.*

Best of all is *antepenultimate* ('third last'). Literally this word means 'before the almost last'. The *antepenult* in the word *usufructuary* is the syllable pronounced 'choo'. What's a *usufructuary*? He's one who enjoys the right of using all the advantages and profits of another person's property. *Fructus* is a Latin word for 'fruit, enjoyment or profit'. When seeds *fructify*, they bear fruit.

Arbor means 'tree' in Latin. That signification is carried forward each year, usually on the last Friday in April, when we plant trees on Arbor Day.

But we have expanded the original definition. An *arbour* now means 'a place shaded by trees, or a bower'. A lovely adjective from this source is *arboraceous* ('wooded or treelike'). And when a young tree starts to spread its branches, it is *arborescent.*

Censor was originally a Roman magistrate appointed to take the census. Later he became what he is today — an official supervising public morals. In modern times we also use the word as a verb meaning 'to ban after examination'. A related adjective is *censorious* ('severely critical'). The verb or noun, *censure,* is a member of this judgmental family.

Clamor is a Latin noun meaning 'a loud call; a shout'. *Clamour* in English has virtually the same import — a loud outcry; an uproar. The parent verb is *clamare* — to call or cry out. From this source we have obtained *acclaim, declaim, exclaim, proclaim* and *reclaim. Claim, claimant* and *clamorous* are other members of this group.

Clangor is also a Latin noun that we have taken over. We have also shortened it to *clang* and lengthened it, as an adjective, to clangorous — noisy and resounding. This family provides a good example of *onomatopoeia.* The sound of the word suits its sense. Other examples are *boom, buzz, cuckoo, hiss, murmur, tinkle* and *whir.* Literally, in Greek, *onomatopoeia* means 'the making of a name'. Its second root has appropriately given us such words as *poem, poet* and *poetry.*

Colour comes right down to us from ancient Rome with its original sense practically intact. It means 'complexion or hue' in Latin. Vergil and Horace used it to signify 'a beautiful complexion'. Another Latin extension of the meaning is 'artful concealment of a fault'. Hence some scholars relate it to *celare,* 'to conceal', and even claim that it is a cousin of *hell!*

Our use of *colour* as a verb does seem to relate to the Romans' idea of artful concealment. People who *colour* a story may be lying, offering excuses or glossing over important facts.

In the *colour* family, the Latin adjective is *coloratus.* The Italians lengthened the feminine form and used it to apply to ornamental passages in music. *Coloratura* is now a part of our language. One of its meanings is 'brilliant runs and trills displaying a singer's skill'. Opera lovers revere *coloratura sopranos* like Beverley Sills and Joan Sutherland.

Creator, curator and *dictator* all have the same meanings today as they did in ancient Rome.

Of the three, *curator* is probably the most fascinating because of its origins and its cousins. It comes from *cura*, the Latin word for 'care'. A *curator* at a museum takes care of all the treasures therein. But let's examine the other offshoots. If a physician finds a *cure* for a patient, he literally took care. When I grew up in Jersey City under Mayor Hague, one of my many uncles had a *sinecure.* He was paid even though he never appeared on the job; literally, his post was without care. Your *manicurist* cares for your hands and your *pedicurist* for your feet. And when you are *secure* you are, literally, free from care.

When I was head recruiter for New York City schools, I was asked to *procure* teachers. Translated, that means 'care in a forward-looking way'. Colleagues gave me a ribbing, because a *procurer* is also a pimp.

A sibling of *procurer* is *procurator.* Originally he was a Roman official who managed the affairs of a province. Today he's a sort of agent or person employed to manage another's estate. In Scotland the *procurator fiscal* acts as public prosecutor. Procuration is synonymous with power of attorney.

Another offshoot is *proctor,* an academic term for an official who maintains order and supervises examinations at a higher institution of learning.

Amazingly enough, even *proxy* stems from our *cura* root. It's a variation of *procuracy,* the office of that Roman above. A *proxy,* too, is an agent, a person authorized to act for another.

It's not hard to see that *accurate* and *accuracy* come to us from this same exciting source. The words can be traced back to the prefix *ad* (changed to *ac*) and the verb *curare.* Translated, they signify 'to take care in relation to'.

Are *curious* and *curiosity* descendants also? Yes, indeed! The Romans broadened the original root into *curiosus* ('full of care'), which eventually came to mean 'too eager'. Hence, *curious!*

Probably the most delightful scion of *cura* and *curare* is that lovely adjective we have stolen from Italy — *pococurante*. Literally and actually, it means 'caring little'.

Now get ready for a real surprise! *Sure, assure, ensure* and *insure* can all be traced back to that fabulous Roman root. Your insurance agent may be amazed to hear that, as advertised, he really does care.

Doctor merits special attention. In Latin the word means 'teacher or instructor'. Its parent verb is *docere* ('to teach') and, like curare, it has given birth to a slew of English words.

Today most people think of physicians and surgeons as *doctors,* but the first meaning of the word in most lexicons is 'a person who holds the highest academic degree awarded by a college or university'.

One of the words stemming from *docere* is *docile* ('teachable; tractable; obedient'). Another is *docent.* He or she is either a college teacher not on the regular faculty or a tour guide at a museum. The latter definition reminds me of *cicerone,* a word we have taken over from the Italians. Because tour guides are so talkative, they reflect that great Roman orator Cicero.

Doctrine and *document* also come from this prolific source.

Dogma is listed earlier in this chapter under words ending in *a.* In Latin it means 'a philosophic tenet or doctrine', just as it does in English. An adjectival offshoot is *dogmatic.*

It should be pointed out that the foregoing words eventually can be traced back to the Greek *dokein* ('to think or seem'). This grandparent is also responsible for the following, among others:

doxology	hymn of praise to God; utterance of thanksgiving
doxological	giving praise to God
heterodox	departing from usual beliefs; inclining towards heresy
orthodox	conforming to the usual beliefs
paradox	seemingly contradictory statement
doxy	opinion or doctrine

Doxy — not from the same root but from Medieval Dutch — can also mean 'trollop or prostitute or loose wench', which gives point to the story that during a debate in the House of Lords, William Warburton (Bishop of Gloucester) whispered to Lord Sandwich: 'Orthodoxy is my doxy; heterodoxy is another man's doxy.'

That Greek verb *dokein* is also responsible, through the Romans' *decere* ('to be fitting'), for such words as *decent, decency, decor, decorate* and *decorous.*

At this point the reader may wonder if the Greeks also borrowed their words. The answer is that they often did. Like Latin, their language is part of the Indo-European family, which includes most of the tongues spoken in Europe and many of those spoken in India and southwestern Asia. As the Greeks conquered other lands, they enriched their own language with words from those countries. For example, when they invaded Persia they learned words of Aryan or Indo-Iranian origin. The Greeks were the first in Europe to make a scientific study of language, chiefly because they felt this would enhance their understanding of other fields of knowledge. Appropriately enough, our word *etymology* is of Greek origin.

But let us return to our list of words ending in *or.*

Dolor meant 'pain, anguish, distress or sorrow' to Cicero and Caesar. Our word *dolour* still carries those definitions. A derivative adjective is *dolorific* ('causing pain or grief'). More commonly used is *dolorous* ('woeful, deplorable, lugubrious').

What we need is a *dolorifuge* — something that banishes or mitigates grief.

Excelsior is the comparative form of *excelsus* ('lofty; high'). In that sense it is the motto of New York State and means 'Higher'. The reader may have guessed that *excel* and excellent come from the same root.

Exterior and *interior* are also comparative Latin forms. One comes from *exter* ('on the outside') and the other from *interus* ('inward'). Inferior also fits into this group. It is the comparative of *inferus* ('low or below'). People with an *inferiority complex* feel they are lower than others.

Fulgor has become archaic, but several of its relatives still sparkle in our dictionaries to remind us of its Latin meaning, 'the flashing thing':

effulgent	shining forth brilliantly; resplendent
fulgence	brilliant lustre
fulgent	dazzlingly bright; radiant
fulgurant	flashing like lightning
fulgurate	to emit flashes
fulguration	lightning flash; spiritual revelation or divine manifestation
refulgence	splendour; brilliance

Junior is a contracted comparative form of *juvenis* ('young'). A few of the other words from this source are *juvenile, rejuvenate* and, through the vagaries of crossbreeding, even *young* itself.

Most people who are *senescent* ('growing old') would rather be *juvenescent* ('becoming young or youthful'). Our salad days are the period of *juvenescence* ('youthful condition').

Lector meant 'a reader' in old Rome and especially 'a slave reading aloud at an entertainment'. Today he is certainly no slave but a professional who gives lectures at colleges and universities. He is also a person who reads the Scriptures aloud at a church service, standing at the *lectern*. Finally, he is a member of one of the minor orders of the Roman Catholic church.

The noun stems from *legere* ('to gather, pick out or read'), and once again we have encountered a fascinating family. Here are some members: *coil, collect, cull, diligent, elect, elegant, intellect, intelligence, lecture, legend, legion, neglect, negligence* and *select*.

Another remarkable offshoot of our root is *sacrilegious* (a word often misspelled with an *e* as the fifth letter because people confuse it with *religious*). The Romans had a noun *oaoriloguo* ('temple robber'). Thus the first definition for *sacrilege* in modern usage is: 'the act of appropriating to oneself or to secular use what is consecrated to God or religion'. That crime has been extended to mean any profanation.

One final gem emanates from *legere*. It is *sortilege*, a synonym for black magic or sorcery. The initial root is *sors* ('lot'). In one of its many senses a lot is an object used in deciding a matter by chance. In Rome an augur (or fortune-teller) would often cast lots and then gather them up again or *sort* them. Thus came to us the original meaning of *sortilege* — prophecy by casting lots.

Liberator means to us precisely what it meant to the Romans. In Latin and in English it is a deliverer. Naturally, *liberty* is a sibling, as well as *deliver* and *liberal*. Strangely enough, *livery* and *libertine* also belong. They come into the picture because of the parent verb *liberare* ('to set free').

Livery has many meanings today, among them:

1. the costume or insignia worn by retainers of a feudal lord
2. the uniform worn by male servants
3. the boarding and care of horses for a fee
4. a livery stable
5. a place where boats are hired out

The word came to us through the French, who often changed a *b* to a *v*. In Medieval English it was an allowance of food or clothes given free to servants.

A libertine in ancient times was a person who had been freed from slavery. In the 1500s a sect of freethinkers arose in Europe. They called themselves the *Libertines*. One of their tenets was that man cannot sin. Hence they indulged in wicked ways. From then on, libertine became identified with a dissolute person.

What about the *liberal arts*? In Latin those academic subjects are *artes liberales* ('arts befitting a freeman'), in contrast to *artes serviles*.

Liber ('free') and *liber* ('book') are sometimes confused. It's easy to see that *library* and *libretto* are derived from the latter, but *libel* must give us pause. It comes from a diminutive *libellus*, meaning 'a little book'. Since such a publication often turned out to be a lampoon*, it gave rise to the idea of a false or malicious statement.

Leaf is also an offshoot of the second *liber,* because the Latin word originally meant 'the inner bark or rind of a tree, or the pith of papyrus'. As is generally known, the leaves of ancient books were made from papyrus.

Another Latin verb that sometimes causes a mix-up is *librare* ('to poise or balance'). From this source we obtain *Libra,* 'the Scales' — a sign of the zodiac and a southern constellation.

Most interesting is the fact that *deliberate* comes from this source. When you deliberate about a problem, you literally weigh it in the scales.

Major is the Latin comparative of *magnus* ('great'). A *major* in the army holds a rank greater than that of a captain. In bridge a *major* suit like spades or hearts has greater weight than diamonds or clubs. And then there is a *major domo* (literally, 'chief of the house'), who is the top steward in a noble household. Nor must we forget *drum majors,* not to mention *drum majorettes.*

Of course *majority* is an esteemed descendant in a democracy. When the *majority* rules, the 'greater' number of people have had their say. And if you have reached your *majority* (full legal age), you are 'greater' than a juvenile.

Mediator is a Low Latin word for an intercessor. The verb

---

* *Lampoon* — a piece of strongly satirical writing, usually attacking or ridiculing someone. The probable source is the French refrain in a drinking song — '*Lampons!*' It means 'Let us drink [or guzzle]!'

mediare ('to be in the middle') and the adjective *medius* ('middle') have sired a goodly number of our words either in whole or in part. Some examples are the following: *mean* (in its arithmetical sense), *medial, median, medium, mizzenmast, intermediate, medieval, mediocre* and *mediterranean*.

Milieu joined the family in France. The first syllable is a shortening of *mid*, and *lieu* is the Gallic variation of *locus* ('place'). Literally, then, the word means 'middle place'. We have taken over one of its extended senses — namely, social surroundings; we use the word to mean 'environment'.

Another French derivative is *moiety*, meaning 'half'.

And now we come to the last list in this chapter on Latin-English words.

minor	rancor (rancour)	squalor	torpor
orator	rigor (rigour)	stridor	tremor
pallor	sapor (sapour)	stupor	tutor
pastor	senator	superior	ulterior
posterior	senior	tenor	victor
prior	spectator	terror	
procurator	sponsor	testator	

Minor is the comparative of the irregular Latin adjective *parvus* ('small'). The superlative is *minimus*, and the neuter form of that has given us *minimum*.

Two delicious words from *parvus* are *parvule*, 'a small pill', and *parvanimity*, 'meanness'. Literally it means the 'state of having a small mind' and it is the opposite of *magnanimity*.

Orator in Latin and English means 'speaker'. Would you believe that *adore* is its next of kin? Both words come from *orare*, a Latin verb with many meanings, among them 'to speak or pray'. *Adore* literally means 'to pray to'. Its verbatim sense persists in such definitions as 'pay divine honours to; revere'. But of course the scope of the verb has been broadened.

From the parent verb we have received other gifts. Among them are *oracle, oration* and *oratory*. The last of that trio has three meanings:

1. skill or eloquence in public speaking
2. a small chapel for prayer
3. a religious society of secular priests, especially the one founded in Rome by Saint Philip Neri in 1565.

From Saint Philip Neri's group we have derived the word *oratorio* — a long dramatic musical opus, usually having a religious theme. The reason is that the priests in the *Oratorio* in Rome often performed such compositions.

From *orare* also come *exorable* and *inexorable.* The former literally means 'to be prayed out', and it is easy to gather the literal sense of its antonym. *Exorable* has become obsolescent, but our linguistic inclination towards the negative has allowed *inexorable* to thrive. It means 'unrelenting', and is often applied to fate, doom, logic and judges.

Finally, there is *peroration* — the concluding part of a speech. *Perorate* means 'to end a speech', but it also carries the notion of declaiming at length, perhaps because so many speakers are long-winded.

To return to *orare,* in case some readers wonder whether *oral* is a derivative, the answer is no. That word comes from *os, oris,* which meant 'mouth' to a Roman.

Pallor means the same today as it did in Horace's era — wanness. Naturally the adjective *pale* is a descendant, and so is *pallid.* But the most enchanting scion is *appal.* Literally, that verb means 'to give wanness to'. If something *appals* you, it makes your face grow suddenly ashen.

Through the Spanish we obtain *palomino* — that cream-coloured horse with a silvery-white or ivory mane and tail. The steed's name comes from *paloma,* the Spanish word for dove, because of its greyish colour. But *paloma* itself is a daughter of our root *pallere* ('to be pale').

Did you know that *fallow* has two altogether different meanings? Probably the more popular one is 'left uncultivated or unplanted'. But the other adjective stems from our root and means 'pale yellow'. Somehow, through the ages, the initial *p* was changed to an *f.* Otherwise the *fallow deer* would be called a *pallow deer.*

One would expect *pall* to come from the root being discussed. It seems to have a wan significance. But its parent is *pallium* ('cover'), akin to *palla* ('a woman's mantle'). One of the meanings of *pall* in English is 'cloak or drape'. In that connection, *palliate* can be defined as 'cover with excuses'. In its most common usage it means 'to ease, allay or alleviate'.

Those whose interest has been aroused are invited to explore the separate derivations of *pallet, palette, pale* (as a noun meaning 'stake') and *palaeolithic.*

Pastor has taken on a religious significance. Today he is a priest in charge of a church or congregation. But in ancient Rome he was a shepherd. The transition is simple to follow. After all, clergymen often refer to their parishioners as 'the flock'.

But the adjective *pastoral* still remains its Latin heritage. Consequently its import has become expanded to signify 'rural'. As a noun it means 'a piece of literature dealing with the country'.

Of course *pasture* belongs to this family, all of which can be traced to *pascere* ('to feed'). Hence *repast* ('meal') joins the clan.

A fascinating offshoot is *pastern* — that part of a horse's foot that lies between the fetlock and the hoof. And an unpleasant cousin is *pester,* which is derived from an Old French word meaning 'to hobble a horse at pasture; to entangle'.

Prior means 'previous' in modern times, and it meant the same to Pompey. Since it also carried the idea of superior, it's not difficult to see why a *prior* is an official at a monastery. But even though he is a superior, he's not supreme. That adjective applies to his boss, the *abbot* — an Aramaic word meaning 'father'.

As expected, *priority* belongs in this group, and so does *a priori,* a phrase that sometimes means 'presumptive'. Thus *a priori* acceptance of a new work of art by a master is based on former experience.

Rigor in Latin and *rigour* in English both mean 'stiffness or severity'. Coroners talk of *rigor mortis* ('stiffness of death'). Of course *rigid* and *rigorous* are part of this group, and *frigid* is a distant relative.

From the French we have received *de rigueur,* a phrase meaning 'prescribed by etiquette, fashion or custom; proper'.

Sapor is another of those words that have survived in meaning and spelling without change, though east of the Atlantic it has become *sapour;* like a number of other words — *colour, honour, rigour* — it was modified by French influence as a result of the Norman Conquest. It has always meant 'flavour'.

I like *saporous* even though it's not often seen. It's a mellisonant synonym for tasty. *Sapid* is another, with its opposite *insipid.*

In old French, sapor suffered a change in the middle. The *p* changed to a *v,* and we inherited *savour,* with the adjective *savoury.*

Well, now, here's another surprise. The parent verb is *sapere* ('to taste, to have discernment; to be sensible'; and finally, 'to know or understand'. Therefore, through those French of long ago we find *savant* in the family. He's a learned person or eminent scholar. To mention still another kinsman, he is *sapient* ('wise'). He certainly is no *sap*!

Sponsor in Latin means 'one who promises solemnly for another; hence, a bondsman or surety'. That seems to be a far cry from the manufacturer who puts up the money for a TV programme. But a *sponsor* in a baptismal ceremony is a godfather or godmother, and those people do solemnly promise to look after the infant whenever needed.

From the parent verb, *spondere* ('to pledge or promise sacredly'), we have been given *respond, responsible, response, spouse, espouse, despondent* and *correspond*. When two people are *correspondents*, they literally make pledges back and forth together.

Squalor meant 'stiffness or roughness' to Lucretius, but the word took on another meaning, 'filthiness'. We also use the word as a synonym for wretchedness, and our adjective *squalid* has come to mean 'miserable or sordid' as well as 'foul and unclean'.

Stridor is derived from *stridere* ('to make a harsh sound'). In Latin and English the noun means 'a harsh, shrill or creaking noise'. Our most common acquaintance with this root is the adjective *strident*. But here are some other relatives, which we appear to be neglecting:

stridulation	a high-pitched, musical sound made by insects like grasshoppers or crickets by rubbing together certain parts of the body
stridulous	squeaky
stridulatory	able to stridulate; stridulous
stridulent	loud, blatant

Stupor originally meant 'amazement' in Latin. It came from the verb *stupere* ('to be astonished; to be struck senseless'). That latter connotation led to the idea of dullness or *stupidity*.

Today we use *stupor* as a synonym for numbness or lethargy. A drug addict or alcoholic has had his senses numbed so extremely that he falls into a state of *stupefaction*.

Our verb *stupefy* carries two meanings: 'to astonish, stun and bewilder' and 'to make dull'. Incidentally, the way to remember how to spell that word is to recall the original Latin verb. Probably the most interesting derivative is *stupendous*, which certainly has no dull significance.

54

The Greek word for numbness or *stupor* was *narke*. From it we obtained the noun or the adjective *narcotic*. A slangy shortening in America is *narc* or *nark* — a government agent investigating drug violations. But in Britain a *nark* is an informer or grass (dating back to a Sanskrit word for 'nose') and in Australia a *nark* is a killjoy or wet blanket.

Tenor comes from *tenere* ('to hold') — a verb that has sired scores of English words. It will be discussed later in this book. To the Romans, *tenor* was 'a holding on or holding out; hence, an uninterrupted course or career'. When we speak of 'the *tenor* of events', we use the word to mean 'course'. Other synonyms are, for example: intent, purport, tendency, and general meaning.

What about *tenor,* the male voice or the singer? The noun may seem to have no relationship with *tenere,* but it does, because the *tenor* voice was originally the one that held the melody in the singing or chanting or hymns.

Terror meant 'great fear' in ancient Rome, just as it does today. Our adjective *terrible* is an offshoot, but its import has been extended along with that of its synonyms, frightful and awful. Consider these two sentences:

I am in terrible trouble.
That singer has a terrible voice.

In the first statement the adjective retains the sense of its Latin root. In the second it means 'very inferior'.

A more astonishing change has occurred in the case of *terrific.* It still means 'causing terror' but is more commonly used to express just the opposite. If a friend reports, 'That horror film was *terrific!*' it would be a safe bet that he was not terrified by it, but enjoyed it immensely.

It may surprise you to learn that *deter* and *deterrent* belong to this fearsome family. Literally, *deter* means 'frighten away'. When a person is *undeterred* by difficulties or setbacks, he's not to be scared away.

Torpor is another of those ancient nouns that have survived the centuries without change in its spelling or meaning. Like *stupor,* it means 'lethargy or apathy'. Its adjective is *torpid,* and the verb *torpify* means 'to benumb'.

Best of all, we have *torpedo.* That was a Latin noun meaning 'numbness'. But it was also the name given to the crampfish or electric ray because of the creature's benumbing sting. Considering the effect of a direct hit by a modern *torpedo,* the person who named that projectile was right on the mark.

Tremor meant all the things to the Romans that it means to us — a shaking, quaking or quivering. Lucretius used it as a term for 'earthquake'.

Naturally *tremble* is in this family and also *tremulous* — quivering, palpitating; hence, fearful or timid. Through Italian we get *tremolo* — a quavering effect produced by rapid reiteration of the same tone.

Additionally, we have inherited *tremendous.* Just as with *terrific,* this adjective represents one of the rare instances in which we turn a negative idea into a positive one. *Tremendous* still means 'dreadful', but in popular usage it's a synonym for the words 'enormous' and — amazingly — 'delightful'.

The same phenomenon has occurred with regard to *wonderful* and *marvellous.* Originally both adjectives were used in the sense of awe-inspiring or astonishing. Although these definitions persist, most of us have forgotten them. Instead we use either of the two words as a substitute for 'excellent'.

Tutor to Horace and his contemporaries meant 'a watcher, protector, defender or guardian'. Today those connotations are present in the definition 'the guardian of a child below the age of puberty or majority'. But more often we consider a tutor to be a private instructor, as at universities perhaps, or at Eton College.

The Romans had *tutelary* gods who watched over them benevolently. The adjective still means 'serving as a guardian'.

Other descendants are tuition, tutelage ('protection or instruction'), *intuitive* and *intuition.* The last duo are in the family because of the parent verb *tueri* ('to watch with care').

Ulterior is the comparative of *ulter, ultra, ultrum* ('beyond'). It means 'further or more remote' in Latin and English. Thus it has come to connote 'beyond what is expressed'. We suspect *ulterior motives* — those that are hidden or undisclosed deliberately.

Note that *ultra* is in this group. It has become a prefix meaning 'beyond, excessive, to an extreme degree'. We use it in such words as *ultrasonic* and *ultraviolet.*

Victor completes our discussion of certain words in the list. As in Caesar's day, it means 'the winner or conqueror'. Boys named *Victor* are not meant to be losers, nor are those named *Vincent.* The parent verb is *vincere* ('to conquer or prevail'). The Queen-Empress Victoria seemed to live up to that linguistic heritage.

56

Remember Caesar's 'Veni, vidi, vici'? He came, he saw, he conquered. He *vanquished* his foes (a derivative from Old French). They were *vincible,* but he seemed to be *invincible.*

Other kinsmen of *victor* include *convict, conviction, convince* and *evict. Victim* is a distant cousin, but *vicious* is not related at all. It can be traced back to *vitium* ('a fault or defeat').

Those ancient Romans were *victors* in more ways than one. They not only conquered other peoples but they became the masters of the western linguistic world.

3   The Wild and the Tame

This chapter has nothing to do with animals. That section will come later. The intent here is to discuss two types of words in our language — those that seem to have no relation to their sources and are therefore 'wild', and the 'tame' words that adhere to their ancestry closely but are nevertheless exciting and fascinating.

Let's begin with some of the mavericks that have strayed far from the fold through semantic changes.

Would you believe that *salary* and *salt* are related? *Sal* is the Latin word for 'salt', and money given to the Roman soldiers for that commodity was called *salarium.* Later that word was applied to any stipend, allowance or pension.

I was once told that *sincere* came from *sine cera* ('without wax') — a plausible idea, but untrue. It's a derivative of *sincerus* ('clean, pure') and can be eventually traced back to the verb *creare* ('to create'). *Procreate* and *crescent* are two of its many cousins.

Vaccination and *pecuniary* have really gone astray. They both relate to cattle. The Latin word for 'cow' is *vacca.* Hence *vaccine* came into our language as an adjective meaning 'relating to cowpox'. When a preparation was found to fight the disease, the adjective also became a noun. The verb *vaccinate* naturally followed.

Incidentally, *vaccary* is a 'tame' word compared with its sisters. It's a cow pasture or even a dairy farm.

As for *pecuniary,* that adjective relating to money comes to us from *pecus* ('cattle'). When a Roman farmer achieved 'wealth in cattle' his status was called *pecunia.*

Peculate ('to steal money or to embezzle') comes from the same bovine root. If we took a *peculator* back to his true origin, we'd have to say he's a cattle thief rather than just any swindler. Similarly, if we wanted to be technical, we'd be forced to conclude that *impecunious* people don't own many steers. But of course the adjective means 'poor or penniless'.

Peculiar also dates back to those cattle. The Romans developed the word *peculium.* In Latin, and in legal English today, the word means 'private property'. Now, if some object or trait belongs to

58

you exclusively, it is *peculiar* to you.

But, as often happens, the meaning of the adjective has devolved. A person who has *peculiar* habits (in the original sense of the word) or who enjoys his privacy is considered to be odd or strange.

The synonym *eccentric* has suffered the same fate. This Greek derivative literally means 'out of the centre of the circle' and is used in that sense by astronomers and mathematicians. But people who are not in the centre of things, or who are off-centre, are regarded as strange. They're *peculiar*, whether they own cattle or not!

At the beginning of the chapter I mentioned *vaccination*. That reminds me of another word, which is often misspelled. When a doctor *inoculates* a child against smallpox, he literally puts an 'eye' into the tot's skin. If you remember that *oculist* and *monocle* are related to *inoculation*, your orthography will be correct.

The problem seems to arise because of the spelling of *innocuous* ('harmless'). That word is also easy to handle if you keep the derivation in mind. It stems from *nocere* ('to harm'): the prefix means 'not'. *Innocent* comes from the same source, and so does *noxious* ('harmful').

An evil cousin is the adjective *pernicious* ('deadly'). It stems from *necere* ('to kill'). Both *nocere* and *necere* owe their origin to the Greeks. In Athens, *nekros* meant 'dead body'.

There are several rather scary words from this root. Here is a selection:

necrology	obituary; list of recently deceased people
necromancy	black magic
necrophilia	erotic attraction to corpses
necrophobia	morbid fear of dead bodies
necropolis	cemetery
necropsy	post mortem

The Romans' equivalent, *corpus*, has been discussed in a previous chapter. Somewhat allied in meaning is *caro, carnis* ('flesh or piece of flesh'). In English, *carnal* means 'bodily or in the flesh'. Because of its non-spiritual import it has come to mean 'sensual or sexual'. *Carnal knowledge* is sexual intercourse.

Some obvious words from the *carn* root are:

carnage	bloody slaughter
carnelian	red variety of quartz; flesh-red colour

carnivorous	flesh-eating
carrion	decaying flesh of a dead body
charnel	(through Old French) a building or place where corpses or bones are deposited; usually called a *charnel house*
incarnate	in the flesh (as in the saying 'the Devil *incarnate*'); personified

But there are some 'wild' words in this group too. Because of its colour the lovely *carnation* has joined the family. And then there is a *caruncle* ('a naked, fleshy outgrowth — as a bird's wattle'). What'll they think of next?

Carnival is probably the most enchanting descendant. Its original English meaning is still in use; it's a synonym for Shrovetide, the period before Lent. The second part of the word comes from *levare* ('to raise or remove'). In old Italian, *carnelevare* meant 'the putting away of flesh', when the fasting period called Lent rolls around.

Since there was much merrymaking just before Lent, *carnival* took on a festive sense, and soon it was applied to any travelling amusement show that appeared at a feast. Some lexicographers, however, suggest that the ending of *carnival* is a shortened form of *vale* ('farewell') — thus, 'farewell to meat'.

Crone is related to *carrion*; hence that withered old hag can truly be said to have decaying flesh.

Among my favourite 'wild' words are *sinister* and *dexterous* (sometimes spelt *dextrous*).

The popular meaning of *sinister* today is 'wicked, evil' or 'most unfavourable'. The Latin adjective meant 'left, on the left hand or side'. But, like many people in our time, the Romans also had their superstitions and prejudices. Since left-handed people were in the minority, they had to be 'awkward or perverse'. Gradually the connotations grew worse. *Sinister* came to mean 'unlucky' and finally 'evil' — a sense that we have retained.

However, a few authorities point out that when Roman augurs began to emulate their Greek predecessors and face north on auspicious occasions, the East (or lucky side) was on their right. Hence the opposite side — or *sinister* — had to be unlucky or evil.

Dexter, in Latin, means 'right, to the right side'. The word remains the same as an adjective in our modern English dictionaries and retains the same sense. But it also means 'auspicious or fortunate'. Considering the above story about the augurs, you can see why *dexter* continues to have a lucky significance. And if you buy the idea of bias in favour of right-handed people, you can see why dexterity came to mean 'skill in using one's hands'.

Anyone who is *ambidextrous* is equally skilful with right or left hand.

Twice in the above paragraphs the word *auspicious* has been used. It deserves to be classified as 'wild' because we no longer think of birds when we use the adjective, yet it has its roots in *avis-spicere* ('to see a bird').

In Rome an *auspex* was an augur, or seer, who watched for omens in the flights of birds. Apparently these diviners found good signs more often than bad ones. In any case, *auspicious* has come to mean 'favourable, boding well for the future, propitious'.

Auspices of course comes from the same source. It has come to mean 'patronage'. If a programme on TV were to be shown under the *auspices* of the Royal Society for the Protection of Birds, that would be a perfect match!

Mention has been made above of *omen, diviners* and *propitious.* Let's take a look at that futuristic trio.

Omen is a Latin word meaning 'prognostic sign'. In English an *omen* is a thing or happening that's supposed to predict what is to come — good or bad. But its adjective, ominous, leaves out the good and clings to the bad. It means 'threatening'.

Diviners are perforce a revered group. Their root is *divus,* the Latin noun for 'a god'. Those soothsayers should not be mixed up with *divines* ('clergymen, theologians, priests'), nor should they be equated with *divas* — from the same root.

But it's fascinating to note that certain farewells — the French *adieu,* the Spanish *adios* — are members of this family. When you bid farewell to your friends in Paris or Madrid, you commend them to God.

Propitious literally means 'seeking forward'. Its parent verb is *petere* ('to seek'). If you examine the word you will see that hope really does spring eternal within the human breast, because it means 'favourable'.

Some 'tame' words from the *petere* root are petition, compete and competitor. It's easy to discern the seeking quality of that trio.

Because *petere* also means 'to rush at', *impetus* presents no problem, nor does that adjectival offshoot, *impetuous.* But *petulant* ('peevish') requires a bit more cogitation, and so do its relatives *perpetual* and *repeat.*

61

The most appetizing member of this Latin family is *appetite* (literally, 'a seeking or rushing toward'). Come and get it!

When *competitor* was mentioned above, I immediately thought of *rival* — and what a 'wild' word that is! The fact that it comes from *rivalis* ('of a brook') seems incredible. Actually, *rivalis* soon became a noun in ancient Rome. It meant 'one living near or using the same stream as another'. Then it came to mean 'a neighbour' and eventually 'one who has the same mistress as another', as in Sheridan's famous play THE RIVALS.

A relation of *rivus* ('brook') is *ripa* ('bank'). From these consanguineous roots we get a strange variety of English words. For example, *arrive* literally meant 'to come to the bank' — hence, 'to reach the shore'. *Derive* carried the idea of diverting a stream from its channel. *River* of course belongs in this immense family. Strangely enough, so does *rive,* and we can even trace the *Rhein* back to those roots. *Rivulet* is a tiny relation. But the most interesting of all is *riparian* ('of, adjacent to, or living on river banks').

Cousins of this tribe, by the way, are *ripe, rip* and *row* (the last meaning 'a line of adjacent seats'). Some words certainly do go astray as time moves on.

Another 'wild' word is *ambulance.* When you think of this vehicle speeding towards a hospital, it's hard to imagine that the word comes from *ambulare* ('to walk'). We owe the word to the French medicos of Napoleon's era. They developed the *hôpital ambulant* (literally, 'walking hospital'), which travelled from place to place on the battlefield to help the wounded. The British, and then the Americans, took over the idea and called the vehicle an *ambulance.*

But the original sense of *ambulare* persists in *ambulatory* and *ambulant.* Those adjectives both mean 'able to walk, itinerant, peripatetic'. Today most postoperative patients are encouraged by their surgeons to be *ambulatory* as quickly as possible. They are urged into *ambulation* ('walking').

Amble ('saunter') and *perambulate* ('walk about') are derivatives. A baby carriage is called a *perambulator* (or *pram* for short) because the infant's mummy strolls around with it.

Itinerant and *peripatetic* appeared a few paragraphs ago. These are interesting words.

Iter ('road') is the Latin root for the first of the duo. *Itinerant* can be used as an adjective or noun, meaning 'travelling from place to place, or traveller'. A travel agent may prepare an *itinerary* for one who is about to *itinerate*.

Peripatetic means 'walking about from place to place or travelling on foot'. As a noun the word means an *itinerant*. When capitalized, *Peripatetic* pertains to the philosophy or methods of Aristotle, who conducted discussions while walking about in the Lyceum of ancient Athens. But his teachings were not *pedestrian* — another 'tame' word that has sometimes a 'wild' connotation. *Pedestrian* (from Latin *pes*, 'foot') means walking, and because walking is considered to be less exciting than speeding around in a vehicle *pedestrian* has come to mean 'prosaic, commonplace, undistinguished, ordinary'.

Exotic is another example of how usage adds to the meaning of a word or changes it radically. In Athens *exo* meant 'outside', so the Greeks developed the word *exotikos* and the Romans transliterated it into *exoticus*. In either case it meant 'foreign'.

We still retain 'foreign or strange' as the definition for *exotic*, but because the unfamiliar excites our curiosity, we have extended the sense of the adjective. It's probable that many people don't realize that *exotic* means 'foreign', but they do know that it has the following connotations:

1. strikingly and intriguingly unusual or beautiful
2. mysterious, romantic, picturesque, glamorous
3. strangely lovely, enticing, exciting.

The *ped* root we met in *pedestrian* has many descendants. Some are easy to recognize — for example, *pedal* and *pedestal*. The *centipede* and the *millipede* are instances of exaggeration; one does not have a hundred feet, nor the other a thousand. But the Latin source is simple to discern.

Expedite doesn't cause a problem either when you dig into its literal meaning — to free one caught by the feet. The definitions 'to hasten or speed up or facilitate' fit the roots perfectly. The same is true of *impede* and *impediment*.

Relatives of *expedite*, by the way, are *expediency, expedience, expedition* and *expeditious*.

A fascinating descendant is *pedigree*. This synonym for family tree came to us via Medieval French. *Pié de grue* meant 'crane's foot'. Because of the resemblance of the lines in a genealogical

63

drawing to the feet of cranes, the French designation certainly seems apt.

Pawn, meaning 'chessman', is one of the 'wilder' words in this family. *Pedo, pedonis* meant 'foot soldier' in the Middle Ages. Later it was used as a term for 'one who has flat or broad feet'. Through Medieval French and English the word was changed to *poon* and then *pown*; finally it made its way to the chessboard as *pawn.* Since the piece can move only one space at a time, its medieval senses are appropriate.

It may surprise you to hear that *pioneer* is next of kin to *pawn,* again through the Latin word for 'foot soldier'. In Medieval France another alteration of *pedo* was *pionier.*

How did our idea that a *pioneer* is an early settler come about? Well, originally he was a soldier who constructed or demolished bridges or built roads for the army. Since he went ahead of the rest of the troops, a *pioneer* soon became identified as one who prepared the way for others.

One of our 'tame' words is Greek-rooted — *antithesis,* 'exact opposite'. Love is the *antithesis* of hate. This word is 'tame' because it reflects its source rather neatly: *anti* ('against') and *tithenai* ('to set or place'). Because of the vagaries of linguistic history, it's astonishing to note that our verb 'do' is related to the verbal root of *antithesis.*

Some other words in this Attic family are *thesis, hypothesis* and *parenthesis.*

Epithet is an interesting derivative. It literally means 'something put on or added'. When we use a word or phrase to describe a person, place or thing, we are employing an epithet. Examples are: Richard the Lion-hearted; Rome, the Eternal City; and the 'ox-eyed one' (Homer's term for Hera).

Apothecary is another offshoot of *tithenai.* The Romans borrowed the Greek word *apothēkē* and came up with *apotheca* ('storehouse'). In the early days, therefore, an *apothecary* was a fellow working in a warehouse. He was literally 'a person who put things away'. Later, people began to employ his appellation as a synonym for shopkeeper. In Shakespeare's day he was a druggist or chemist. As Romeo drinks the poisonous potion he cries: 'O true apothecary!/Thy drugs are quick.'

While checking on *apothecary* I have discovered that *boutique* is in this family. Now, that's really a 'wild' one, but not so hard to fathom if you remember the French penchant for changing some letters into other letters. Go back a paragraph and gaze on that Greek storehouse. Drop the initial letter and change the second letter from *p* to *b*. It begins to make sense, especially when the idea that an *apothecary* was once a shopkeeper is kept in mind.

In case you have lost track, this section of the chapter began with *antithesis* and *antithetical*. Last but not least of the relations that I have chosen to include is *bibliotheca* ('a library or collection of books').

The first root of that word has given us a cluster of delectable entries in our dictionaries. Aside from *bibliomania, bibliophile* and *bibliophobe* (covered in other chapters), here are some other gems to add to your treasury:

Biblicist	scholar specializing in the Scriptures
biblioclast	destroyer or mutilator of books
bibliofilm	microfilm for photographing pages of books
bibliognost	person having thorough knowledge of books
bibliogony	production of books
biblioklept	one who steals books
bibliolater	a book worshipper
bibliolatry	worship of the Bible; extravagant devotion to books
bibliomancy	divination by books, especially the Bible
bibliopegist	bookbinder
bibliopole	bookseller
bibliotaph	person hiding or hoarding books
bibliotherapy	guidance in psychiatry through selected reading
bibliotist	expert in handwriting and in determining authenticity of authorship

If you really examine the above list and then refer to your lexicons for words related to the second roots, you will find a host of other words that we have inherited from the Greeks. For instance, I can think of *iconoclast, agnostic, idolater, epitaph* and *psychotherapy*. The *mancy* source alone has given us scores of words like *chiromancy, hydromancy, pyromancy* and so on. The diviners do seem to be multifarious and multitudinous.

But let us return to our Latin extractions. *Companion* captivates me. Literally, it means 'bread fellow' or 'one who breaks bread with another'. *Panis* ('bread') is the basic root.

Some *companions*, however, are not necessarily buddy-buddy. They have been *incarcerated* in the same cell block. That verb comes from the Romans' *carcer* ('prison or gaol').

Americans spell that word *jail.* Why? They preferred to accept a variation of the Middle English *jaiole,* while the English adopted the Norman French *gaole.*

Incidentally, as you follow the discourse in this book, notice how often our immediate ancestors have tended to shorten words as much as possible. In the above instances a final vowel has been dropped, and in *jaiole* another vowel has been eliminated.

Would you suspect that *cancel* bears any relationship to *incarcerate*? Indeed it does! The Latin word *cancer* means 'lattice', and it's an alteration of *carcer.* Then came the diminutive *cancelli* ('screens usually made of latticework') — a word that has found a niche in our language. When writers, editors, musicians et al decided to omit a passage, they drew horizontal and vertical lines over it, thus forming a pattern that looked like a lattice. In other words, they *cancelled* the passage.

Note that another Latin *cancer* means 'crab'. As a sign of the zodiac it retains that sense. The Romans borrowed it from the Greek noun *karkinos,* the source of our word *carcinoma* ('cancerous growth').

Additionally, *candidate* deserves attention because it has such an astonishing background. It comes from *candidatus* ('clothed in white'). Apparently the Romans who sought public office wanted people to picture them as pure as the driven snow.

Candid comes from the same root. The parent verb is *candere* ('to shine'). In English the adjective is still sometimes used as a synonym for white, but because that so-called colour is associated with purity and clarity, *candid* is commonly employed to mean 'frank, very honest, forthright or even blunt'. Would that all our *candidates* spoke with *candour.*

Candle and *incandescent* are members of this radiant clan. *Incense* and *incendiary* are cousins through a related verb, *cendere* ('to burn').

At this point let me comment on the fact that colour bias seems to be built into our language. Consider the following words and definitions extracted from various reputable dictionaries:

black	soiled; dirty, evil; wicked; harmful; disgraceful; sorrowful; dismal; gloomy; disastrous; sullen; angry (as black looks); deep-dyed (as a black villain)
blackball	exclude socially; ostracize

Black Death	deadly disease in the fourteenth century
blacken	speak evil of; defame; slander
blackguard	contemptible scoundrel; villain
Black Hand	lawless Sicilian secret society
blackheart	disease of potato tubers
blackleg	member of a trade union who works during a strike
blacklist	list of persons who are disapproved of or who are to be punished or discriminated against
blackmail	practise extortion
Black Maria	police van for transporting prisoners
black mark	unfavourable mark on one's record
black market	place or system for selling goods illegally
Black Mass	blasphemous parody of the Mass by worshippers of Satan
black sheep	person regarded as less respectable or successful than the rest of the family or group

There ought to be a way to eliminate some of the above. Maybe we should boycott them. Someone has suggested a better way — change the first syllable to *white*, or if that's too drastic, use a variety of hues. Thus a villain would become a *bluegard*, or an extortioner a *purplemailer*. It certainly would be colourful.

Some readers may regard the foregoing paragraphs as *supererogatory* — a high-sounding adjective if I ever saw one. It means 'going beyond what is needed or expected'. The related verb is *supererogate* ('to do more than duty requires'). It can be analysed as follows: *super* ('above'), *e* ('out'), *rog* ('ask'), *ate* (common suffix for English verbs). Now, I suggest that you put the parts together in terms of the meaning. You will see that it is one of our 'tame' words.

Subpoena is a conformist too. Literally, it means 'under penalty'. Anyone *subpoenaed* to appear in court must do so or pay the penalty.

What's most interesting about that word is that it has not been changed to *suppoena*. The retention of the *b* is rare; the change to *p* in other cases is common — for example:

supplicate	to petition earnestly; from *sub-plicare* ('to fold'). When you supplicate you 'fold under' or bow.
supplant	to take the place of; from *sub-planta* ('sole of the foot'). The Romans developed the verb *supplantare* ('to put under the sole of the foot; to trip up').
support	to carry the weight of; from *sub-portare* ('to carry')

In fact, one might even expect *subpoena* to have been changed to *suppena*, because diphthongs are often shortened to one vowel in the transition to English. *Penal, penalize* and *penalty* are examples. They all come from the same source as *subpoena*.

Other words in this group include *pain, impunity, penologist* ('specialist in criminal reform or gaol management'), *punish, penance* and *penitentiary*.

But *pen* and *pencil* have no relation to the above or to each other. Early writing instruments, such as quills, were made from feathers. The Latin word for feather was *pinna* (an alteration of *penna*). *Pencil* comes from *penis,* the Latin word for 'tail'. The diminutive of that word is *pencillus.*

Before we leave words that start with *pen,* a few more deserve mention. In Latin, *paene* means 'almost', and *insula* means 'island'. I live on a *peninsula* in Massachusetts. It's not quite an island because of a little piece of ground, no wider than ten feet, that serves as a road to my home. In winter, whenever the fury of the storms and the height of the tides combine, my wife and I become *isolated.* That's a verb derived from *isola,* the Italian noun for 'island'.

I was about to say 'We become *insulated,*' and I would have been correct, because that word may be used as a synonym for *isolated.* But in modern times we tend to think of *insulation* as material that retards the passage of heat out of a house or deters the cold blasts from entering. It forms an *insular* or *islandish* barrier.

Penultimate is another delightful word from our *paene* root. It means 'next to the last'. If you reach the *penultimate* chapter of this book, you will have almost completed your perusal.

The geographical significance of *peninsula* reminds me of *Orient* and *Occident.* One comes from *oriri* ('to rise') and the other from *occidere* ('to sink or set'). Since the sun rises in the East and sets in the West, it is no accident that *Orient* and *Occident* are proper nouns today.

Sanguinary means 'bloody, bloodthirsty, murderous', but *sanguine* has come to mean 'confident or optimistic'. Why has the latter become one of our 'wild' words? Well, a ruddy complexion, in medieval physiology, suggested a warm, passionate or cheerful temperament. The idea has persisted to this day. If you are *sanguine* about the future, you have high hopes; but if you think that *sanguinary* events await us, you foresee bloodshed.

Consanguinity ('blood relationship') belongs in this group, as does its adjectival form. Cousins, for example, are *consanguineous.*

This leads us to *primogeniture* ('the condition or fact of being the first to be born of the same parents'). The roots are *primus* ('first') and *gignere* ('to beget'). In law this word has much importance. It applies to the exclusive right of the eldest son to inherit his father's estate.

Contumely has a very interesting background. Lexicographers assume that it is rooted in *tumere* ('to swell') and in earlier years meant 'puffed-up, arrogant speech'. Today the word means 'insult or humiliation' — Hamlet speaks of 'the proud man's *contumely*'. It is not to be confused with its relative *contumacy,* defined as 'stubborn rebelliousness, disobedience or insubordination'.

Let's look at some of the kin:

tumescent	swelling up
tumid	swollen, bulging; hence, pompous or bombastic
tumour	bodily swelling
tumefacient	causing swelling
tumefaction	a swollen part
detumescence	a lessening of a swelling

But here are some of the 'wilder' relatives:

tuber	fleshy part of an underground stem, as a potato
tuberculosis	infectious disease
protuberate	to bulge
truffle	fleshy fungus regarded as a delicacy

As you can see, linguistic nuances and variations have caused us to rove around in this chapter. *Rove* is related to archery. In Medieval English, *roven* meant 'to shoot at random'. The expression *at rovers* signified 'haphazardly', and *rover* itself meant 'a random mark at an uncertain distance used as an archer's target'.

Incidentally, some philologists point out that *rover* is a Middle Dutch synonym for robber. That makes sense, because one of the definitions for *rover* is 'pirate'.

The mention of pirates somehow calls up the adjective despicable, and the discussion on roving suggests *peregrine* to me. Let's take them in order.

Despicable means 'contemptible or vile'. The root of the adjective is *despicere* ('to look down upon').

Peregrine is from *peregrinari* ('to travel'). As an adjective it means 'roving or alien'. There is also a *peregrine* falcon, which is famous for its swiftness and its migratory habits. The basic root of this word is *ager* ('field'). Literally, it can be taken to mean 'beyond the borders of the field (or home)'.

Now let me cite some of the members of this widely distributed unit. Through Old French we get *pilgrim.* Then of course there are *agriculture* and *agrarian.* The wild ass called the *onager* belongs, as does *acre.*

But I like *peregrinate* and *peregrination* best of all. They remind me of an activity that has always entranced me and millions of others — travel.

Because of this book I have been *procrastinating* my proclivity toward *peregrinism.* In other words, I have been putting off the pleasure until the future. The Latin word for 'tomorrow' is *cras.*

I don't mean to be *maudlin* about the matter, but the *crux* of the situation is that I would *decline* abroad and would be unable to withstand the *vicissitudes.* I'd be in such a dither that the *stewardess* on the plane would probably advise that I turn back as soon as I deplaned.

Admittedly, that's a devious way to introduce six words into this chapter, but it does permit me to elucidate concerning a fascinating octad. Now let us pursue them seriatim.

Maudlin means 'weakly emotional or tearfully sentimental, especially from too much liquor'. The word dates back eventually to Mary Magdalene, from the practice of representing her in paintings as a weeping penitent. The connection in the spelling comes from *Maudelyne* in Medieval English.

Crux now means 'a puzzling problem or pivotal point'. In Caesar's day it signified 'a cross used for torture'. We get the word *crucial* from it.

Decline has several meanings today. One of them is 'to refuse an invitation'. In that sense it seems faithful to its original Latin sources: *de* ('away') and *clinare* ('to incline'). But it also means 'to deteriorate', because of a semantic change that ocurred years ago when the French developed *decliner* ('to sink') from the Latin root.

Vicissitudes are shifting circumstances; ups and downs. The word is derived from the Romans' *vicis* ('turn or change'). At first it may seem incredible that *vicar* is a relative. But the first meaning of that word is 'a person who acts in place of another; a deputy'. Today in various religions a *vicar* is a minister, parish priest or church officer. The Pope is called the *Vicar of Christ* because Roman Catholics believe he is God's earthly representative.

A kindred adjective is *vicarious* ('performed, received, enjoyed or suffered in place of another'). Sports fans who watch athletes receive *vicarious* thrills.

Vice-Presidents fall into this same category. They are, in truth, deputies for the elected chiefs. *Viceroy* ('deputy for a sovereign') is another member of the family.

Finally, *vice versa* ('conversely') belongs in this group. In Latin that phrase signifies 'the position being changed'.

Dither is a variation of *didder,* a dialect British word meaning 'quiver, shake or tremble'. We now use it to signify 'a state of strong excitement or agitation'. It should be noted that *dither* may also be used as a verb meaning 'to shake, waver or vacillate'.

Stewardess is the last and most interesting word in my paragraph about travelling abroad. *Steward* and *stewardess* have been ameliorated by the passage of time. A steward originally meant a 'sty ward' or 'keeper of the pigs'. Later he elevated himself to become the person in charge of the affairs of a large household or estate. He then got into the restaurant business as the man in charge of food and drink. Subsequently he expanded his scope to become a sports official. At sea he became an attendant looking after passengers' comfort. Finally he underwent a sex change and took to the air.

Feminists think these aircraft attendants should still be called *stewards.* On the whole I am in favour of the feminist movement. Just as our language discriminates against blacks, it may be subtly violating women's rights. But I am not sure how far we should go. Should we call Jane Fonda an *actor* rather than an *actress*? What about *waitress, seductress, temptress, countess, hostess, priestess, mistress, seamstress,* and so on? Where do we draw the line?

As for *trix,* I can see my way clear. Amy Johnson was just as fine an aviator as any man of her time. *Aviatrix* seems unnecessary, and so do *janitrix, spectatrix* (and its companion *spectatress*), *inheritrix, executrix, proprietrix* (and *proprietress*), *rectrix, curatrix,* and *administratrix.*

Whether or not *suffragettes* become just plain *suffragists* in the near or distant future, their heritage is fascinating but puzzling. Some authorities surmise that the word goes back to *suffragari* ('to use a broken piece of tile as a ballot').

That sounds correct, because *fra(n)gere* meant 'to break in pieces' in ancient Rome. However, other philologers opt for *sub* plus *fragor* ('loud noise or applause'), because of the early practice of voting by acclamation. Perhaps both sets of scholars are right.

Finally, have you ever seen a *saxifrage*? It's a perennial plant that grows in the crevices of rocks: *saxi* ('rock') and *frage* ('break'). Literally, this lovely flower is a 'rock breaker'. Therefore it's not surprising that it's also called a *breakstone*.

4 Roots, Branches and Twigs

A game I invented when I was an English teacher in Frederick Douglass Junior High School in New York, as a way of building the vocabulary of the young Harlemites in my class, was the Latin-English tree. First you draw a tree, and at its base you write in a Latin root — say *port,* from *portare* ('to carry'). Then, on the branches and twigs, you put in all the words you can think of that are derived from that root — *porter, report, portable, transport,* etc, etc. Here are some of the roots I doled out to my class, and some of the branches that grew from them:

ROOTS	SOME BRANCHES
duc, duct ('to lead')	duce, reduce, product, induction, deduce, duct, conductor, abduct, ducal, duchess, duke, introduce, seduce, educe, conducive, educate, viaduct, aqueduct
voc, voke ('to call')	invoke, provoke, revoke, evoke, convoke, vocal, vocation, vocabulary, vocalize, provocative, avocation, advocate, equivocate
dic, dict ('to say')	diction, edict, predict, dictaphone, dictator, addict, indict, indicate, contradict, dictionary, verdict, dictum, benediction, jurisdiction, valedictory
scrib, script ('to write')	scribe, scribble, inscribe, subscribe, prescribe, describe, transcribe, ascribe, script, Scriptures, circumscribe, postscript, inscription, prescription, description, transcript, conscription
mov, mot ('to move')	move, remove, remote, motion, motor, movement, commotion, emotion, demote, promote, motel, motivate, automotive
ven, vent ('to come')	advent, avenue, adventure, circumvent, convene, convent, convention, event, eventual, intervene, invent, prevent, revenue, supervene, vent, venture
spec, spect ('to look at')	spectacle, spectator, inspection, respect, suspect, prospect, speculate, introspection, retrospect, aspect, spectrum, circumspect, expect, perspective

ROOTS	SOME BRANCHES
vert, verse ('to turn')	verse, version, revert, reverse, convert, converse, invert, inversion, subvert, supervision, introvert, extrovert, pervert, perversion, contravert, divert, diversion, versus, vertigo, transverse, universe, avert, anniversary, controversy, adverse, adversary
tend, tent ('to stretch or strive')	contend, tend, tendon, tent, attend, attendant, attention, tense, distend, extend, intend, pretend, pretense, ostensible, extensive, intention, portend, portent
pon, pose ('to place')	component, compose, composition, composure, composite, depose, repose, suppose, supposition, impose, purpose, proposal, dispose, disposition, expose, exposition, exponent, postpone, transpose, interpose, position, preposition, positively, proposition

One thing leads to another when a classroom project really makes a hit. The next step was to show the importance of the prefixes and suffixes. I called them 'our twigs'.

Conductor and *composer* provided the initial impetus. I explained that the prefixes meant 'together' and that *con* always changes to *com* before the letters *b, f, m* and *p.* The 'one who' idea carried by *or* and *er* was easy for the boys to see. They had already been exposed to *porter.*

Here are some of the prefixes we discussed:

PREFIX	MEANING
con, com, co, cog, etc.	together, with, jointly
re	back, again
mis	badly, mistakenly, wrongly, incorrect
a, ab	not, away
de	down
dis, di, dif, etc.	away, not, apart
in, ig, im, etc.	very, into, not, without
per	through, throughout
pro	before, forward, on behalf of, in place of
sub, suf, sup, sur	under, beneath, below, somewhat
ad, ac, ag, ap, etc., *ob, oc, op,* etc.	against, toward, to
e, ef, ex	out of, away from, outside

74

PREFIX	MEANING
trans	across
ante	before
post	after
retro	backward
inter	between, among
intra, intro	within
super, sur	above, over and above, higher, extra

Sometimes prefixes can fool us. Note that *sur* (last on the above list) is an alteration of *sub* ('under') and a shortening of *super* ('above, over'). In such words as *surrogate* and *surreptitious* the prefix means 'under'. But in *surmount, surrealism, survey, surname, surplice* and *surplus*, for example, it's an abridgement of *super*.

Probably the most interesting word in this group is *surplice*. Today it's a loose, white, wide-sleeved outer vestment worn by the clergy and choir in some churches. But originally it was worn by clergymen of northern countries over their fur coats. In Medieval Latin it was called *superpellicum* ('over a fur coat').

And here are several of the suffixes:

SUFFIX	MEANING
tion, sion, ment, ness, tude, ation, ition	the act of or the state of
ive, al, ic	pertaining to
ous	full of; having
ate	to make or cause
ant, ent	one who; doing
ance, ancy, ence, ency	the quality or state of

Here are a number of words that emerge, using the root *grad, gress* ('to step, walk, go') and combining it with some of the above prefixes and suffixes:

WORD	LITERAL MEANING
aggressor	one who steps against
congressional	pertaining to the act of walking together
degradation	the act of stepping down
digression	the act of stepping away
graduation	the act of going
ingress	a walking in
progress	step forward

75

WORD	LITERAL MEANING
regress	step back
retrograde,	step backward
retrogress	
transgression	the act of stepping across

That last word merits attention. When we commit a *transgression,* we sin. Literally, we have stepped across the boundaries between right and wrong.

I have deliberately omitted *egress* from the above because of a story connected with it. As I recall the tale, P. T. Barnum had erected a large tent in a small town and had filled it with strange animals. The local people were enchanted. However, they hung around inside so long that there was little room for new customers to join the throng. So Barnum took down the *Exit* sign and replaced it with *To the Egress.* Thinking that some exotic bird lay behind that flap in the tent, the crowd swarmed forward — and found themselves stepping outside.

Now let's try another. The root is *nomen, nomin,* from *nominare,* ('to name').

WORD	LITERAL MEANING
agnomen	a name added to
cognomen	a name going along with
denomination	the act of putting a name down
ignominious	having no name
misnomer	incorrect name
nomination	the act of naming

Some of the above words may need further explanation. An *agnomen* is a nickname, and a *cognomen* is a family name or surname, such as Kelly or Cohen. In ancient Rome it was the third word in a person's name. For example, Cicero was the *cognomen* of Marcus Tullius *Cicero.* Incidentally, the accent for both of the above words falls on the second syllable.

Denomination has undergone a semantic change. It has taken on a religious significance in popular usage and is synonymous with sect.

Ignominious and *ignominy* are very interesting words. If a person has no name (perhaps he's illegitimate), he sometimes suffers from public shame and dishonour. Hence the adjective has come to mean 'disgraceful or despicable'.

Now let's see how well *you* can do with some other Latin roots. Here are some basic Roman underground growths that need 'branches' and 'twigs' to fill them out in our language. If you will consult the Appendix (pp. 220-1), you will find my own orchards.

ROOT	MEANING
ag, act	do, drive, impel
cad, cas	fall
cap, capt, cept	take, seize
clud, clus	close, shut
cur, curr, curs	run
fac, fact, fect	do, make
frag, fract	break
leg, lig, lect	choose, read
mit, miss	send
pend, pens	hang, weigh, lay
plic, pli	fold
sed, sid, sess	sit, seat
sent, sens	feel
solv, solu	loosen, free
ten, tin, tent	hold, contain
volv, volu	roll, turn

The above, of course, is only a sampling of the many Latin roots that have gained strength through the centuries and have flowered in our language. Some of them have departed a bit, through usage, from their original intent. Those are like sprouts that form new and different buds from the main source, but it is amazing how many have blossomed without much change. It cannot be said too often that our linguistic to the Romans is beyond comprehension.

5   The French Connexion

In 1066, at sunset on Senlac Hill, an errant arrow struck King Harold II in the eye, and he succumbed to the wound. His Anglo-Saxon soldiers, already losing to the forces of the Duke of Normandy, fled from the field. Thus William the Conqueror won the Battle of Hastings and marched on London.

William brought not only troops with him; he brought thousands of words. Although English remained the language of the peasants, the influence of the conquerors over a period of almost three centuries soon seeped through; willy-nilly the common people began to Gallicize their language.

And so today French leads all the Romance languages in affecting English speech and writing. Some philologers estimate that almost one-third of our words come from French.

Now let us review the historical events above, with stress on the French phrases and words that have permeated our languages.

While examining French words and phrases that we have assimilated, I began to notice that they fell mainly into eight categories:

Clothing and Fashion	War and Diplomacy
Food and Drink	Gambling
The Arts	L'Amour
Shelter and Furniture	Miscellaneous

In the list below and those to follow, words marked with a tick will be discussed.

CLOTHING AND FASHION

appliqué	boutonnière	casaque	chine
bandeau	√ brassiere	cerise	√cloche
barrette	bretelle	chapeau	cloqué
beige	broché	chic	coiffeur
bon ton	burnoose	chichi	coiffure
bouclé	camisole	√chiffon	coque
bouffant	cap-a-pie	chignon	corsetiere

costumier	ecru	moiré	sabot
couturier, -iere	froufrou	nacré	sachet
√cravat	√guimpe	negligee	samite
crepe	lamé	panache	soutache
cretonne	lapin	passé	soutane
√crinoline	lingerie	peignoir	svelte
crochet	mannequin	picot	toque
√culotte	marquisette	plissé	√trousseau
décolleté	modiste	rabat	√voile
dishabille			

Brassiere comes from *bras* ('arm'). Actually, in French it means 'an infant's undergarment or child's bodice or shoulder strap'. The noun dates back to the Old French word *braciere* ('armour for the arm; an arm guard').

Our word *bracer* is from the same root. In archery that's a leather guard worn on the arm holding the bow.

Chiffon is the French diminutive of *chiffe* ('an old rag'). As every woman knows, it's now a lovely sheer, lightweight fabric.

It's also intriguing to note that *chiffon* has another meaning to chefs. It denotes 'light and porous, as by the addition of stiffly beaten egg whites'. If you have ever tasted *lemon chiffon pie,* you will attest that it bears no resemblance to tiny dirty tatters.

I think you will be surprised to learn that the chest of drawers called a *chiffonier* (or *chiffonnier*) was originally the French word for 'ragpicker'.

Cloche literally means 'bell or bell jar'. It's a bell-shaped glass vessel used for covering plants or food. But it's also a woman's hat shaped like a bell. Incidentally, the word is related to clock.

Cravats have an interesting history. They were originally scarves worn by Croatian mercenaries in the French army. Since *Cravate* meant 'Croatian' to the French, the name was applied to the distinctive neckwear. In fact, in the seventeenth century the French decided to imitate the Croatians. They dressed a regiment of the cavalry in *cravats.* The idea then took hold in Paris, whence it spread throughout the world. As its popularity extended, somewhere along the line *cravat* became a synonym for necktie.

Crinoline, like many other words, came to the French via their Italian neighbours. In Milano the word was *crinolino* and literally meant 'horsehair flax'. Interestingly enough, the material is still sometimes partly made of horsehair, though cotton is sometimes substituted. It's a coarse, stiff cloth used for hoopskirts.

Culottes are trousers for females, made full in the legs to resemble skirts. Actually, *culotte* in French means 'a little backside'. In English it can also be defined as 'hair on the thighs of an animal, such as a Pomeranian dog'.

But the derivative word that is most fascinating is *sansculotte* (literally, 'without breeches'). This is a term of contempt applied by the aristocrats to the republicans in the poorly clad French Revolutionary Army, who rejected knee breeches in favour of pantaloons because they wanted to be different from the elite.

Guimpe and *wimple* are related words. The latter is the head covering worn by nuns who haven't kicked the habit. The former (pronounced *gamp*) is a blouse worn under a jumper, or a yoke insert for a low-necked dress. A trimming for upholstery is called *gimp*; it has the same ancestry. Gimp is also a thread or yarn used for embroidery.

Every bride knows that a *trousseau* is the special wardrobe that she assembles for her marriage. But I wonder if she knows that it really means 'a little bundle'. Worse yet, the word is a cousin of *truss* — a supportive device used to prevent enlargement of a hernia. The eventual Latin root is *torquere* ('to twist'). A bride would be horrified to know that her lovely collection of clothes, linens and accessories is related to *torment, distort, torture, extort* and *contortion*.

Voile is the French noun for 'veil'. In English it has assumed the meaning of 'a sheer fabric'. The transition is not difficult to fathom.

And now let us consider some of the words that have filtered into our language because the French are so adept in the culinary art and in preparing beverages that please the palate. (Wine lovers will please excuse the omissions, which are mostly place names anyway.)

FOOD AND DRINK

à la carte	casserole	√croissant	madeleine
apéritif	√chowder	croquette	menu
au jus	cocotte	√crouton	meringue
√au naturel	compote	daube	moule
√baba au rhum	consommé	√demitasse	√mousse
bisque	√convive	filet	mouton
blancmange	coq au vin	flan	muscat
blanquette	coquille	√fondue	parfait
bombe	côtelette	√frangipane	potage

80

√bonne femme	coupette	frappé	purée
boudin	crème d'ananas	gateau	ragout
bouillabaisse	crème de bananes	√gigot	rechauffé
bouillon	crème de café	glacé	rissole
brioche	crème de cassis	√gourmand	rotisserie
√brochette	crème de moka	√gourmet	sauce
brut	crème de noyau	grille	sauté
√café	crème de violette	jujube	vermouth
canapé	crémerie	macédoine	vichysoisse

Au naturel means 'in a natural condition — hence, naked or nude'. To a French chef it signifies 'cooked plainly, or without dressing'.

Baba au rhum is a fruity cake soaked in rum. This popular pastry literally means 'little old woman with rum'. *Baba* is a borrowing from the Poles. A related word is *babushka* (a Russian grandmother). The term is kind of a pet name like 'granny' in English

Bonne femme ('good housewife') is a term used for home-style cooking. If you see *filet de sole bonne femme* on the menu in a French restaurant, it might be a good idea to try the fish.

Brochette means 'little pointed tool or little spit'. We use the word to mean 'skewer', but we also apply it to the meat that is broiled on a skewer. *Broach,* by the way, is a related word.

Café ('coffee or coffeehouse') was borrowed from the Turks. Their word was *kahve.* The broadening of the meaning of *café* is remarkable. First, the beverage itself; next, the little lunchroom where it was served; and finally, let's not forget that *cafeteria* belongs in this family.

Chowder comes to us via *chaudière,* the French word for 'pot or the contents of a pot'. The word can be traced back to *caldus* or *calidus,* the Romans' adjective for 'hot'. *Cauldron* is a cousin.

One might think that *chow,* our slangy synonym for food, is a member of the *chowder* family, but the experts guess that it has a Chinese origin. It's possibly related to *chow mein* ('to fry flour').

Convive means 'guest' to the French. They inherited the word from the Latin *convivia* ('one who lives with another and eats with another'). The parent verb is *vivere* ('to live').

In English, *convives* are fellow banqueters, or comrades at the table. You can spring that one on your friends the next time you attend a formal dinner. Of course *convivial* and *conviviality* are next of kin.

Other descendants of *vivere* are *viva, vivacious, vivid, revive* and *survive.*

Victuals is in the family too, by way of the past participle, *victus.* Finally, through a complicated series of semantic changes, *quick* turns out to be the oldest relative of them all.

Croissants are well named. They are rich, flaky rolls formed in the shape of a crescent. *Croissant* is the French word for 'crescent'.

The rolls originated in Vienna. Chefs created them to celebrate the defeat of the Turks in 1689. The Turkish emblem is a crescent. Hence the Viennese were symbolically devouring their enemies.

Croutons are those small, crisp pieces of toast or fried bread that are often served with soup or salads. In French, *croûton* means 'crust or hunk'. It's an alteration of *crusta,* a Latin noun for 'the skin, rind, shell, crust or bark'.

Demitasse is a small cup of coffee, usually taken black. This postprandial beverage is well named. Literally, it means 'half a cup'.

Fondue (sometimes spelt *fondu*) is a treat that grows ever more popular with each passing year. Primarily, it is a dish made by melting cheese in wine, with a little brandy and seasoning added. Then cubes of bread are dipped into the mixture. The word is derived from the past participle of the French verb *fondre* ('to melt').

Frangipane is another word that the French borrowed from the Italians. A nobleman named Marquis Frangipani invented a perfume that became popular from the sixteenth century on. His *frangipani* imitated the lovely odour of red jasmine. Then a clever chef created a desert of almond cream flavoured with *frangipani,* or jasmine perfume. The dish was called *frangipane.* Then the creamy delicacy was inserted into pastries as a filling, and that is perhaps the most popular conception of the word.

When you order a *frangipane* you are asking the waiter to bring you a tart — a small open pie with a sweet filling. Slangsters got hold of the word 'tart' and cunningly changed it to mean 'a loose woman or prostitute'. *Tarting up* is furnishing or attiring or decorating in a cheap or showy way.

Gigot is a leg of lamb or mutton. It's the diminutive of *gigue* ('a fiddle') and was named for its shape. Incidentally, a *gigue* is also a jig or lively dance movement.

An interesting offshoot is the *gigot sleeve* on a woman's garment. Its shape resembles a leg of mutton.

Gourmand and *gourmet* are often confused. The former is a glutton, and the latter is discriminating about what he eats and drinks. Synonyms for *gourmet* are epicure and connoisseur. In Old French the spelling was *groumet*. In those days he was a vintner's young assistant or wine taster.

Mousse literally means 'froth' in French. It is derived from the Latin adjective *mulsus* ('mixed with honey or sweet as honey'). The word has at least three definitions in English:

1. frothy dessert
2. purée of fish or meat lightened with gelatin or whipped cream or both
3. light, spongy, creamy food, usually containing gelatin, cream or whites of eggs. (In this sense it is often spelt *mousseline*.)

It grieves me to report that *mildew* is a relative of this delicious dish.

Next, let us turn to the Gallic influence on English words that pertain to such arts as the theatre, music, dance, painting, literature and connected fields. Again, only a sampling is listed below.

THE ARTS

allemande	chansonnier	coupe	√gouache
apache dance	chassé	courante	√harlequin
√aperçu	clarinet	cramignon	√ingenue
arabesque	clavecin	craquelure	motif
artiste	clavicor	crèche	ormolu
√atelier	clavier	critique	pastiche
√ballet	√collage	danse macabre	polonaise
bal masqué	comedienne	danseuse	√potpourri
bas bleu	concert	debut	précis
√bassoon	√connoisseur	denouement	première
beguine	conservatoire	dilettante	√protégé
√bibelot	√conte	eloge	revue
√bijou	contredanse	encore	roulade
brisé	corps de ballet	étoile	salon
√burlesque	coryphée	√étude	tableau
cabriole	côtelé	√farceur	taupe
√cénacle	cotillion	√fugue	√timbre
√chanson	couac	genre	valse

Aperçu is an outline or brief sketch. A relative is perceive. The eventual Latin root is *capere* ('to hold').

Atelier has an unbelievable history. The grandparent of this artist's studio meant 'a shaving or splinter'. Thereupon *astelier* emerged. That noun was originally a woodpile, then it became a construction yard, and finally a workshop. The second letter was dropped as time went by, and the word became associated with painters and architects. Note the latter; they do deal with wood.

Ballet is a diminutive of *bal* ('dance'). When you waltz in a *ballroom,* you are in the same league, but not when you watch a *ball game.* That's from an entirely different root.

Bassoon is a woodwind instrument with a deep tone. The French took *basson* from the Italians' *bassone* and we added an extra vowel. The word is related, of course, to *basso.*

Bibelot means 'a trinket' in French and in English. We also use the word to signify 'a miniature book especially of elegant design or format'. *Bible* and *bibliography* are among its kinsmen.

Bijou is a Parisian's jewel. We have taken over that meaning completely. Have you ever heard of *bijouterie*? That's a synonym for trinkets or jewelry. I would like to think that it's one of the gems in this book.

Burlesque today is associated with striptease acts, but 'twas not always so. We took the word from the French, who had borrowed it from *burlesco,* the Italian adjective for 'comical'. Originally such shows features comics in baggy pants who performed low comedy. A *burlesque* is also a literary or dramatic opus that ridicules what is usually considered serious and dignified.

A *cénacle* is a coterie of writers or other artistic people. Literally, it is the scene of the Last Supper. The word can be traced back to the Romans' *cena* ('dinner').

Cenacle (without an accent) is a retreat house, named for the Society of Our Lady of the Cenacle, a congregation of nuns founded in France in 1826 to direct retreats for women.

Chansons are songs. The parent verb is the Romans' *cantare* ('to sing'). Note again how the French liked to change *c* to *ch*. Naturally, *chant* comes from the same root. Other directly related words include *chansonnier* ('cabaret singer'), *chansonette* ('little song'), *chanteuse,* chanticleer, chantey ('song originally sung by sailors in rhythm with their work') and chanteyman.

Some relatives, via Italy, are *cantabile, cantata, canto* and *canzone.*

84

Among the other members of this prolific family, we find *accent,* *canorous* ('musical'), *cant* ('whining or singing speech used by beggars, etc. — hence argot, jargot, secret slang'), *canticle, cantor, descant, enchant, incantation, incentive* and *precentor.*

Oddly enough, *canary* does not belong in this group. Its Latin root is *canis* ('dog')! The Canary Islands, to which the bird is native, were called *Canariae Insulae* ('Dog Islands'), because large dogs were once bred there.

Collage literally means 'a pasting'. It's an artistic composition made with bits and pieces of materials pasted together in seemingly haphazard fashion. Newspaper clippings, pressed flowers, ticket stubs, etc. are often used in this medium.

Collage is not to be confused with *montage.* The latter is a photographic process for making composite pictures. Its source is the French verb *monter* ('to mount'). When a number of separate exposures are made on the same negative, that art is called *photomontage.*

Connoisseurs are people with expert knowledge and discrimination in particular fields, especially the arts. The word dates back eventually to *cognoscere,* the Latin verb meaning 'to know thoroughly'. Some relatives are *acquaint, cognition, notice, notify, notion, notorious, quaint* and *recognize.*

You may ask how *quaint* got into this family. After all, in spelling and meaning, it seems to be a total stranger. Well, in Old French it was spelt *cointe* and meant 'expert or elegant'. Medieval Englishmen changed it to *queinte.*

In Elizabethan times the word meant 'skilled in the use of language'. A line from Shakespeare reads: 'How *quaint* an orator.' Gradually the idea of skill came to be associated with uniqueness. Some other definitions for it today are 'picturesque, old-fashioned, singular, naïve, illogical, artificially unfamiliar and different in a pleasing way.'

Conte is another example of how semantic changes through the centuries seem to make strange bedfellows. Who would believe that this short adventure tale has any relationship to *pavement* or *amputate?*

Conter ('to relate') is the French parent of *conte.* But the grandparent is *computare,* the Latin verb meaning 'to reckon with'. Other kinfolk are *account, computer, count* (as a verb), *counterman, deputy, disputation, impute, putative* and *repute.*

The Latin verb *putare* had a variety of meanings. One of them

85

was 'to strike, strike off, prune or trim'. Another was 'to reckon, think or count'. Hence it's easy to see how *amputate* and *compute* are descendants of the same root.

Pave and *pavement* come in via a Latin alteration of the parent verb. To the Romans, *pavire* meant 'to ram down, beat or strike'.

Etude means 'study' in French and in English. To musicians it's a practice piece or exercise. However, it also contains the idea of dwelling on a special point of technique and being performed for artistic value, as the études of Chopin and Schumann.

Farceurs are jokers or wags. They are also actors in or writers of *farces*. The parent Latin verb is *farcire* ('to stuff'). Consequently, one can readily understand why *farce* means 'forcemeat or stuffing'. But why is it also defined as 'a light, satirical or humorous drama'? The answer is that in medieval days the travelling troupes stuffed a boisterous, comical diversion between the acts of the principal presentation in order to give themselves a breather, change scenery and perform other chores. Today any ridiculous situation or display is called a *farce*.

Fugues are complicated polyphonic musical compositions. Literally, they are 'flights' of music. *Fuga,* the Latin noun meaning 'fleeing', is the source. Its other scions include *centrifugal, fugitive* and *refuge.*

A most interesting cousin is *subterfuge* (literally, 'a fleeing below'). When you use deceptive artifices, you retreat into underhanded tricks. Some of the Watergaters were masters of *subterfuge.*

The adjective *febrifuge* means 'serving to reduce a fever'. A perennial European herb called the *feverfew* was reputed by old wives to have that power. Does the plant come from the same root? Yes! *Febris* ('fever') is the first source, changed through the Anglo-French. Fuga is the second source. The Anglo-French loved their *v*'s and *w*'s!

My favourite member of the tribe is *fugacious,* meaning 'lasting for a short time; of unsubstantial nature; evanescent; wandering'.

But all 'acious' words entrance me. They have a delightful ring to them. When I hear *perspicacious* used instead of shrewd, a thrill goes through my spine. And how about *audacious, capacious, fallacious, loquacious, sagacious, tenacious, vivacious* and *voracious*? Aren't they all as delicious as a piece of French pastry?

Take *salacious,* for example. The very sound is exciting, unlike its synonym, pornographic. That adjective has a harsh, unmusical tone.

Then there are *pertinacious, pervivacious* and *contumacious.* How nice they sound compared with stubborn and insubordinate! *Gouache* (pronounced 'gwash') is a method of painting with opaque watercolours. The French borrowed the word from the Italians' *guazzo* (literally, 'a puddle'). Readers who have followed this text thus far may not be surprised to learn that the term is descended from Caesar's *aqua* ('water'). What amazes me as I write this book is the fact that thousands upon thousands of words from the ancients have undergone tremendous structural changes as different nationalities and cultures have adapted them to their own languages and purposes.

Harlequin, if capitalized, means 'a conventional buffoon of the commedia dell'arte traditionally presented in a mask and parti-coloured tights'. However, as a common noun the word has taken on a few other connotations:

1. any clown
2. a small duck with distinctively patterned plumage
3. a variegated textile pattern

As an adjective *harlequin* can be defined as follows:

1. bright, parti-coloured; spangled like the dress of Harlequin
2. like spectacles with frames that flare in an upward slant like the slits of Harlequin's mask
3. comic, ludicrous, colourful

This word, like so many others, has gone through a multitude of aberrations. It can be traced to a Medieval Latin term, *Herla rex* — a mythical king identified with Woden.

Ingénues are ingenuous. They are artless, innocent young women. Hence they are actresses who play such roles. If one takes their roots literally, these girls must be very, very young. The parent verb in Latin is *gignere* ('to beget') and the prefix means 'not'. Therefore, *ingénues* are so immature that they can't have children.

Potpourri (pronounced 'pō-pǒo-rē') is a combination of miscellaneous, and often incongruous, elements (originally, a stew). An anthologist who has compiled literature from various sources can

87

be said to have published a *potpourri*. But the basic meaning is 'a mixture of dried flower petals and spices kept in a jar to scent the air'.

For a change, the French borrowed this word from the Spanish. *Olla podrida* is literally 'a rotten pot', but it has come to mean 'a stew' and, by extension, 'an assortment or miscellany'.

Some unpleasant cousins of *potpourri* are *purulent, pus, putrefy, putrid* and *suppurate*.

Protégé goes back to the Latin verb *protegere* ('to protect'). A *protégé* is a man under the care and protection of an influential person, such as a sponsor, teacher or patron.

Timbre is a distinctive quality of tone or sound. In Medieval French it meant 'a bell struck by a hammer', and in Old French it was a drum. The root is the Greek word *tympanon,* from which we also get *tympanum* ('ear drum'). A *tympanist* plays the kettledrums in an orchestra.

Americans sometimes use the spelling *timber,* but it has no relationship with trees or wood. The source of its look-alike can be traced to Sanskrit and Greek words meaning 'to build'.

The fact that *timber* ('lumber') and *domicile* are related linguistically seems appropriate. But it may strike you as odd that *dame, domino, madame* and *madonna* can claim the same ancestors as the *timber* wolf.

The list that follows is by no means a complete one, but it should indicate that we have indeed brought the French into our homes.

SHELTER AND FURNITURE

√armoire	√chauffer	Limoges
auberge	chauffeuse	maître d'hotel
√boudoir	chiffonier	marquetry
√cabriole	√concierge	oriel
√chaise longue	√console	√pension
chalet	étagère	√portiere
√chandelier	√hospice	potiche
√château	jalousie	taboret
	√kiosk	

Armoire is a warlike word that has been tamed. Although it's a large ornate cupboard or wardrobe, its eventual Latin source is *arma* ('weapons'). Can you picture Caesar taking off his armour at home and placing it in his *armarium* ('closet')?

Boudoir comes from the French verb *bouder* ('to pout or be sulky'). Originally it was a room to which a person could go if he or she felt sullen, depressed or unsociable. Today it's a bedroom or a woman's private dressing room.

Cabriole is a style of furniture leg that curves outward at the top and then descends in a tapering reverse curve that ends with an ornamental foot. It literally means 'leap or caper' and was named for its resemblance to the foreleg of a capering animal.

Chaise longue (literally, 'long chair') is a couch or sofa.

Chandeliers ornamented French homes long before Edison came on the scene. Hence it's understandable that those lighting fixtures are literally candlesticks. Their close kin are *candelabra* ('decorative candlesticks having several arms or branches').

Two other members of this family are *chandler* and *chandlery*. The former is a seller of candles, or, nowadays, of any specific goods (*corn chandler*, for instance). The latter is his store.

The most common definition for *château* is 'a country house, especially one resembling a castle'. Appropriately, *castle* is a related word. In Old French it was spelt *chastel*. The Latin root is *castellum* ('a castle, fort or citadel'), from the verb *castrare*.

It will probably shock you to learn that *castrate* is linguistically akin to *castle* and *château*. In ancient Rome, *castrare* meant 'to emasculate — hence, to deprive of strength; to restrain or check'. The latter definitions fit nicely with *castle*, a fortified place to check the forces of the enemy.

A *chauffer* is a portable stove, not to be confused with *chauffeur*. Originally the latter was a stoker employed to keep the heat going. Many early cars ran on steam, so the *chauffeur*'s new job was to heat up the engines. A *chauffeuse*, by the way, is not only a female employed to drive but also a low-seated French chair near the hearth.

Concierges are doorkeepers; they are also custodians or head porters at apartment houses and hotels. Would they be pleased to learn that their heritage is *conservus*? It's the Latin noun for 'fellow slave'.

Most of us know that the verb *console* means 'to comfort'. Does the noun from the French have any relationship? Indeed it does! *Consoles* were originally *consolateurs* in France; these were carved human figures used to support cornices. They were also rails used in choir stalls. When the singers stood up to perform, they had a place to lean for support. Note the similarity between *support* and *console.*

Hospices are shelters or lodgings for travellers, students or the destitute; they are often maintained by monastics. They are similar in meaning and derivation to *hostels* and *hotels.*

The source, as usual, is a Latin word. *Hospes* meant 'guest or host'; the Romans couldn't make up their minds, probably because they thought that *hospitality* ('friendliness') was a reciprocal duty.

At any rate, it's fascinating to note that *hospital* belongs in this family. It was originally a sort of *hospice,* or place for travellers to rest. But in 1048 the shelter provided by monks for pilgrims in the Crusades was filled with so many people who had fallen ill on the journey that *hospital* came to mean 'a place to care for the sick and injured'.

Kiosk, or *kiosque,* is a word that the French borrowed from the Turks. In its original sense it was a summer house or open pavilion. The French thought of it as a bandstand. To the British it is a stand where merchandise is sold or information is provided. Though once a summer structure only, it is now a stand for all seasons.

The story is told that an American in Paris saw the sign *Pension* on one building after another. Told that they were boarding houses, he commented: 'I didn't know there were so many retired Frenchmen'.

The French and other Europeans developed their meaning for the word from the fact that a *pension* ('fee') had to be paid for their children who boarded away from home as students.

The Latin root is *pendere, pensus* ('to weigh or pay or hang').

Portieres are heavy curtains usually hung in doorways. The French word *portier* means 'doorkeeper', and *portière* is its feminine form. Literally, the curtains are feminine doorkeepers.

Next let us turn to those French-English words that deal with international relations, whether evil or beneficent. In this category the French have given us scores of words. A few are listed below.

WAR AND DIPLOMACY

aide-de-camp	caisson	cuirassier	oubliette
ambuscade	√camouflage	√debacle	paladin
arrière-ban	cartel	√détente	perdu
attaché	casque	√entente	√poilu
avant-courier	chargé d'affaires	espionage	politesse

banquette	congé	esprit de corps	rapport
barrage	√cordon sanitaire	étape	rapprochement
bayonet	corps	√grenadier	reconnaissance
beau sabreur	corps d'élite	kepi	√sabotage
bivouac	corps diplomatique	√laissez-faire	√saboteur
√boche	√corvette	matériel	sortie
√cadet			

Boche is French slang for a German soldier. This derogatory term arose in World War I. It is a contraction of *tête de caboche* ('head of cabbage' — hence, 'hard head').

Most of us think of *cadets* as young men (or young women) training to be officers. Actually, the first meaning of *cadet* is 'a younger son'. But in former times such a scion had no chance to inherit his father's estate, and it became usual for the younger sons to make a living by joining the army.

The word is derived from *capitellum* ('little head' in Latin). The Gascons, in southwestern France, developed *cupdet*, and thence it was shortened to *cadet*. The grandparent is *caput* ('head') — and what a large family that word sired! Here are some of its members: *cap, cape, capital, capitol, capitulate, caporal, caprice, captain, cattle, chapter, chief, decapitate, kepi, kerchief, mischief, precipitate* and *recapitulate*.

Caddies are also members of the group, via *cadet*. They were originally errand boys in Scotland. And from *caddie* the British developed *cad*. This ungentlemanly fellow was a menial helper centuries ago. Then he became associated with rowdyish town boys, as distinguished from the hardworking students at local institutions. The transition to his present status is simple to comprehend.

Camouflage is a derivative of *camouflet* ('a puff of smoke; a smoke bomb'). In French, *moufler* means 'to muffle or cover up'. And so when soldiers use *camouflage* to conceal themselves they are really blowing out a screen of smoke and covering up.

Cordon sanitaire has two meanings:

1. a barrier restraining free movement of people or goods to keep a disease from spreading
2. a belt of countries isolating another nation in order to check its aggressiveness or lessen its influence.

91

Corvettes are fast warships. The word is probably derived from Middle Dutch *corf* ('a basket or small ship').

Debacle means 'the breaking up of ice' in a river. As a result, the second definition is 'a violent flood'. Finally our most common association with the word evolved. Today a debacle means 'a calamitous failure or collapse, or an overwhelming defeat'.

Détente literally means 'an easing'. It has taken on an international significance and now refers to a relaxation of tension between nations. Its cousin *entente* means 'understanding' in French. This word also has acquired a diplomatic connotation. It has come to mean 'an understanding or agreement between or among nations'. In 1904 the *Entente Cordiale* was signed and it developed into the *Triple Entente* between Great Britain, France and Russia.

Grenadiers were originally soldiers who carried and threw *grenades*. The British applied the word to a special regiment attached to the royal household. The noun now also refers to deep-sea fishes of the cod family.

Of greatest interest is the fact that the French named the *grenade* after the pomegranate because of its original shape. In fact, *granade* is an obsolete synonym for pomegranate, and survives in the sweet syrup *grenadine*.

Laissez-faire means 'let (people) do (as they please)'. It is the policy or practice of non-interference, domestically as between governments and industrialists, internationally as between nations.

Less known, but perhaps more apt, is *laissez-passer,* a permit or pass allowing officials of one country to travel in another.

An *oubliette* is a dungeon with a trapdoor in the ceiling as its only opening. Via Latin ancestors, *oblivion* fittingly is in the same family.

Poilu actually means 'hairy or virile' in French. The term was applied to any French soldier in World War I. He was the counterpart of one of General Pershing's *doughboys* or a British *Tommy.*

Sabotage and *saboteur* have fascinating histories. In French a *sabot* means 'a wooden shoe'. This footwear was commonly worn by peasants. Since the upper classes considered such lowly persons to be awkward and slipshod, the verb *saboter* was created. It meant 'to botch the job, to be clumsy and careless'.

Some philologers think that *sabotage* arose from the fact that the peasants threw their wooden shoes into the machinery at factories. My own opinion is that the first *saboteurs* were peasants who rebelled against the oppression of their masters. They didn't need to throw their shoes; the fact that they wore them was enough to cause the landowners to label them as deliberate damagers of property.

Next, here is a small selection of words, some of which have been transferred from Paris and Monte Carlo to London, Las Vegas, Reno and Atlantic City, among other places. All the words in this win-or-lose category will be discussed.

GAMBLING

baccarat	craps	parimutuel
bagatelle	croupier	roulette
boule	écarté	vingt-et-un

Baccarat is a card game similar to chemin de fer and twenty-one. The origin of the word is not certain. Possibly it came from a town of the same name in eastern France. However, the French call the game *baccara*.

Bagatelle means 'a trifle'. The French borrowed it from the Italian noun *bagatella,* which has the same meaning. The game *bagatelle* is played on an oblong table with a cue and usually nine balls. In recent years it has been associated with pinball.

Finally, the word signifies 'a short piece of light verse or of music for the piano'.

The Latin root is *baca* ('berry'). That seems to fit, because a tiny berry is a mere nothing.

Boule literally means 'ball' in French. It's a game similar to roulette. The word also is used as a synonym for a pear-shaped synthetic sapphire.

Craps comes to us via the Creoles in Louisiana. They borrowed the name from an obsolete English slang word, *crabs,* which meant the lowest throw in an old dice game called 'hazard'. It's interesting to note that today a player who throws two aces 'craps out'.

Croupier displays the Gallic sense of humour. Its French root is *croupe* ('rump') and it originally meant 'rider on the rump behind another rider'. Drolly, the French applied it to the original *croupiers,* who were advisers standing (or maybe sitting) behind the players at the gaming tables. The practice still exists in baccarat and chemin de fer, but today a *croupier* is usually an attendant who collects the losers' bets and pays the winners.

Ecarté is a game for two, played with thirty-two cards — sevens up through aces. The word is the past participle of *écarter* ('to discard'). The game is well named, because all the cards dealt may be discarded and replaced from the pack.

Parimutuel literally means 'a mutual stake'. It's a system of betting (as at a horse race) in which the winners share the total stakes minus a small percentage for the management. All racetracks are now equipped with *parimutuel machines* that register and indicate the number and nature of the bets and then compute the payoffs. In Britain they are called totalizators, or 'totes'.

Roulette owes its origin to *rota* ('wheel' in ancient Rome). The Late Latin diminutive *rotella* is the immediate ancestor.

Aside from being a casino game, with a lively little ball bouncing around inside a spinning bowl, *roulette* is a small toothed wheel attached to a handle, used to make the perforations in sheets of postage stamps. By metonymy the incisions themselves have come to be called *roulettes.*

As a verb the word means 'to make dots, marks or incisions'.

Vingt-et-un is the game of 'twenty-one' or 'pontoon'. Literally, it means 'twenty and one'.

Leaving the casinos, we now turn to the boudoirs. Here is a small list of words on the tender passion, French style.

L'AMOUR

√accouchement	√billet-doux	√débauchée	√oeillade
affaire d'amour	coquetry	√divorcée	√paramour
√amourette	√coquette	√fiancé	√rendezvous
beau	√courtesan	√odalisque	roué

Accouchement comes from the verb *accoucher,* which first meant 'to put to bed' and soon acquired an association with childbirth. *Accouchement,* therefore, is confinement for giving birth to a baby. An *accoucheur* is a male attendant at childbirth, and an *accoucheuse* a midwife.

Our word *couch* comes from the same root, *collocare* ('to place together or lay together').

Amourette is a trifling or short-lived affair. The woman involved in such a brief encounter is also an *amourette*.

Billets-doux are literally sweet short notes — hence, love letters.

Doux has some sweet cousins. Among them are *dulcet* and *dulcimer*. The former means 'melodious' and the latter is a musical instrument that looks rather like a xylophone.

Coquette has an entertaining background. It's a diminutive of *coq* ('cock'). The noun *coquet* has become obsolete in English. Too bad! It meant 'a little cock — hence, a flirtatious man'. But the female of the species has survived, and so has *coquet* as a verb meaning 'to flirt, trifle or dally', and *coquetry* means 'dalliance or flirtation'.

Courtesans are ladies of the court, but not straitlaced ones. In truth, they are high-class prostitutes or kept women. Their ancestry can be traced back to *cohors,* the Latin noun for 'an enclosure or court, a fenced-in multitude — hence, a company of soldiers'.

Relations include *cohort, cortege, court, courteous, courtesy, courtier, curtain* and *curtsy.*

Debauchees are dissipated persons, libertines or people given to sensual excesses. *Debauch,* if followed to its source, means 'to separate branches from a trunk'. Thus the word has taken an evil connotations, such as 'to lead astray, corrupt, seduce, deprave, debase'.

Divorce came into our language, via Medieval French, from *divortere* and *divertere.* Those Latin infinitives mean 'to turn oneself in a different direction, or to go different ways'. A *divorcée* is a divorced woman; her erstwhile partner is a *divorcé.*

It's strange to think that *divertissement* ('amusement') and the dissolution of marriage should be closely related.

Fiancés must be trusted by their *fiancées.* Their titles stem from the French verb *fier* ('to trust'). The eventual root is *fidere* — the Romans' verb meaning 'to trust or confide in'.

Some of the many members of this trusting tribe are *affiance, affidavit, confederate, confidence, defy, diffident, faith, fealty, federal, fidelity, fiduciary, infidel, infidelity, perfidious, perfidy* and good old *Fido* (a dog I trust).

Odalisques are concubines or female slaves in harems. The French developed the word from their association with the Turks.

Oeillade might eliminate all the contestants in a spelling bee, unless they happened to be versed in French. The immediate parent is *oeil* ('eye'). The definition of the verb is 'to eye amorously; to ogle'.

The Roman ancestor is *oculus* ('eye'). As you can see, it has suffered quite a Gallic face-lift.

An *oeil-de-boeuf* is a round or oval window — literally, 'eye of an ox'.

Best of all is the *trompe l'oeil* ('trick the eye'). It's a painting or other representation that creates such a strong illusion of reality that the viewer at first thinks it's three-dimensional.

Paramour, when analysed, means 'by way of love'. In Middle English it was an adverb. Today it means a lover or mistress.

Rendezvous should probably have been placed in the category containing military words, because one of its primary meanings is 'an assembly of troops, ships or planes'. However, since *coquettes, courtesans, debauchees* and *paramours* do arrange *rendezvous,* it seems appropriate to include it here. The word actually means 'present yourself or yourselves'. This translation certainly sounds like the order for a general or an admiral. But in fact *rendezvous* means 'a meeting or the place where the meeting occurs'.

Finally, we come to an olio of French words that have found their way into our everyday speech and our prose and poetry. Naturally, this mixture is the longest list of all, but it must be emphasized that it only scratches the surface. Keep in mind that almost one-third of the entries in our dictionaries have a French connection. That adds up to over 100,000 in an unabridged lexicon.

MISCELLANEOUS (*a* through *c*)

abattoir	√bonhomie	caporal	contour
abbé	bouquet	capsule	√contretemps
√accolade	bourgeois	carillon	cortege
adieu	bourse	carousel	coterie
aplomb	briquette	cassette	cougar
apropos	√brochure	√causerie	coulee
√argot	√brouhaha	chagrin	couvade
√au revoir	bruit	chevrotain	Creole
automobile	brunette	chicanery	cretin
avocet	√buccaneer	civet	crevasse
badinage	√cabal	√cliche	critique
bastille	√cabotage	clientele	croquet
baton	cache	clique	crosier
beau geste	cachet	cloture	crotchet
√bizarre	√cajole	commune	cupel
blasé	camaraderie	concessionaire	curé
bloc	√canard	confidante	cuvette
boîte			

WORD	DEFINITION	DERIVATION
accolade	1. ceremonial embrace 2. ceremony for conferring knighthood 3. award; bestowal of praise	*accoler* ('to embrace'); from Lat. *ad collum* ('to the neck')
argot	1. secret jargon of criminals 2. slang	*argoter* ('to beg'); probably from *ergot* ('claw') — hence, 'to get one's claws into'
au revoir	goodbye (temporarily)	*au* ('to the'), *revoir* ('seeing again'); from Lat. *revidere* ('to see again')
bizarre	odd; queer; grotesque; fantastic; unexpected and unbelievable	It, *bizarro* ('angry, fierce, strange'). Sp. *bizarro* ('bold, knightly'), Basque *bizar* ('beard')
boîte	small nightclub or cabaret	*boîte* ('box')
bonhomie	good nature; amiability	*bon* ('good'), *homme* ('man')
brochure	pamphlet; booklet	*brocher* ('to stitch')
brouhaha	hubbub; commotion	probably imitative; possibly from Heb.
buccaneer	pirate	*boucanier* ('user of a *boucan* — a Brazilian roasting grill'); originally applied to French hunters of wild oxen in Haiti
cabal	1. small group engaged in intrigue 2. junta 3. intrigue; plot	*cabale* ('club of plotters'). The word was popularized in England because of the initials initials of the ministers of Charles II — Clifford, Arlington, Buckingham, Ashley and Lauderdale.
cabotage	1. coastal navigation and trade 2. air transport within a country 3. the right to engage in navigation near a foreign coast	*caboter* ('to sail along the coast'); from Sp. *cabo* ('cape')
cajole	1. coax with flattery 2. wheedle	*cajoler* ('to chatter like a jay in a cage — hence, to wheedle or coax'); blend of *cavus*, the root for 'cage' and *gaiole* ('bird-cage'). *Jail* and *gaol* are relations.

WORD	DEFINITION	DERIVATION
canard	1. fabricated, malicious report 2. groundless rumour 3. aeroplane with a horizontal stabilizer forward of the wings	*canard* ('a duck'). In Med. Fr., *vendre des canards à moitié* meant 'to sell half ducks — hence, to deceive or cheat'.
causerie	1. informal discussion; hat 2. short, conversational piece of writing	*causer* ('to chat'); from Vulg. Lat. *causare* ('to complain')
cliché	1. stereotype printing plate 2. trite expression; platitude	*clicher* ('to stereotype'); from Ger. *klitsch* ('clump; claylike mass'). Original meaning of *clicher* was 'to pattern in clay'.
clique	1. small exclusive circle of people 2. snobbish group	*cliquer* ('to click'). In Med. Fr. *clique* meant 'a clicking sound'. Later sense may have come from secrecy of exclusive groups; also possibly an alteration of *claque* ('group of frowning followers').
contretemps	1. awkward mishap 2. embarrassing occurrence 3. syncopation	*contre* ('opposite'), *temps* ('time').

And now here is our second group of miscellaneous English words borrowed from the French. This list will start with words that begin with *d* and will continue through those that begin with *n*.

√debris	√elegant	√gauche	mal de mer
debutante	elite	gaucherie	matinee
√déclassé	enfant terrible	gout	mélange
derange	essence	guillemot	métier
detour	√fainéant	habitué	milieu
√de trop	fete	hauteur	moraine
diligence	fiacre	idée fixe	√morgue
distrait	√fleur-de-lis	impasse	mot juste
√dossier	flux	√jardiniere	√naïve
√doyen	fringe	lagniappe	naïveté
√éclat	gaffe	levee	noel
élan	gasconade	√malaise	√nuance

WORD	DEFINITION	DERIVATION
debris	1. rubble; litter; ruins 2. heap of rock fragments deposited by a glacier	Old Fr. *debrisier* ('to break apart')
déclassé	1. lowered in rank or social position 2. of inferior status	*dé* ('down'), *classe* ('class')
de trop	1. superfluous; unwanted 2. too much; too many	*de* plus *trop* ('too much')
dossier	1. dossier of documents, records, and reports on a single subject 2. file	*dossier* ('bundle of documents with a label on the back'); from *dos* ('back')
doyen	1. senior member of a group 2. person uniquely skilled by experience	*doyen* ('dean'); from Late Lat. *decanus* ('chief of ten')
éclat	1. brilliant success 2. dazzling display 3. approval; acclaim; fame	éclat ('splinter; fragment; explosion; ostentation')
elegant	1. characterized by dignified richness and grace. 2. tastefully luxurious 3. refined 4. impressively fastidious in manner and taste	*élégant* ('tasteful; stylish'); from Lat. *e* ('out') and *legere* ('to choose')
fainéant	lazy, idle person; do-nothing	present participle of *faindre* ('to feign or shirk'); literally (he) does nothing
fleur-de-lis	1. iris 2. coat of arms of former French royal family (Charles V et al)	'flower of the lily'
gauche*	1. lacking social grace 2. awkward; tactless	literally, 'left' in Fr. — hence, 'gawky, ungainly'; from Fr. *gauchir* ('to become crooked or warped')

* *Gauche.* Compare this with 'sinister' in Chapter 3; note the same prejudice against left-handers.

jardiniere	1. ornamental bowl, pot or stand for flowers or plants 2. garnish for meat consisting of several vegetables	*jardinière* ('female gardener')
malaise	1. vague feeling of physical discomfort or uneasiness 2. vague awareness of moral or social decline	*mal* ('bad'), *aise* ('ease')
morgue	1. place where bodies of unidentified persons are kept . newspaper's reference library, containing back numbers, photographs, clippings, miscellaneous information	*morgue* ('haughtiness, stolidity, impassivity')
naïve	1. unaffectedly or sometimes foolishly simple 2. childless; artless; unsophisticated 3. not suspicious	fem. of *naïf;* from Lat. *nativus* ('natural')
nuance	1. slight or delicate variation in tone or colour 2. shade of difference	*nuer* ('to shade'); from Lat. *nubes* ('cloud')

Herewith is the last group of words borrowed from the French.

√outrageous	√portmanteau	savant	triste
parvenu	poseur	√Scaramouch	verjuice
√pastille	√pourboire	seneschal	vis-à-vis
√patois	puissant	√sobriquet	visa
√penchant	raconteur	√soi-disant	voyageur
√persiflage	réclame	soiree	√voyeur
pique	riant	√soupçon	vrille
piton	√risqué	√toupee	√wagon-lit
plaque			

100

WORD	DEFINITION	DERIVATION
outrageous	1. exceeding limits of decency or reasonableness 2. very offensive or shocking 3. violent; unrestrained 4. extravagant; fantastic	*outre* ('beyond'); from Lat. *ultra*; derivation not related to 'rage'
pastille	1. aromatic or medicated lozenge 2. small cone used for fumigating or scenting the air 3. paper tube causing fireworks to explode	*pastille* ('lozenge'); from Lat. *pastillus* ('little roll or lozenge'), via *pascere* ('to feed')
patois	1. provincial or local dialect 2. specialized vocabulary of a group; jargon	Old Fr. *patois* ('uncultivated speech'); akin to *patoier* ('to shake paws; behave crudely')
penchant	1. strong liking or fondness 2. inclination; taste	*pencher* ('to incline'); from Lat. *pendere* ('to hang')
persiflage	1. light, frivolous or flippant style of speaking or writing 2. such talk or writing; banter	*persifler* ('to banter'), via *per* ('through') and *siffler* ('to whistle, hiss, boo')
portmanteau	travelling bag	*porter* ('to carry') and *manteau* ('cloak, coat')
pourboire	tip; gratuity	*pour* ('for'), *boire* ('drink')
risqué	1. very close to being indecent or improper 2. daring; suggestive	past part. of *risquer* ('to risk')
Scaramouch	1. stock character in old Italian comedy, depicted as a braggart and poltroon 2. boastful coward; scamp; rascal	from *Scaramouche*, via It. *Scaramuccia* (literally, 'a skirmish')
sobriquet	1. nickname 2. assumed name	from Med. Fr. *soubriquet* ('tap under the chin; nickname')
soi-disant	self-styled	*soi* ('self'), *disant* ('saying')

WORD	DEFINITION	DERIVATION
soupçon	1. slight trace, as of a flavour 2. hint; suggestion 3. tiny amount; bit 4. literally (from Fr.), 'suspicion'	from Med. Fr. *sospeçon,* via Lat. *suspicio* ('suspicion')
toupee	hairpiece; a man's wig	*toupet* ('tuft of hair; forelock')
voyeur	Peeping Tom	from *voir* ('to see'), via Lat. *videre* ('to see')
wagon-lit	1. European railway sleeping car 2. compartment in such a car	*wagon* ('railway coach'); from Dutch *wagen* ('cart'), Fr. *lit* ('bed')

Almost every English word and phrase listed or discussed in this chapter is spelt exactly the same in French, except that accents have been dropped occasionally in Anglicization, thus altering pronunciation slightly. And remember that my presentation of such words represents only a mere sampling.

6   Imports from Spain and Italy

Just as William the Conqueror's men had spread French throughout England after their victory at Hastings in 1066, so the armies of the Spanish *conquistadores* (Coronado, Pizarro et al) brought their language to the New World. Subsequent Spanish settlements in the Southwest, West and South of the United States — as well as in countries below the border — have caused thousands of their words to seep into everyday English, especially as spoken in America.

The Italians, on the other hand, were too busy fighting one another, and made few conquests outside their own country. The result is that our language reflects Italianate words and phrases less than any other Romance language.

Apart from wars and invasions, there are two other factors to be considered. The Renaissance is one. The other — particularly where what H. L. Mencken has called 'the American language' is concerned — is immigration. In the great European revival of art, literature and learning that took place between the fourteenth and sixteenth centuries, Italy was the initiator, and consequently a goodly number of the words and phrases of that great land were absorbed by the British. The effect of immigration has been more recent. During the last three decades the influx of Puerto Ricans, Cubans, Mexicans, Dominicans and other people of Hispanic background into the United States has been tremendous, and many of their words have crept into the language.

As an aside, let me point out that a melting pot such as the United States, with a relatively short history, is far more likely to accept and absorb the expressions of foreigners than a land with a more ancient background. This is a difference between the Americans and the French. Recently a Parisian statesman tried to ban the importation of English words into France; he deplored the adulteration of his native language. In contrast, Americans openly welcome all comers.

As in the case of the French imports, our Hispanic borrowings can be divided into various categories:

> Geographical Terms and Outdoor Places
> Mammals, Fish, Birds and Insects
> Bullfighting
> Food and Drink
> Clothing and Shelter
> Dances
> Miscellaneous

Please note the difference between the above groupings and those related to the French. The world of fashion is missing, as are the areas of war and diplomacy. In the arts, except for the dance, the pickings are meagre. The same can be said for furniture and for relations between the sexes. On the contrary, sports and geographical entries, as well as bestial words, far outnumber the contributions of the French.

Let us begin with a sampling of words that fall into the first category. In the list below and those to follow, words marked with a tick will be discussed.

GEOGRAPHICAL TERMS AND OUTDOOR PLACES

abra	√canyon	√mescal	saguaro
agostadero	coquito	√mesquite	sapodilla
√alamo	cuesta	montaña	savanna
arado	√estancia	noria	√sierra
arroyo	gaucho	nutria	silo
boca	√lasso	palmetto	solano
bosque	llano	pampas	√tornado
buckaroo	loma	patio	vaquero
cajón	√machete	pelota	√vega
√cañada	√marijuana	playa	yucca
√canoe	mesa		

Most of us know about the *Alamo,* a Franciscan mission built circa 1722 at the present site of San Antonio, Texas. And some of us are aware that Davy Crockett and Jim Bowie died there when Santa Anna's forces finally stormed into the building. But I wonder how many people know that an *alamo* is a poplar or cottonwood.

To a westerner a cañada is a little canyon or creek. The word is an extension of caña, meaning 'cane; small hollow object'. *Canada,* the country, has an altogether different background. It's from a

French-Huron word, kanáda, meaning 'village or settlement'. *Canoe* has a Spanish-Carib background. To a South American the boat is a *canoa*. Columbus recorded the word *canoa* in his log in 1493.

Canyon is derived from an American Spanish noun cañón (pronounced 'canyon'), meaning 'a long tube or hollow'. The ultimate ancestor is the Romans' canna ('reed').

To Hispanic Americans an *estancia* is a ranch or farm. To a Madrileño the word means:

1. room; stopping place; habitation
2. day in a hospital or fee paid for it
3. stanza

The noun is related to *stanchion* ('an upright bar, beam or post used as a support'). Some experts trace *estancia* and *stanchion* back to the Latin verb *stare,* meaning 'to stand'.

Lasso is an alteration of *lazo* ('a loop, noose or snare'). It's fascinating to note that *lace* is in the same family.

A *machete* is a large heavy-bladed knife used to cut down sugar cane or dense undergrowth. It's the diminutive of *macho* — a word that has recently come into common usage.

What's a *macho*? Well, the word has many meanings. Of course it means 'male'. It's also a screw, hook, bolt, tap, spur, buttress, abutment or sledge hammer. That last definition probably gave rise to *machete*.

Interestingly enough, in colloquial Spanish a *macho* is a blockhead. In English he's a strong, virile fellow who has lots of *machismo*.

Marijuana is a native American Spanish word blended with a personal name, *Maria Juana*. The plant is a wild tobacco or type of hemp. The dried leaves and flowers are used for smoking, especially when formed into a kind of cigarette. The common slangy name for this *Cannabis sativa* plant is 'pot'.

Mescal and *mesquite* are alterations of words in the Nahuatl language. The Nahuatls were various people of ancient origin ranging from southeastern Mexico to parts of Central America. Among them were the Aztecs, whose proud empire was destroyed by the Spanish conquest. Again, it is fascinating to note that the victors not only foist words from their language on to the victims but are also the beneficiaries of the vocabulary of their captives.

At any rate, *mescal* is a cactus, a drug that is also called peyote,

105

and a Mexican liquor distilled from the fermented juice of certain agaves. That other intoxicant, tequila, is also a product of the century plants.

In Spanish, *mesquite* is spelt *mezquite.* It's a shrub or small tree. Its pods are used as fodder. Vast pastures in south-west U.S.A. and Mexico are covered with *mesquite grass.*

Sierra has two basic meanings in Spanish. It's either a saw or a mountain range. We combined the two. Our definition is 'a mountain range having a saw-toothed appearance'. The eventual root is *serra,* the Latin noun meaning 'a saw'.

Tornado is the past participle of *tornar,* the Spanish verb meaning 'to turn or return'. A related Hispanic noun, which got twisted up, is *tronada* ('thunderstorm').

In Spanish a *vega* is a lowland or plain. Hence Las Vegas would have been called Les Plaines if the French had beaten the Spanish to the punch.

And now let us turn to our Spanish legacy in the area of the second category. The following is only a small sample of our inheritances.

MAMMALS, FISH, BIRDS AND INSECTS

alpaca	guacharo	merino	√puma
barracuda	guanaco	√mosquito	√rodeo
bonito	√guano	palomino	tapir
√chinchilla	√iguana	pinto	√tuna
√cockroach	junco	pompano	vicuña
condor	√llama	porgy	

Lexicographers are puzzled about the origin of the name of that tiny rodent called the *chinchilla.* Some guess that the Spanish borrowed it from the Aymara, an Indian people of Bolivia and Peru. But my favourite explanation is that the word is a diminutive of *chinche* ('bedbug') — a good illustration of South-of-the-Border humour.

Chinchilla, aside from being the costly fur of the rodent, is a breed of domestic cat with long, soft, silver-grey hair. It's also a heavy cloth used for overcoats. In that sense it's probably named for *Chinchilla,* the Spanish town in which it was first made.

Some readers may recall the 1934 hit song 'La Cucaracha'. Translated, that's 'The Cockroach'. English-speaking folks anglicized *cucaracha* rather wittily.

Guano isn't a mammal, fish, bird or insect, but it seems to fit under this heading. It's the manure of sea birds.

The Arawaks of South America and the West Indies had a word, *iwana,* which the Spanish changed into *iguana* and passed on to us. It's a big lizard.

In a Puns and Anagrams crossword puzzle, the clue for the *llama* was: 'Does the young of this animal call for its Mmama?'

Seriously, this cousin of the *alpaca, guanaco* and *vicuña* was first named by the Quechua, a group of Indian tribes dominant in the former Inca empire. Again, the captors borrow from the captives!

Mosquito is a Spanish and Portuguese diminutive of *mosca* ('fly'). The Latin ancestor, with the same meaning, is *musca.*

Puma is another word that the conquering Spaniards took from the Quechua people. A puma is a cougar, is a catamount, is a mountain lion, is an American lion. Move over, Gertrude!

Rodeo is included in this list because one of its meanings in Spanish is 'cattle ring'. As in English, it also means 'round-up'. Other Hispanic definitions are 'detour' and 'subterfuge'. In Madrid, 'to beat about the bush' is *andarse con rodeos.*

Tunu is a strange anagram of *atún,* the Spanish word for the fish that's also called *tunny.*

Here's a new one for you. A *tuna* is also a prickly pear. The origin is also Spanish.

Several words from our next category, 'Bullfighting', have become familiar.

How many chess players know that *checkmate* is related to the Spanish *matador,* 'killer', which is derived from the Arabic? *Checkmate* comes from Arabic *Shāh māt,* 'The king is dead.'

Picador comes from the Spanish verb *picar* ('to prick'). The picador is a horseman who uses a lance to prick the neck muscles of a weakened bull.

The Latin ancestor of *toreador* is *taurus* ('bull'). The Spanish noun is derived from *torear* ('to fight bulls'). *Torero,* also from *taurus,* is a generic term for any bullfighter, but is often used as a synonym for *matador.*

Here is an abbreviated list in an area in which we have gained a great number of words from our friends in Spain and Mexico.

FOOD AND DRINK

abalone	cassava	frijol	√ sarsaparilla
atole	chicle	guava	taco

banana	chili con carne	maize	tamale
√barbecue	√coconut	√olio	tapioca
bodega	coquina	panada	tequila
√cacao	√cuba libre	√pimiento	√tomato
√cantina	enchilada	√potato	√tortilla

The Taino, an extinct Indian people of the West Indies, have given us a word that delights every picnicker. *Barbecue* is literally 'a framework of sticks'. If any of those Indians were alive today, they would be amazed to see the use of charcoal. The Spanish word for our outdoor party is *barbacoa*.

Cacao is still another word that the *conquistadores* appropriated from the Nahuatl. *Cocoa* is our modification of this chocolate producing bean, although we have accepted *cacao* too.

The French borrowed the Italian word *cantina* ('wine cellar') and changed it into *cantine,* and we promptly altered the French spelling into *canteen.* But the Spanish also borrowed *cantina* from the Italians. In Spain *cantina* means *canteen,* but to the American Spanish a *cantina* is 'a saloon or barroom'.

Incidentally, this word is a good example of the importance of the diacritical mark called a tilde. Cantiña is the colloquial Spanish word for a popular song.

Coconut (sometimes spelt *cocoanut*) has an interesting history. It's derived from the Spanish-Portuguese word *coco.* In Lisbon a *coco* is a bogeyman. Hence philologers assume that the resemblance of the coconut to a grotesque head gave rise to its name.

A *Cuba libre* is a tall rum-and-cola drink mixed with lime juice. Literally it means 'free Cuba' and originally it was a drink of water and sugar quaffed by the rebels during the Cuban war of independence. I wonder what intrepid bartender was the first to lace the beverage.

Olio means 'oil' in Spanish. But the English word with the same spelling is a corruption of *olla* ('pot'). The Spanish developed a stew called *olla podrida* ('rotten pot'). All kinds of meat and vegetables were tossed into the pot. Hence the American variation, *olio,* came to mean 'a miscellaneous mixture; hodgepodge; potpourri'. Another connotation is 'a musical medley'.

At least two groups of lexicographers state that there is no difference between *pimiento* and *pimento.* They are realistic, because most people use the two interchangeably. But a purist would say that a *pimiento* is a garden pepper used as a garnish or a stuffing for olives, while *pimento* is allspice or a vivid shade of red.

Those Taino Indians of the West Indies (see *barbecue,* above) are also responsible for *potato.* Their word was *batata*; the Spanish changed it to *patata,* and we gave it the *o* sounds.

Batata has survived in English. It's the *sweet potato.*

Why do the experts accept 'sass-pa-ril-a' as the first pronunciation for *sarsaparilla?* Well, they had to yield to popular usage. And now when a person orders the drink, he merely asks for a 'sass'.

Its tropical ancestors are *zarza* ('bramble') and *parrilla* ('little vine'). It's really a tropical American spiny, woody vine of the lily family. The dried roots were formerly used in medicine. Then an extract led to the popular carbonated drink.

Tomato is another of those words that were originated by the Nahuatl. Their word was *tomatl.* The Spanish changed it to *tomate.*

Tortilla is the Spanish diminutive of *torta* ('a cake'), which goes back to Late Latin: *torta* ('twisted loaf').

And now we come to some items relating to clothing and shelter.

CLOTHING	SHELTER
√chaps	adobe
√mantilla	cabana
poncho	fonda
rebozo	√hacienda
serape	posada
√sombrero	presidio
	√pueblo
	ramada

Chaps are those extra leather trousers, without a seat, worn by cowboys. The word is a shortening of the Mexican noun *chaparejos* or *chaparajos,* so named because the trousers offer protection from *chaparro.*

What's *chaparro?* In Spain it's an evergreen oak, but in the south-western States it's *chaparral* — a dense thicket of shrubs and thorny bushes. Hope you chaps understand.

Mantilla is the diminutive of *manta* — a shawl or cape made of coarse cotton; also a horse blanket. The *mantilla* is a woman's lacy scarf worn over the hair and shoulders.

Sombreros are well named, because these broad-brimmed hats provide shade for their wearers. The root word is *sombra* ('shade'), and that noun is a neat combination of the Latin words *sub umbra* ('under the shade').

Hacienda suffered an initial change from the original somewhere along the line. In Old Spanish it was spelt *facienda* ('employment or estate'). The Latin ancestor is the same word, but to the Romans it meant 'things to be done'. Isn't it interesting to discover that Cicero's agenda have been transformed into a modern ranch, plantation or large estate?

A related word from the same root is *fazenda,* a Brazilian coffee plantation. It's a Portuguese variant of Cicero's *facienda.*

The Spanish not only introduced the horse to the Indians but also gave at least one large group a name that has stuck. The *Pueblos* are American aborigines of New Mexico and Arizona; they include the Hopi and the Zuñi. Today we even call the dwellings and the villages of these Indians *pueblos* — such is the weight of Spanish influence.

In Spain a *pueblo* is a town, village, settlement, people or nation. The first two definitions are commonly used in the Southwest and West of the United States. In fact, a city in Colorado bears the name.

Our penultimate category is 'Dances'. Here are half a dozen to be discussed: *cha-cha, conga, fandango, rumba, seguidilla* and *tango.*

The *cha-cha* is a dance of Cuban origin. Some dictionaries now give *cha-cha-cha* as an alternative. Having attended a few weddings lately, I predict that the triple *cha* will eventually win out. All the dancers at those feasts kept chanting 'cha-cha-cha'.

Have you ever danced in a *conga* line? I used to get a kick out of it. Although we have inherited the dance from the Cubans, it really has an African origin. *Conga* is the Spanish feminine of *Congo.*

The drum employed to accompany the dance is also called a *conga.*

Fandango may be a Spanish derivative of *fado,* the Portuguese folk song. At any rate, it's a lively dance performed by a man and a woman with castanets, in triple time.

Interestingly enough, the word has taken on several other connotations:

1. tomfoolery, especially in public affairs or other matters of serious import.
2. a ball or party featuring dancing in the southwestern United States.

110

A related English word is *fandangle,* meaning 'an ornate or fantastic ornament', or 'nonsense; tomfoolery'.

The name Xavier Cugat and *rumba* seem to be wedded like man and wife. Blacks from Africa brought the dance to Cuba, and Mr. Cugat helped to import it into the U.S. and thence to Europe. The word is derived from *rumbo* ('carousal; spree; ostentation').

Seguidilla is another fast Spanish dance accompanied by castanets. Aside from also being music for that dance, the word means 'a stanza of four or seven short lines, sung to *seguidilla* music'.

The root verb is *seguir* ('to follow'), from the Latin *sequi.*

Tango means 'I touch' in Latin, but the dance for two does not date back to the Romans. Instead, it's an American Spanish alteration of the African word *tamgu* ('to dance'). I have also recently learned that *tango* is a variety of *bingo,* which is a variety of *lotto,* which is a variety of *housey-housey.*

Finally, here is a small collection of words from various sources which we have borrowed from the Spanish

MISCELLANEOUS

√bastinado	√comrade	√guitar
√bonanza	dinero	√mestizo
√cigar	√gringo	√peccadillo

Bastinado comes from *bastón* ('stick'). It's a blow with a stick or a form of corporal punishment once practised in Asia; the victim was placed face down and his ankles were tied between two poles. Then the soles of his feet were cudgelled.

One would think that *baste,* when it means 'beat soundly', belonged to the same family, but the resemblance is only coincidental. The verb stems from *beysta,* an Old Norse word.

In Spanish, *bonanza* means 'fair weather', and its figurative connotation is 'prosperity or success'. The latter idea caught on in the U.S.A., especially among western miners. A *bonanza* is a very rich vein or picket of ore or the mine in which such a strike is made. Finally, it has come to mean 'any source of wealth or profits'.

The Mayans had the noun *sik* ('tobacco') and the verb *sikar* ('to smoke'). The Spanish conquerors did some borrowing again and developed *cigarro.* We dropped the last two letters to form *cigar.* And of course the diminutive became *cigarette.*

It may seem strange, but *comrade* and *camera* are relations.

111

Their ultimate common ancestor is the Greek noun *kamara* ('vaulted chamber').

Centuries ago the Spanish created *camarada* ('chamber mate'), and the French changed it to *camarade*.

Originally, in English, *comrades* were men who shared the same sleeping quarters. Soon that sense was extended — comrades became men who shared the same fortunes and experiences. As soldiers, they were *comrades-in-arms*.

Today our usual synonym is companion or associate. Communists are known to address one another as 'comrade' — a usage not confined to them but quite common in trades unions and other working-class movements.

Gringo is often used disparagingly by Spaniards and Latin Americans to indicate a white foreigner, especially a Briton or person from the United States. The word is an alteration of *griego* ('Greek'). You know the expression 'It's Greek to me,' meaning 'It's incomprehensible.' Well, the Spanish had the same kind of idea. The *griegos* became any strangers, whether Greek or not.

Actually, the Spanish cannot claim that *guitar* is their legacy to us. The French, Arabs and ancient Greeks had a hand in the evolution of the word. Here's the history: French — *guitare*; Old Spanish — *guitarra*; Arabic — *gītār*; Greek — *kithara*.

A *mestizo* is a man of mixed parentage; in western United States and in Latin American lands he's the offspring of a Spaniard or Portuguese and an American Indian. The female of this species is a *mestiza*. The Latin ancestor is *miscere* ('to mix').

Peccadillo comes from the Spanish diminutive of *pecado* ('sin'). Literally it means 'a little sin'. Hence it denotes any slight offence or petty fault. The Latin root is *peccare* ('to sin').

A taradiddle ('fib') is a *peccadillo*.

Picaroon has a great sound. In fact, many 'oon' words delight me. Consider such mellisonant nouns as *poltroon, doubloon, bassoon, macaroon, pantaloon* and *honeymoon*. Then there is *rigadoon* — a once popular lively dance for two.

But the *picaroon* isn't really a sweet fellow at all. He's a pirate, rogue or tramp. His root is *picaro*, the Spanish word for 'scamp or knave'.

Picaroon has two other meanings: 'a pirate ship' or 'to act as a pirate'.

We have invented an equally pleasant-sounding adjective —

picaresque (from *picaresco*). The word is often applied to a certain kind of fiction featuring roguish, witty heroes.

Let us now turn our attention to Italian imports. From the beginning it must be emphasized that the French borrowed extensively from the Italians and then passed their adoptions along to us. As a random example, take *peruke* ('wig'). We extracted the word from the Medieval French *perrugue*. But the French had already appropriated it from *perruca* or *parruca*, which meant 'head of hair or wig' in Old Italian.

As I noted earlier in this chapter, the Italians monopolize the area of musical directions. Besides those that actually give direction to the performer, too numerous to list here, Italian has endowed us with scores of other words in the area presided over by Euterpe (the ancient Greeks' Muse of music). Some of them are listed below. Ticks here and in lists to follow indicate words that will be discussed.

MUSICAL TERMS

√a cappella	√cantabile	contratempo	√prima donna
allegretto	cantata	√crescendo	ritornello
√alto	√canzone	√diva	romanza
aria	capriccio	√fagotto	scena
arietta	√cavatina	falsetto	√scherzo
arioso	cello	fantasia	segno
√arpeggio	√coda	√maestro	√segue
basso	coloratura	mezzo-soprano	√sonata
√basso profundo	√concertino	obbligato	√stanza
√bel canto	√concerto	√ocarina	tempo
√bravura	contrabass	√pastorale	√toccata
√buffa	√contralto	√piano	tremolo
√buffo	contrapuntal	√piccolo	vibrato
caccia	contrapuntist	√pizzicato	viola
cadenza	contrapunto	√ponticello	violoncello

A cappella (sometimes wrongly spelt *a capella*) literally means 'in chapel style'. Translated, that comes out as 'unaccompanied by musical instruments', because it has been the custom of priests in the chapel and many choirs to go it alone.

In Italian, *alto* literally means 'high'. In English it's the highest adult male voice; also, the part in choral music between the soprano and the tenor.

In Italian, *arpeggiare* means 'to play on a harp'. As a result, *arpeggio* means 'the playing of the notes of a chord in quick succession', as on a harp. The chord so played is also a synonym.

Basso profundo (more correctly, *profondo*) means 'low, deep'. A man with such a voice can really stir you, especially when he sings a song like Kern's 'Ol' Man River'.

Bel canto literally means 'beautiful song'. It's a style of singing characterized by brilliant vocal display and purity of tone.

In Italian, *bravura* means 'bravery'. In music it's a brilliant passage or piece that displays the performer's skill and technique.

A related word is *bravo*. You hear it shouted at operas, concerts and plays when the performer has pleased the audience immensely. Some purists yell *brava* if the performer is a female.

Strangely enough, a *bravo* is also a hired killer, an assassin or desperado!

Buffo means 'comic' in Italian. Most opera fans know that the *buffo* is the singer, usually a bass, who plays a comic role. If the comic is a woman, she's a *buffa*. You can guess what *opera buffa* is.

Buffoon and *buffoonery* are members of this family.

Cantabile comes from the Late Latin *cantabilis* ('worthy to be sung'). As an adjective *cantabile* means 'melodious, flowing, song-like'. As a noun it's the music composed in that easy style.

The word has no relation to a *Cantabrigian* — a native of Cambridge, England or Cambridge, Massachusetts, and hence a student at Cambridge or Harvard. The popular short form is *Cantab*.

A *canzone* is a lyric poem of Provençal or early Italian troubadours. It's also an ode suited to a musical setting, or the setting itself, resembling that of a madrigal.

Derivatives are *canzonets* ('short, light, graceful, sprightly songs').

Cavatina has a fascinating background. Its Latin ancestor is *cavare* ('to extract or dig out'). In Italian it means 'a little separate song'. To English-speaking music-lovers it's an operatic solo that is simpler and briefer than an aria, or a solo song that is part of a larger composition. In other words, true to its Roman heritage, it's an extract.

A *coda* is a musical passage formally ending a composition or section of one. Appropriately enough, it stems from *cauda*, the Latin noun for 'tail'. If the finale is a brief one, it's called a *codetta*.

The musical composition called the *concerto* is characteristic of the sixteenth and seventeenth centuries. Typically it has three movements. A short one is a *concertino*. A *concerto* is written for a soloist, or soloists, playing with an orchestra. The eventual Latin root is *con-certare* ('to strive together'), which is just what the players do.

In the nineteenth century an English physicist named Sir Charles Wheatstone invented the *concertina* — an instrument that looks like a small accordion.

Contralto literally means 'against high'. The word has come to mean 'the lowest female voice or a singer possessing such a voice'.

Crescendo comes from *crescere,* the Latin verb meaning 'to grow'. During a *crescendo* the music is growing in volume.

Considering the Italians' great love for music, especially opera, it seems fitting that a prima donna or leading female singer should be called a *diva*. In Italian, that word means 'goddess'. (See *prima donna,* below.)

A *fagotto* is a bassoon, or an organ stop. The player is a fagottist. There's also a *fagottino* — a tenor bassoon or tenoroon.

The word is related to *faggot* ('a bundle of sticks'). I don't know why — or maybe I should just say I forgotto. But let me not forget the *contrafagotto,* or contrabassoon, the largest member of the oboe family.

Maestro comes from *magister,* the ancient Romans' word for 'master'. In the world of music a *maestro* is a great composer, conductor or teacher.

A *maestro di cappella* is a choirmaster.

An *ocarina* is a small, simple wind instrument or toy of the flute class. It's originators apparently thought it resembled a little goose, because that is what the word literally means in Italian.

Pastorales can be musical or literary. They are operas or cantatas with rural themes, or pieces of prose on the same subject.

What an interesting background the *piano* has! Its name is a short form of *pianoforte,* which literally means 'soft and loud'. Unlike its predecessor the harpsichord, its volume can be varied by the player.

The *piccolo* is also well named. The word for that tiny flute literally means 'small' in Italian.

Pizzicato means 'plucked'. A note or passage played by plucking the strings of instruments is called a *pizzicato*. The word is also a musical direction.

The bridge of a stringed instrument, such as the violin, is called the *ponticello*. The first part of the word dates back to the Latin *pons, pontis* ('bridge'), and the ending is a diminutive.

Most exciting is the fact that *ponticello* also means 'the change in an adolescent boy's voice'. In truth, he has formed a little bridge between puberty and manhood.

Prima donna literally means 'first lady'. (See *diva,* above.)

In Italian a *scherzo* is a jest or sport. Hence the word aptly describes the movement in a sonata or symphony in which the music is lively and playful in three-four time.

When defining *segue* for a crossword puzzle, I like to use the clue 'musician's transition', because that's exactly what it is. The idea is to continue playing without a break from one part of the composition to the next. The Latin root is *sequi* ('to follow'). *Sequential* is a close relative. You can see how that adjective belongs with *segue.*

Sonata literally means 'sounded' (as distinct from 'sung'). The composition is for only one or two instruments and may have from one to five movements. Beethoven was a master of the form.

Stanza in Italian means 'a stopping place'. The Latin source is our old friend *stare* ('to stand'). In English a *stanza* is a group of lines of verse forming one of the divisions of a poem or song. Note that word 'divisions'. It really is a stopping place.

Toccata comes from the past participle of the Vulgar Latin verb *toccare* ('to touch'). It's a composition in free style usually for the piano, organ or harpsichord, often employed as the prelude to a fugue. The form was originally designed to show off the artist's technique. It was invited to show his 'touch'.

Another area in which the Italians have bestowed a great number of words and phrases upon us is that of eating and drinking. The following is a partial list.

FOOD AND DRINK

√artichoke	fra diavolo	polenta	√spaghetti
√broccoli	√gnocchi	prosciutto	tortoni
cacciatore	√linguine	provolone	√trattoria
√cauliflower	√macaroni	√ravioli	√tutti-frutti
cioppino	√maraschino	√ricotta	veal scaloppini
√coffee	√minestrone	√rigatoni	√vermicelli
√cannelloni	√mozzarella	√risotto	zabaglione
chicken tetrazzini	√pasta	√salami	ziti
espresso	pistachio	√scampi	zucchini
√fettucine	√pizza	√semolina	

116

Artichoke doesn't sound Italian at all, but we derived the word from the people in Lombardy. They called the plant *articiocco* (pronounced 'ar-tee-chó-ko'). We brutalized that lovely word to make it seem as if we're telling little Arthur that he can't swallow the vegetable.

Broccoli literally means 'a little sprout'. The plant is a relative of the cauliflower.

There's also a colour called *broccoli brown* and a *broccoli rab* is an Italian turnip. The term is a modification of *broccoli di rapa* ('flowering tops of the turnips').

Cauliflower is *cavolfiore* in Italian (literally, 'cabbage flower'). The Latin root *caulis* means 'cabbage'. The plant *cole* is a linguistic cousin of *cauliflower*.

In Italian, coffee is *caffè*. And in French of course it's *café*. The word can be traced back to the Turks and Arabs.

Cannelloni is an Italian dish of large-sized macaroni stuffed with forcemeat or a cheese mixture. The name was chosen because the casings for the dough are tubular. Literally, *cannelloni* means 'small tubes'.

Related words are *cane, canal, canyon, canister, channel* and even *kennel*.

Fettucine are literally 'little ribbons'. They are broad, flat noodles served with sauce or butter. A Roman chef has gained fame because of his special way of preparing the noodles with a creamy sauce. He named the dish after himself: *fettucine alfredo*.

By now you must realize how metaphoric yet realistically expressive and humorous the Italians are, especially in their nomenclature. Take *gnocchi* — small dumplings of a paste often made with cheese or riced potato and served with a sauce. They look a bit like knots in wood, and the word is an alteration of *nocchio*. What does that mean? A knot in wood!

Here are some other Italian expressions that should give you a chuckle. The literal meanings are in parentheses.

essere una buona forchetta	to be a hearty eater ('to be a good fork')
essere in forse	to be of two minds ('to be in maybe')
quattro gatti	scanty attendance ('four cats')
asino calzato e vestito	a perfect ass ('an ass with shoes and clothes on')
come il cacio sui maccheroni	just about perfect ('like the cheese on macaroni')

Typical of this drollery is the word *linguine*. Literally, they are 'little tongues' — and that's what they look like to anyone who has a poet's imagination. The singular is *linguina* — but who would want only one of those delectable bits of pasta?

Probably the most interesting word in this list is *macaroni*. It's a form of pasta having a diameter of .11 to .27 inches and is not to be confused with *spaghetti, linguine* or *vermicelli,* which are thinner.

The immediate source of the word is *maccarone,* a Neapolitan term for 'dumpling or small cake'. Some lexicographers claim that it can be traced back to the ancient Greek *makar* ('blessed'). In later Greek texts (200–600 A.D.) *makaria* was literally 'a blessed cake'.

In the eighteenth century, *macaroni* took on another connotation in Britain — a dandy who adopted foreign mannerisms. The affections of those fops must have been more Italianate than Gallic, or they would have been called *macaroons.* Yes, those cookies are a French borrowing from *macaroni.*

When Yankee Doodle 'stuck a feather in his hat and called it *macaroni*', he became a fop wearing a plume. If the metre had allowed, the word 'himself' would probably have replaced 'it'.

A related adjective is *macaronic,* used to describe prose or verse in which vernacular words are mixed with Latin. The carol 'In Dulci Jubilo' is a famous example.

The Italians took the adjective *amarus* ('bitter') from the ancient Romans and changed it to *amaro.* Then they dropped the initial letter and developed *marasca* ('wild cherry'). The diminutive became *maraschino,* that special kind of cherry that is usually added to a Manhattan cocktail. *Maraschino* is also a sweet liqueur made from the fermented juice of the *marasca.*

If you have never tasted *minestrone,* you're in the minority. This rich, thick Italian vegetable soup has been gaining popularity for many decades. The word is an augmentation of *minestra* ('thick soup').

But the derivation is most interesting! The parent verb is *minestrare* ('to dish up'), and the Latin ancestor is *ministrare* ('to serve or dish up'). It's fascinating to think that *minestrone* and *minister* are close relatives.

Italians love diminutives, and I think this says something about their character. Such words as *falsetto, operetta* and *bambino* abound in their language. *Mozzarella* is a good example. It's the diminutive of *mozza* ('a kind of cheese'). The verb is *mozzare* ('to cut off'). The cheese is moist and rubbery, but it's an important ingredient of such popular dishes as *lasagna* (literally, 'the noodle') and *manicotti* (literally, 'muffs or sleeves'), and in the preparation of *pizza* and *ravioli*.

Pasta is the flour paste or dough used in making *macaroni*, *spaghetti, ravioli* and other such foods, and hence is the generic term for them. Without any alteration in meaning or spelling, the word was taken from a Late Latin noun. The ultimate root is the Greek verb *passein* ('to sprinkle').

In the 1930s few people of non-Italian ancestry knew what a *pizza* was. Now it has become a favourite snack. *Pizza parlours* and *pizzerias* have mushroomed. The original dish featured cheese and tomatoes baked on a thin layer of dough. Now there are dozens of varieties of *pizza,* with anchovies, sausages, mushrooms and other garnishes.

The etymology of the word is in doubt. Some experts believe that it comes from Old Italian *pizza* ('a point'). Others trace it to Medieval Greek *pitta* ('cake or pie').

The Italians' penchant for naming things according to their resemblance to other objects is revealed once again in *ravioli*. To the originators of the dish the small casings of pasta filled with chopped meat or cheese looked like little turnips. *Rava* means 'turnip' in Italian dialect, and the diminutive is *raviola*. The Latin ancestor is *rapum* ('turnip or beet'). Another derivative is the plant called *rape* — not to be confused with the sexual crime, which dates back to the Romans' *rapere* ('to seize').

Ricotta is also well named. This cheese is made from the whey of other cheeses. Its literal meaning is 'cooked or boiled again'. The Latin verb *recoquere* is the immediate ancestor.

Another perfect designation is revealed in the derivation of *rigatoni*. These large casings of pasta bear ridges. *Rigato* is the past participle of *rigare* ('to mark with lines'). Again, note the ending. In this case the size is exaggerated.

Risotto is rice sautéed in oil with a mixture of finely chopped onions and garlic with seasonings. It is then diluted gradually with broth until it is tender and moist. It is most often served with Parmesan cheese.

Salami is the Italian plural of *salame* ('preserved meat or salt pork'). This highly spiced sausage can be traced back to *sal,* the Roman noun for 'salt'.

119

Scampi are large prawns — in Britain, Dublin Bay prawns.

Semolina is a granular milled product of durum wheat, used in the making of pasta and, sweetened, as a pudding. It is the diminutive of *semola* ('bran') and can be traced back to the Latin *simila* ('finest wheat flour') — a word probably borrowed from the Assyrian *samīdu* ('fine meal').

Spaghetti, the most popular form of pasta, is another of those diminutive nouns that express so much so well. *Spago* is a cord in Italian. Hence *spaghetti* are literally 'small cords'.

Somewhat derisively, the slangsters have come up with a phrase for a cowboy film made in Italy; they call it a *spaghetti* western. Spaghetti Junction, the complex road intersection in Birmingham, is another derisive nickname, comprehensible at once to any motorist who has ever traversed it.

A *trattoria* is a small, inexpensive Italian restaurant. Here are its roots:

trattore	('innkeeper')
trattare	('to handle or manage')
tractare	('to treat' — Latin)

So the next time you trot over to a *trattoria* you can expect a treat.

Tutti-frutti has a nice ring to it, and the ice-cream has a nice taste. It means 'all fruits'.

Perhaps you won't want to eat *vermicelli* when you hear that this pasta literally means 'little worms'. Not to worry; the imaginative Italians chose that name because the strings of pasta are so thin.

Now let us turn our attention to the contributions to our language from the Italians in all of the arts besides music — an area already covered. Below are many of the words in that category.

THE ARTS

√ amoretto	√ gesso	√ patina	√ sestina
√ amorino	impasto	√ Pietà	stanza
ballerina	√ impresario	√ Punchinello	√ stucco
canto	√ intaglio	√ putti	studio
caricature	√ libretto	replica	√ tempera
cartoon	literati	rilievo	√ terra cotta
√ chiaroscuro	majolica	√ saltarello	√ terrazzo
extravaganza	√ novella	scena	√ terza rima

√fantasia	√ottava rima	√scenario	√tondo
√fresco	√ovolo	√sepia	torso
gala			

An *amoretto* is an infant cupid, such as those found in Italian art of the sixteenth century. The noun is a diminutive of *amore* ('love'), which comes of course from the Latin word *amor*. *Amorino* is another diminutive of the same word. It has come to mean 'cherub'.

The Italian verb *caricare*, derived from Vulgar Latin, means 'to overload'. That's just what a *caricature* does, whether it's an artist's exaggerated drawing or a writer's satirical piece about a person.

When I was growing up I loved *cartoons* and always thought they were simply synonymous with caricatures and comic strips. Then I discovered that *cartoon* has another meaning. It can be an artist's full-size preliminary sketch of a design or picture to be copied, for example, in a fresco, mosaic or tapestry.

The word comes from *cartone* ('a pasteboard') and is an augmentation of *carta* ('card'). The Latin root is *charta* ('leaf of papyrus'). If you have always wondered why *Magna Charta* could also be spelt *Magna Carta,* now you know.

Chiaroscuro has been taken over in English without the slightest change. Literally, it means 'light and shade'. It's a style of painting using those two opposites to produce a dramatic effect and the illusion of depth.

Fantasia literally means 'fancy' in Italian. In addition to its musical uses, it can be a poem or play in which the author's fancy roves without restriction. It's also an Arab performance featuring dancing and various kinds of shenanigans on horseback, including rapid rhythm gunshots and shouts. Walt Disney's film Fantasia helped to popularize the word.

Fresco is the art of painting with water-based pigments on wet plaster. 'Wet' is significant because one definition of *fresco* is 'fresh'.

Gesso is the Italian word meaning 'gypsum or plaster of Paris prepared for use in painting, sculpture or bas-reliefs'. Our painters and sculptors have embraced the word in its entirety.

Another Italian word that we have adopted without change in sense or spelling is *impresario* — a manager or conductor of an opera or concert company. We have extended the use a bit to mean the director of TV shows, art exhibitions and even sports contests.

The Italian root is *impresa* ('enterprise'), and the Vulgar Latin grandparent is *imprendere* ('to undertake'). Incidentally, let's not look down our noses at Vulgar Latin. Actually, the Romance languages developed mostly from that colloquial form of the parent tongue. I keep reminding myself that today's colloquialisms are tomorrow's accepted, dignified words.

The chief meaning of *intaglio* is 'an engraving or incised figure in stone or other hard material'. The Italian verb is *intagliare* ('to engrave, carve, cut'), an offshoot of a Late Latin verb *taliare* ('to cut').

You can see why tailor is a relative.

Libretto is the diminutive of *libro*, which evolved from *liber*, the Latin word for 'book'. Today the 'little book' is the text for an opera, oratorio or other long choral work.

It's interesting to note that the text of a musical comedy is also called 'the book', as differentiated from the music itself, which is 'the score'.

Novella and *novel* are cousins. Both are derived from *novus*, the Latin adjective for 'new'. *Novelty* is of course in the same family.

Ottava rima (literally, 'eighth rhyme') is a stanza of eight lines, with a rhyme scheme of *abababcc*. The English form has ten or eleven syllables in each line.

Sometimes *octave* and *ottava rima* are used as synonyms.

Ovolo, a convex moulding known to all crossword puzzle fans, dates back to the Romans' *ovum* ('egg'), because of its elliptical shape.

Patina originally meant 'tarnish' in Italian, and in Medieval Latin it was a shallow dish or pan. In English it is defined as 'the green film that forms on copper or bronze by long exposure to a moist atmosphere'. Because it is valued aesthetically, it is often produced artificially, as by treatment with acids.

We have extended the use of the word; it now applies to the thin coating or colour change resulting from age. Antique collectors delight in the *patina* on wood or silver.

An accepted variation is *patine*. I first met that word when I read THE MERCHANT OF VENICE. Lorenzo says:

> 'Sit, Jessica. Look how the floor of heaven
> Is thick inlaid with *patines* of bright gold.'

The passage in which those lines appear is one of the most beautiful and thought-provoking in all of English literature. If your curiosity is excited see Act V, Scene 1.

A *Pietà* is a representation of the Virgin Mary mourning over the body of Christ after the Crucifixion. In Italian the word means 'pity'. The Latin root is *pietas* ('piety').

Punchinello has a fascinating history. This buffoon in puppet-shows got his name from Neapolitan dialect. His eventual ancestors are *pulcino* ('chicken') and the Latin noun *pullus* ('pullet').

The British adopted him; he became the quarrelsome, hook-nosed husband in the Punch and Judy shows. Sometimes that grotesque character put one over his wife, and then he was as pleased as Punch.

Putti are cherubic little angels or cupids used in painting and sculpture, especially during the Renaissance. If you visit St. Peter's Basilica in the Vatican, you will see many a *putto* on the gigantic columns.

Saltarello (sometimes spelt *saltarella*) sounds salty, and in a way it is — but not because of its linguistic background. It's a lively Italian dance featuring hops and skips, and it's also the music for that ballroom exercise.

The Latin root, fittingly, is *saltare* ('to jump or leap').

Scenario is an Italian adaptation of the Late Latin adjective *scaenarius* ('of the stage'). It has evolved into a synonym for screenplay, or outline of the plot of a play or film. Naturally, the people who write such material had to have a name, so we dubbed them *scenarists*.

Sepia has several meanings:

1. a dark-brown ink or pigment originally prepared from the fluid secreted by the cuttlefish
2. a sketch or picture using the above pigment
3. a dark reddish brown colour
4. a photographic print in the above colour

The Italian noun is *seppia* (they love to add extra consonants!), but the Latin root is *sepia* ('cuttlefish').

The Italian word *sesto* ('sixth') has given us *sestina,* a form of poem having six six-line stanzas and a tercet. What's a tercet? It's a group of three lines that rhyme. Here's my tercet; you can curse it.

> In the creative, poetic arena
> I confess I have never seen a
> Completely delightful *sestina.*

123

In defining the word 'plaster' for a crossword puzzle, I was once tempted to write, 'Don't get *stucco* on this one!' Sober judgment prevailed and I refrained.

This word that we borrowed from the Italians originally comes from an Old High German noun, *stukki,* or *stucki* ('crust, covering, fragment'). At any rate, the material is used to decorate walls, whether interior or exterior. Even the Romans used it; their word was *tectorium.* It is a mixture of pulverized white marble and plaster of lime, with water added.

Relatives of *stucco* include *stock* and *stoker.*

Tempera is a medium used by painters, consisting of pigment usually mixed with egg yolk to produce a dull, opaque finish. This Italian import can be traced to *temperare,* the Latin verb meaning 'to mix in true proportion'. Most lexicographers assume that the ultimate root is *tempus* ('time').

Of special interest is the fact that *temper, temperament, temperance, temperate* and *temperature* all belong in this Roman tribe.

In Italian, *terra cotta* means 'cooked earth'. This hard, waterproof clay is a standby for potters and builders. The word also means 'a shade of orange'.

Terrazzo is a flooring material made of marble or other stone chips set in cement or marble and polished when dry. Literally, this mosaic form means 'terrace' in Italian.

Terza rima was the verse form used by Dante in his Divina Commedia. The rhyme scheme is rather complicated: *aba-bcb-cdc,* etc. There are other variations.

A *tondo* is a round painting or sculptured medallion. The word is a derivative of the Latin adjective *rotundus* ('round'). Guess what English word is a relative!

Strangely enough, in the areas of clothing and shelter we have only a small inheritance from Italy. Most of the imports in the first category have been transmitted to us by Roman Catholic officials.

CLOTHING

biretta	a square cap with three or four projections and a tassel on top
mozzetta	a prelate's short cape having a small hood
zucchetto	an ecclesiastic's skullcap

campanile	a bell tower
casino	a. a place for gambling, dancing, entertainment
	b. a card game (also spelt *cassino*)
	In Italy a casino is a small country house; it's the diminutive of *casa*.
cupola	a. a rounded roof or ceiling
	b. a small dome on a roof
	c. a dome-shaped structure
	The word is derived from *cupola* ('a little tub')
loggia	a roofed open arcade or gallery on the side of a building and usually facing an open court.
pergola	an arbour, usually with an open roof and often featuring latticework
seraglio	a. a harem
	b. palace of a sultan
	The Italian word is *serraglio,* meaning 'an enclosure or paddock'. It can be traced back to the Latin noun *sera* ('a bolt or lock').

Finally, we come to an interesting conglomerate group of words and phrases borrowed from Italy.

MISCELLANEOUS

agio	√ciao	√inferno	pococurante
√alfresco	√cognoscenti	√influenza	√punctilio
amore	√credenza	lava	√regatta
autostrada	√ditto	√lira	√salvo
bambino	fascist	√madonna	scarp
banco	fata morgana	√mafia	sequin
√belladonna	felucca	major-domo	sirocco
braggadocio	√fiasco	√malaria	√stiletto
buffalo	generalissimo	manifesto	umbrella
√cameo	√ghetto	mohair	√vendetta
camorra	√gondola	√motto	vista
caprice	√graffito	√nuncio	viva
carnival	grotto	√padrone	volcano
√carton	√imbroglio	paparazzo	√zero
√catafalque	inamorata	pellagra	√zingana
√cavalier	inamorato	piazza	√zingaro

Alfresco (sometimes spelt as two words) literally means 'in the cool'. In Italian or English the adjective now carries the idea of being outdoors or in the open air.

125

Belladonna is a poisonous plant of Europe or the United States. Another term for it is 'deadly nightshade'. Why, then, should it carry such a lovely name (literally, 'beautiful lady')? The reason is that it has been used as a cosmetic for dilating the eyes.

Because *cameo* is a finely carved gem, the word has recently acquired two other definitions:

1. a minor but well defined role, usually played by a noted actor
2. a fine bit of descriptive writing

Carton, like *cartoon*, is from *cartone*, the Italian word for 'card or pasteboard'.

What a strange history *catafalque* has! First of all, the word can be defined in several ways:

1. an ornamental, rather elaborate structure for solemn funeral rites in churches
2. a pall-covered empty coffin used at Roman Catholic requiem Masses after the burial
3. a hearse

The Italian source is *catafalco* ('funeral canopy'); the French borrowed the word and Gallicized the spelling. But the ultimate ancestors are a mixed breed: *kata,* from Greek, 'down', and *fala,* from Latin, 'a wooden tower'.

Cavalier is directly from the French, but the Italians deserve more credit, because their word *cavaliere* was transported to Paris centuries ago. The ancient Roman root is *caballus* ('horse'). Via the same routes, *cavalry* and *cavalcade* have come into our language. *Cavalcade* originally meant only 'a procession of horsemen or carriages'. Then it became any sort of procession, and finally evolved into a synonym for any sequence of events.

There are so many meanings for *cavalier* that I cannot give them all. Chiefly, the chap is a man-of-arms on horseback, or a knight. Hence he's also a gallant or a lady's dancing partner. In British history he became a supporter of Charles I against Parliament.

Possibly because he was a Royalist or aristocrat, the fellow took on a pejorative sense when he was turned into an adjective. If someone gives you *cavalier* treatment, you're getting what is known in the streets as 'a fast brush-off'.

Finally, as one who loves lyrics, I am compelled to mention the *Cavalier* poets: Herrick, Carew, Suckling, Lovelace et al. They

126

were so named because of their association with the court of Charles I.

Ciao, the Italians' informal greeting or farewell, has become popular with the jet set and others. The word is pronounced like a G.I.'s meal — 'chow'.

The *cognoscenti* are the experts or people in the know, especially in the fine arts. A *cognoscente* can presumably distinguish an original Cézanne from a fine copy. The Latin root is *cognoscere* ('to know'). Relatives include *incognito* (from Italian, too), *cognizant*, *recognize, connoisseur, notion, acquaint* and *quaint*.

Credenza has a delightful etymology. This buffet, sideboard or bookcase without legs originally meant 'belief or confidence' in Italian and goes all the way back to the Romans' *credere* ('to believe'). The word is derived from the practice of placing a nobleman's meal on a buffet or sideboard to be tasted first by a servant. If he didn't die on the spot, the lord of the manor believed it was safe to take a bite.

Some words in this Latin family are *credo, credulous, credence, credit, credible, miscreant, recreant* and a host of others.

In the Tuscan dialect *ditto* means 'said'. It's from *dictus*, the past participle of *dicere* ('to say') in Latin. Thus the first meaning of the word is 'the aforesaid'.

Fiasco has an interesting history. This ambitious project that turns out to be a complete failure literally means 'bottle' in Italian, and in fact it can also be used in English to mean 'a bottle of wine'.

No expert is sure how this container for Chianti took on the connotation of 'a complete failure'. I wonder if it is possible that Italian glassblowers coined that definition when they were unsuccessful in their attempts to form a bottle of a certain ornamental shape. It sounds like a good story, but it's probably far off the mark.

In any case, our word *flask* is directly related to *fiasco*.

Ghetto, according to one group of philologers, originally meant 'foundry' in Italian. The section occupied by Jews in Venice had once been the site of a cannon foundry.

Jews were *ghettoized* in many European cities. In other words, they were forced to live in one area only. Today a *ghetto* is any section occupied by a minority group.

Naturally, *gondola* has a Venetian origin. The name of that long, narrow flat-bottomed boat so beloved by tourists is considered by some lexicographers to be an alteration of *dondolare* ('to rock and roll')! Others conjecture that it can be etymologically traced back to the Greek word *kondy* ('drinking vessel').

Aside from being a canal boat, a *gondola* is also a flat-bottomed river barge, a chair or couch with the back sweeping up like the end of the Venetian boat, the car attached to a dirigible or balloon, and, in the U.S., a topless freight car on the railway.

Loving diminutives as they do, the Italian *gondoliers* also invented the *gondoletta*.

Graffito literally means 'a scribbling', from *graffio* ('a scratch'). The ancient Greek ancestor is *graphein* ('to write'). Hence you can readily see that *graffito* has scores of kin.

But the closest relative is *sgraffito*, a method of making designs, as on murals and ceramics. It is also the decoration or pottery produced by this method.

The plural of *graffito* is commonly used to mean 'scrawled words or pictures written in public places such as pavements, walls, phone booths and lavatories'.

The archaeologists who uncovered Pompeii were amazed to find *graffiti* on the walls. Visitors to New York City are also astonished to see the exteriors (and interiors) of most subway cars covered with gaily coloured designs, apparently executed surreptitiously while the cars are parked in the railway yards.

Imbroglio originally meant 'a confused heap'. Thus one might say, 'An imbroglio of manuscripts and letters lay on the editor's desk.' But the word is more often used today to mean 'a confused and violent altercation'. *Embroil* is one of its relations.

Dante's INFERNO deals with Hell. An *inferno* is any hellish place; it's also a conflagration. The Latin root is *infernus* ('situated beneath; lower'). Since Pluto ruled the lower world, called Dis by the Romans and Hades by the Greeks, and since our flaming hell is also reputed to be down under the earth, you can see how such a tepid word as *infernus* gave rise to a hot one — inferno.

The adjective *infernal* not only means 'hellish or diabolical' but has developed into a synonym for 'damnable, outrageous'. We say, 'He's an *infernal* nuisance.' Bombs used to be called *infernal machines*.

The Italian astrologers gave us *influenza*. Literally, it means 'influence', but the notion arose that the cause of the disease was influenced by the stars.

Many a *lira* glistens under the waters of the Fountain of Trevi in Rome. The plural of this Italian coin is *lire*. The word comes from

Latin *libra* ('balance or pound'). If horoscopes interest you, then you probably know that *Libra* ('The Balance') is a zodiacal constellation between Virgo and Scorpio. Anyone born between September 23 and October 22 is a *Libra*.

Madonna literally means 'my lady'. The title is usually applied to the Virgin Mary. Thousands of artists have painted *Madonnas* through the centuries.

In Sicilian dialect, *mafia* means 'boldness, bluster, swagger'. Thus arose the name *Mafia* (or *Maffia*) for that notorious secret society of terrorists and bandits. The members are called *Mafiosi*.

Malaria is literally 'bad air'. The name originated because people once believed that the miasma from swamps was responsible for the disease. They overlooked the mosquitos that bred in those fens!

In Italian, *motto* means 'word'. In French, *mot* has the same meaning, and *bon mot* ('good word') is a witticism. The common ancestor is the Latin *muttum* ('a grunt or muttering').

A *nuncio* is a permanent official representative of the Vatican to a foreign government. *Nuncio,* or *nunzio,* means 'messenger', from the Latin *nuntius*.

Padrone means 'patron', from the Latin *patronus*. Today the word has several meanings:

1. boss or chief
2. landlord or innkeeper
3. master of a Mediterranean trading ship

The word should not be confused with *padre,* which means 'father' or 'priest' in Italian or Spanish. The *padre* in the armed forces is the chaplain.

All of the above words ultimately owe their heritage to *pater,* the Latin noun for 'father'.

Even though *punctilio* means 'an instant of time' or 'a small detail', in common usage it refers to a point of etiquette or conduct in a ceremony, or the observance of petty formalities. The adjective *punctilious* is a derivative.

The Italians and Spanish share the honours for *punctilio.* The former evolved *puntiglio,* the latter *puntillo.* Both mean 'a little point'. The Latin ancestor is *punctum* ('point').

Henley-on-Thames, and all those other *regattas,* have attracted worldwide interest, but few of us know that the first *regatta* was the *regata* at Venice, in which the gondoliers raced. This dialectal word came from *regalar* ('to compete') and literally meant 'a striving for mastery'. In modern usage a *regatta* is any race involving various kinds of vessels — for example, sculls, yachts, speedboats.

Salvo is a modification of the Italian *salve* ('Be safe!'). The Latin grandparents are *salve* ('Hail!'), *salvus* ('safe') and *salvere* ('to be in good health').

In a way *salvo* can be compared with *goodbye* ('God be with you'), because the original meanings of both words have been generally forgotten through usage.

When a head of state is greeted, he's given a twenty-one-gun salute. That's a salvo. When Ian Botham hits a century, the crowd at Lord's gives him a salvo, whether they know it or not. But it's no salute or cheer when a warship fires a *salvo* at the enemy.

The ancient Romans used a needle-like device for writing on wax tablets. The instrument was a *stilus*. Today we call it a *stylus* or *style*.

Who would think that a tool used for peaceful, creative ends could become such a dangerous weapon as a *stiletto*? This 'little dagger' has a French-derived cousin, *stylet* — equally ominous.

However, *stiletto* and *stylet* do have their more constructive aspects. The former can be a sharp instrument for making holes in cloth; in Britain it's a woman's spike heel. *Stylet* to a surgeon is a slender probe.

Vendetta is the Italian alteration of the Latin *vindicta* ('vengeance'). This blood feud is typified in Romeo and Juliet. Some of the many relations include *vindicate* and *vindictive*.

The Arabs really deserve the basic credit for *zero*. Just as they have given us our numerals, they sent *sifr* ('cipher') to Italy. There it was changed to *zero*. English adopted it via French *zéro*.

Zingana means 'zebrawood'. That's a tropical tree or shrub with a striped appearance, used in cabinet work. In Italy a *zingana* is a female Gypsy; a male Gypsy is a *zingaro* or *zingano*.

If you have guessed by now that the Italians are high on my list of favourite people, you are *corretto*. After all, I married a *bella signorina* whose father was born near Napoli and whose mother came from Sorrento. Beyond that, she makes a great dish of *manicotti,* and her *bistecca alla pizzaiola* is out of this world.

7 Words from Everywhere

English is not just a linguistic mixture of the Romance languages and Anglo-Saxon; it contains a mélange of the vocabulary of scores of groups from every continent on our planet. Open-heartedly, and almost naïvely, English speakers — especially the Americans — have become the most avid adopters of foreignisms in the history of civilization.

The fact that we engaged in two great wars with the Germans during the first half of this century caused a great number of their military words to enter our vocabulary. Here is a sampling; the words ticked will be discussed.

Anochluss	√ flak	√ panzer
√ Big Bertha	√ Gestapo	√ putsch
√ blitz	Junker	√ rucksack
√ blitzkrieg	√ Luftwaffe	√ stalag

Big Bertha was a large German gun used in World War I. It's an alteration of *dicke Bertha* ('fat Bertha') and was named for Bertha Krupp. The Krupp Works at Essen supplied the Germans with military equipment in both wars.

Any large, cumbersome machine or tool may now be called a *Big Bertha*. Certain cameras and lenses that are excellent for long-range photography also bear the frau's name.

Blitz is a short form of *Blitzkrieg*, which literally means 'lightning war'. Any sudden overwhelming attack is a *blitzkrieg* or *blitz*.

Flak (sometimes spelt *flack*) is an abridgement of *Fliegerab-wehrkanone*, a combination of three words meaning 'aircraft-defence-gun'. The first word begins with *Fl*, the second with *a*, and the third with *k*. The original meaning of *Flak* was 'anti-aircraft gun'.

Today *flak* is used to mean 'strong, abusive criticism'. Some lexicographers label that definition as slang, but it's predictable that it will be legitimized in the future.

Gestapo is another of those acronymic names. The German parent is *Geheime Staatspolizei* ('secret state police'). If you

131

examine those words carefully, you will find *Ge-Sta-Po* in neat sequence.

We have not only taken over the word as a noun with evil connotations but have also used it attributively. Sometimes police are accused of employing *Gestapo* tactics.

The *Luftwaffe* was Hitler's air force. The first syllable means 'air' and the second means 'weapon'.

Panzer means 'armour'; the German *panzer* divisions in World War II were armoured divisions. As a noun in English, *panzer* has come to mean 'tank'. The original German word is *Panzerkampfwagen* ('armoured battle-wagon').

Putsch means 'a sudden rebellion'. The Germans borrowed it from Swiss dialect, where it means 'a push or blow or thrust'.

The resemblance between *putsch* and *push* is only a coincidence. The latter can be traced to *pulsus,* the past participle of the Latin verb *pellere* ('to beat'). *Pulse, pulsation, repulsive* and *compulsion* are a few next of kin.

A *rucksack* is a form of knapsack — a bag for carrying supplies while on a march. The first syllable of *rucksack* is a dialectal form of *Rücken* ('back').

Stalag is another of those abridgements. The origin is *Stammlager* ('base camp').

Again a coincidence arises. The German prison camp has no relation to *stalagmite,* which dates back to the Greeks' *stalagmos* ('a dropping').

Have you every had trouble distinguishing a *stalagmite* from a *stalactite*? Both are deposits of carbonate of lime in caves. The first builds up from the floor, and the second hangs from the ceiling. A good mnemonic is *g* for ground and *c* for ceiling.

Next, let's look at just a few delicious imports from Germany related to food and drink and kindred areas:

kaffeeklatsch	√lager	rathskeller	√schnitzel
√kirsch	marzipan	√sauerbraten	√strudel
√kohlrabi	√pretzel	√sauerkraut	√wurst
√kümmel	√prosit	√schnapps	zwieback

Kirsch is a short form of *Kirschwasser* (literally, 'cherry water'). It's a dry, colourless brandy distilled from the fermented juice of morello cherries.

The Germans borrowed *kohlrabi* (we lowercase it) from the

Italians' plural *cavoli rape* ('cole rape'). This garden vegetable is related to cabbage.

Kümmel means 'caraway seed'. It's a colourless liqueur flavoured with caraway seeds and such aromatics as anise and cumin.

Lager (or *lager beer*) comes from *Lagerbier* ('beer made for storage'). In German, *Lager* means 'storehouse'. True to its name, the beer is aged in refrigerated storehouses or cellars for several months.

Pretzel is from *Brezel*. But that German noun finds its ultimate source in the Romans' *brachium* ('arm'). The original *pretzels* — and those today that are still shaped like the letter B — resembled a pair of folded arms.

Prosit is also from Latin. Literally, it means 'may it be good'. For some reason the Germans took a fancy to the word. When they raise their steins and shout 'Prosit!' their toast conveys 'To your health!'

By the way, *stein* should probably have been included in my list. It's an abridgement of *Steingut* ('stoneware').

Sauerbraten and *sauerkraut* may be taken up together because they both begin with a German word meaning 'sour'. *Braten* means 'roast', and this meat dish is a standby in German homes and restaurants. *Kraut* means 'cabbage'.

Schnapps (or *schnaps*) is a strong Holland gin. It is also any of various distilled liquors. In German, *Schnaps* means 'a dram or nip'. Our verb *snap* is a relation.

Schnitzels are veal cutlets, German style. The parent is *Schnitz* ('a piece cut off'). *Schnitzel* is the diminutive form. If it comes from Vienna, it's a *Wiener Schnitzel*. *Wien* is the German name for Vienna and is pronounced 'Veen'.

Strudel has a fascinating background. Literally, this pastry means 'whirlpool'. The name was chosen because of its spiral cross section. Our word *stream* is a relation.

Wurst is the best for many lovers of sausages. *Bratwurst* is a highly seasoned sausage made of veal or pork. *Brato* means 'lean meat'. *Knackwurst* is also very spicy. The initial syllable stems from *knacken* ('to crack or split or make a crackling noise').

And now let us review a few of the German phrases and words that are familiar to many of us:

Achtung!   'Attention!'
Auf Wiedersehen   'Till we meet again' or 'Goodbye'

Ausländer	Foreigner; outsider
Danke schön	'Thank you very much'
Gesundheit!	'To your health!' (This can be a toast or consoling word to a sneezer.)
Unter den Linden	Main street in Berlin (literally, 'under the limes')
Wie geht's?	'How goes it?' 'How do you do?'
Wunderbar!	'Wonderful!'

German and Austrian psychologists and psychiatrists have made many contributions to our language. Here are just a few:

Angst
Gestalt
Weltschmerz

Of the four, *Angst* seems to have become the most commonly used, perhaps because of such problems as inflation, the energy crisis and the hustle and bustle of our cities. Or maybe we have adopted the word because it sounds so much like *anxious, anger, anguish.* At any rate, *Angst* is a feeling of anxiety or a gloomy, often neurotic, state of depression or fear.

The Danes can claim partial credit for the word. Incidentally, the plural is *Angste*, and in English the singular and plural are sometimes spelt with a lowercase *a*.

Gestalt psychologists popularized the German word that literally means 'shape or form'. They studied behaviour from the standpoint of response to configurational wholes. Their thesis is that we see an object or hear a melody not as a collection of parts or separate notes but as a whole or unit.

Weltschmerz literally means 'world pain'. It's a mood of sentimental sadness or pessimism about the state of the world.

Many German breeds of dogs have become our pets. Among them are the *poodle, schnauzer* and *spitz.*

Poodle comes from *pudeln* ('to splash'). *Puddle* is a related word.

In German, *schnauzen* means 'to growl or snarl'. But if you own a non-snarling *Schnauzer,* you might prefer *Schnauze* as the real source; it means 'snout'.

Spitz means 'pointed' in German. The thin, pointed rod that we call a *spit* is a related word. Dogwise, a *spitz* is a small dog with a sharp-pointed muzzle, or *Schnauze.*

Finally, let's look at a selected olio of words transmitted from German to English. Those with ticks will be discussed.

alpenglow	√ Frau	√ kitsch	turnverein
alpenhorn	√ Fräulein	√ lieder	umlaut
alpenstock	√ glockenspiel	Lorelei	verboten
autobahn	kegler	schloss	verein
bund	√ kaput	schneider	wanderlust
√ edelweiss	√ kindergarten	√ schuss	Wunderkind
√ ersatz			

The Alpine plant called *edelweiss* has petal-like leaves that are white and woolly. It is well named: *edel* means 'noble or precious' and *weiss* means 'white'.

Ersatz comes from the German verb *ersetzen* ('to replace'). In English it means 'artificial or synthetic' and conveys the idea of substituting something inferior for the real thing.

Frau means 'wife or married woman' and is the German equivalent of Mrs. The word comes from Old High German *frouwa* ('mistress'). From there it can be traced back to a basic Indo-European word *per,* and it is part of an immense family. Among the members are *fore, before, forefathers, far, fare* and *first.*

Fräulein is the diminutive of *Frau.* She's an unmarried woman.

Glockenspiel, when translated backward, means 'play bells'. This percussion instrument produces a series of bell-like tones when struck with small hammers. *Clock* is a related word; it is so called because the first *clocks* were bell-like in form.

A goner is a person who is *kaput.* He's finished, ruined, done for. The word is sometimes spelt *kaputt,* and that form is the exact duplication of the German adjective meaning 'lost or ruined'.

The Berliners borrowed the word from the Parisians. *Capot* means 'not having a single trick in the game of piquet'. The original meaning of *capot* is 'a hooded cloak'.

Kindergarten literally means 'a garden of children' — a lovely word indeed! What amazes me is that we did not change the *t* to a *d* somewhere along the line.

In German, *Kitsch* is 'arty trash' — from *kitschen* ('to smear or slap together, as a work of art'). The original meaning in German dialect was 'to scrape up mud from the street'.

Hence *kitsch* is shallow, pretentious, inferior artistic or literary material slickly calculated to have popular appeal.

Lieder (pronounced like 'leader') is the plural of *lied* — a German song, either a popular song or an art song, such as those composed by Schubert.

Schuss is a straight downhill run in skiing. As a verb it means

135

'to ski straight down a hill at full speed'. In German, one meaning of the word is 'gunshot'. When you *schuss,* you literally shoot down the slope — as fast as a bullet.

And now let us review some of our words that are of Russian origin. Communism has provided us with such words as *commissar* (since 1946, a minister), *oblast* (U.S.S.R. subdivision), *Presidium* (chief, permanent administrative committee) and *soviet* (council).

From pre-Lenin eras we have obtained *czar* (or *tsar* and *tzar*), *czarina* (or *tsarina* and *tzarina*), *pogrom, ukase* and *cossack,* among others.

A *pogrom* is an organized persecution and massacre of a minority group. The *czars* often prompted such attempts to wipe out the Jews. *Czar,* by the way, can be traced back to Caesar.

A *ukase* is an imperial decree or arbitrary proclamation, such as used to be issued by the czars.

The *Cossacks* were members of a favoured military group, especially in the Ukraine. The word *kazak,* or *kozak,* was of Turkish origin; it conveyed the idea of a free, independent person or vagabond or adventurer.

Our culinary heritage from Russia is more pleasant. Three samples are *borsch, samovar* and *vodka.*

Borsch (or *borscht*) is a beet soup, served hot or cold, often with sour cream.

Samovar literally means 'self-boiler'. It's a copper urn used in Russia for making tea.

Vodka is the Russian diminutive of *voda* ('water'). I am reminded that the French call brandy *eau de vie* ('water of life'). *Vodka* looks like water and also looks like gin. At any rate, this Russian liquor is distilled from rye or wheat and has a sneaky kick to it.

Here are three Russian imports of the beastly variety: *beluga, Borzoi* and *corsac.*

A *beluga* is a large white sturgeon or dolphin. Sometimes the latter is called 'the white whale'. Was Moby Dick really a *beluga*? In any case, the Russian source is *byeluga,* from *byely* ('white').

Borzoi means 'swift' in Russian. A dog of this breed is large and long-legged, like a greyhound. The head is narrow and the coat is silky. It's called 'Russian wolfhound' because it was trained to pursue wolves.

The *corsac* (or *corsak*) is a bushy-tailed fox of central Asia. Its other name is 'Afghan fox'.

The Steppes are vast Russian grasslands — from *step* ('lowland'). To the north is the *tundra,* another treeless plain. The Russians borrowed the word from the Lapps' *tundar* ('hill').

Siberia may not have any hepcats, but it can boast of steppe cats. The usual name for such an animal is *manul.* It's a small wildcat that also inhabits parts of Mongolia and Tibet.

The *telega* and the *troika* are two of the vehicles that help the Siberians to get around. The former is a four-wheeled springless wagon, and the latter is a carriage or wagon drawn by a team of three horses running abreast. The source is *troe* ('three').

We have enlarged the connotation for *troika.* It can mean 'a triumvirate or group of three people with authority'.

Among the words we have absorbed from Moscow's space programme are *Sputnik* and *Lunik.* When Sputnik I was launched in October 1957 it caused quite a stir because the Russians had outdone the United States. Theirs was the first artificial satellite placed in orbit. *Lunik,* by the way, had a dog as passenger, but it wasn't a *Borzoi.*

Probably the most popular of Russian-originated musical instruments is the *balalaika.* You may remember seeing it in the movie DR. ZHIVAGO. It looks like a guitar with a triangular body. Etymologically it may be akin to *balabolit'* ('to chatter').

It may surprise you to learn that we borrowed *intelligentsia* ('intellectuals') from the Russians. Of course the word ultimately has a Latin origin. *Intelligere* means 'to perceive or understand'. The verb is a combination of *inter* ('between') and *legere* ('to choose').

Any wealthy farmer who exploited the peasants in the pre-Communism years was called a *kulak.* The word means 'fist' — hence, 'tightwad or pinchpenny'. In the 1920s most *kulaks* refused to collectivize their farms, and many of them were liquidated.

Bolshevik almost literally means 'the larger majority'. The Bolsheviks formed the Social Democratic party, which led to the creation of the Communist party after power was wrested from the Czar in the 1917 revolution. Troublesome people are sometimes called 'Bolshies'.

Now we turn to words we have borrowed from Japan and consider a logical grouping: *judo, karate, jujitsu* and *sumo.* All four can be regarded as means of self-defence, although the last is merely a Japanese form of wrestling.

Judo actually means 'soft or gentle art' and is a refinement of *jujitsu,* which has the same literal sense. The practitioners of the art use no weapons; instead they employ the principle of turning the opponent's weight and strength against him. Like engineers, they study leverage and take advantage of their knowledge of it.

Karate literally means 'empty or open hand'. If you have ever seen a *karate* expert chop a solid block of wood in half with the side of his hand, you'll agree that the art is well named. Sharp, quick blows with the feet are also employed.

Incidentally, the Chinese relative of *karate* is *kung fu* (literally, 'boxing principles').

It's ironic that the Japanese yelled 'Banzai!' when they charged against Allied forces in World War II. The cheer means 'May you live ten thousand years!' Of course, during a *banzai attack* they were cheering each other rather than their foes.

The suicide attacks by Japanese pilots familiarized us with another Japanese word — *kamikaze.* It translates into 'divine wind'. We now use the word as a synonym for suicidal.

Hara-kiri (sometimes spelt *hari-kari*) is in a class with the above; it's a ritual suicide by disembowelment. Literally, it means 'belly cutting'. The practice was formerly employed by the *samurai,* who were the warrior aristocracy of feudal Japan. They performed the act to avoid execution or disgrace.

A *geisha* is literally an 'art-person'. She looks her best in a *kimono,* a word that to a Japanese means simply 'clothes'.

Mikado, as every Gilbert and Sullivan buff knows, is the former title of the emperor of Japan. The word means 'exalted gate' — another example of metonymy, or the use of a name for something associated with it. The 'exalted gate' refers to the entrance to the Imperial Palace. A comparable usage today is to speak of the White House when we mean the U.S. President.

Maru is familiar to navy men and other sailors. It's a Japanese merchant ship. The word is often appended as a suffix to the names of ships, as we use *SS* before the name of a steamship. *Maru* actually means 'circle'.

While we're in the Far East, let's take a look at just a few of the words that we have inherited from China.

Naturally, because of the great popularity of Chinese restaurants, foods with oriental names have become known to millions in the west. *Chop suey** (alteration of *tsa-sui* — 'various pieces') and *chow mein** (ch'ao mein — 'to fry flour') are the most familiar. *Won tons* grow more popular each year. They are dumplings filled with minced pork and spices. The derivation is *wan t'an,* a word from Cantonese dialect meaning 'pastry'. The dumplings are especially delicious as a basis for *won-ton soup.*

While eating Chinese food, many people try to master the skill of using *chopsticks.* Those implements are linguistic creations of pidgin† English. In Chinese the original word means 'the quick ones'.

Rice and *tea* are of Oriental origin. The former has a long linguistic historic and eventually dates back to Sanskrit, a language that is still used in the ritual of the Northern Buddhist church. *Tea* is derived from *t'e,* a word in the dialect of the Chinese at Amoy. It's a corruption of the Mandarin *ch'a.*‡

Wok is another word associated with food. This bowl-shaped metal cooking pan is often used with a circular stand to hold it steady. Its popularity is so recent that the word is not listed in many dictionaries, but you can be sure it will be an entry in future editions.

Mandarin is the chief and official dialect of China and is spoken by most of the people. Oddly enough, the word does not have a Chinese origin. It has come to us via the Portuguese and is related to the Latin verb *mandare* ('to command'). But ultimately its etymological history can be traced back to Sanskrit.

As a common noun mandarin has a number of meanings. Among them are:

1. a high public official in the Chinese Empire
2. any person belonging to an elite group, especially one respected by the literati or intellectuals

---

* According to no less a culinary expert than Craig Claiborne, *chop suey* and *chow mein* are not authentically Chinese.

† *Pidgin* is a concocted word supposedly based on the Chinese traders' pronunciation of their noun for 'business'. It's a simplified form of speech, mixing two languages. *Pidgin English* is used as a trade language in Far Eastern and South Pacific ports. The French equivalent is *bêche-de-mer.*

‡ In Britain, *cha* means 'tea' and is usually altered to *char.* 'A cuppa *char*' is a slangy expression for 'a cup of tea'. In America, *cha* means 'rolled tea'. It is also spelt *chaa, chais* and *tsia.*

3. a pompous, pedantic official; a bureaucrat
4. a small, sweet orange (probably from the colour of the Chinese official's robe) or the tree that bears the fruit.

There is also a *mandarin duck,* as well as *mandarin oil.* The latter is obtained from the peel of the orange and is used in perfumery.

The versatile Chinese have originated everything from gunpowder to games. *Mah-jongg* and *fan-tan* are two of the pastimes we have imported.

In the 1920s *mah-jongg* became a craze throughout the western world, but its popularity has greatly diminished. The name literally means 'house sparrow'; it's taken from the figure on one of the tiles.

Fan-tan was originally a Chinese betting game played with small objects such as beans. Then it developed into a card game. Since seven is a key card, the game is also called 'sevens'.

Finally, here is a small potpourri of words we have inherited from the Chinese:

WORD	DEFINITION	LITERAL MEANING
kowtow	show submissive respect	'knock head' (on the ground).
pongee	soft, thin light brown silken fabric	'domestic loom'
sampan	small Chinese boat	'three-plank'
tong	Chinese association, political party or secret society	'hall, meeting-place'

Travelling southwest from China, we come to India. Largely because of the long British occupation of this land, we have been endowed with a rich mine of words, some of Hindi or Urdu origin and others Anglo-Indian.

In the area of clothing and fabric alone we have acquired many words. Some of them are listed below. The literal meanings are indicated only when they are of interest.

WORD	DEFINITION	LITERAL MEANING
bandanna	large, coloured handkerchief	'a method of dyeing'

140

cummerbund	waistband; broad sash	'loins band': from Pers. *kamar* ('loins')
dhoti	Hindu's loincloth or fabric for it	
khaki	twilled cloth, used for soldiers' uniforms; the brown colour of it	'dust-coloured; dusty'; from Pers. *khak* ('dust; earth')
puttee	covering for the lower leg	'bandage'
sari	woman's outer garment in the Indian sub-continent	
seersucker	striped, crinkled fabric	'milk and sugar'; from Pers. *shir u shakar*

I have deliberately omitted *chintz* from the above list because it merits special consideration. This glazed cotton fabric, often featuring flowery designs, has acquired a pejorative adjectival significance. Because *chintz* usually has a flamboyant, ornate look, *chintzy* has come to mean 'gaudy, tawdry, cheap'. Incidentally, *chintz* is not an inexpensive fabric; it doesn't really deserve such denigration.

India has also bestowed upon us a largess of designations for people in various walks of life. Here are some of them:

WORD	DEFINITION	LITERAL MEANING
begum	Moslem queen, princess or high-ranking lady	'lady'; from Turk. word for 'princess;
coolie	unskilled labourer receiving little pay	'hired servant'; from *koli*, ('caste of Gujarat')
dacoit	robber	'attacker'; from *daka* ('attack')
guru	religious teacher	'heavy, weighty' — hence, 'venerable'
maharajah	former Indian prince	'great king' and
maharani	and princess	'great queen'; from Sans.
mahout	elephant driver or keeper	'of great measure'; from Sans.
pandit, or pundit	wise or learned man	'learned person'; from Sans.
pariah	outcast	'drummer'; from Tamil *parai*
rajah	prince or chief	see *maharajah*
rani	princess	see *maharani*

sahib	sir, master	'master'; from Ar. *sahib*, ('friend')
swami	pundit, seer, master, lord	'lord'; from Sans. *svamin*, ('lord')
yogi	Hindu ascetic; mystical person	'one practising *yoga*'; from Sans. 'union, yoking'

Brahmin deserves special attention. Actually, the word is a variation of *Brahman,* a priestly member of the highest Hindu caste. Hence in our language a *Brahmin* is a cultured intellectual of an established upper-class family. Since such a person is exclusive, the word has come to be equated with snob.

What is most fascinating and ironic is that the original word Brahman now means 'a breed of domestic cattle'. If a *Brahmin* is called a *Brahman,* he may have a beef.

In the area of shelter, here are two of the words imported from India.

Bungalow is an Anglo-Indian variation of the Hindus' *bangla.* In the subcontinent it's a low one-storied house usually having a wide porch. In Britain the term specifies a single-storied house such as is sought after, for example, by people wanting small holiday homes near the sea or by the elderly who have difficulty with stairs.

Veranda (sometimes spelt *verandah*) is another Anglo-Indian word. Its source is the Portuguese *varanda* ('balcony'). The grandparent is the Latin noun *vara,* meaning 'a wooden trestle or forked pole for spreading out nets'. That's a long way from our present definition of *veranda:* 'an open porch or portico; piazza, gallery or balcony'.

In the field of food and drink, a sampling from India follows:

Curry is another of those strange etymological coincidences that I have noted before. As a verb the word has nothing to do with India. Its source is Vulgar Latin, whether it means 'to groom a horse' or 'to flagellate'. And when flatterers *curry favour,* their source is Medieval English.

But *curry,* the spicy dish in a hot, piquant sauce — there are countless varieties — goes back to the Tamils of southern India and Sri Lanka, whose word for 'sauce' was *kari.*

A favourite dish at the Indian restaurants that have sprung up all over Britain is meat or vegetables cooked by the *tandoori* method, on a spit in a clay oven. *Tandoori* is from Urdu *tandoor,* an oven.

My father always drank a *hot toddy* when he wanted to ward off a cold. Little did I realize that he was quaffing brandy or whiskey mixed with hot water, sugar and spices.

Toddy is an Anglo-Indian word from the northern part of the country. The Hindi *noun* was *tari* ('fermented sap of the palmyra tree'). That juice is still used as a beverage, minus the alcohol.

Two musical instruments of Hindu origin are *sitar* and *tom-tom*. The former, which looks like a lute, has been made famous by Ravi Shankar. As for *tom-tom* — one would think that the American Indians or Africans originated that drum. However, it's a variation of *tam-tam*, a name given to it by the Indian peoples because of the sound it makes.

One might also assume that the *topee* (or *topi*) had an African origin, because that helmet worn as a sunshade was so often used on safaris in the Dark Continent. But the headgear is another Hindi export.

That swiftest of beasts, the *cheetah*, has a Hindi heritage, *cita*. The ultimate root is *citrakāya*, a Sanskrit noun meaning 'tiger'. Actually, the *cheetah* looks more like a leopard.

Catamarans were originally rafts or floats. Now they have also developed into boats with two hulls. Even more fascinating is the fact that a new definition for the vessel has evolved. A *catamaran* can mean 'a quarrelsome woman'. Why, I don't know.

At any rate, the Tamil people have the word kattumaram, which literally means 'tie' plus 'log or tree'. That fits, because the original rafts were made of two or more logs lashed together.

By the way, in Canada a *catamaran* is a big sled used for hauling wood. As in so many other cases, there seems to be no end to the varied uses of certain words.

Dinghy stems from the Hindi word *dingi* ('little boat'). It was, and is, a rowing boat or sailboat for passengers or cargo on sheltered coastal waters of India. Nowadays it means a wide variety of different small boats, with or without sails.

Finally, here is a miscellany of words from India:

bangle	cushy	purdah
banyan	ditty bag	suttee
cheroot	ghat	tatty
chit	howdah	tonga
chukker	juggernaut	tulwar
cowrie	mugger	tussah

143

Bangles are bracelets, anklets, armlets or any ornamental circlets of gold, silver, glass, plastic or almost any rigid material. The source is a Hindi word, *bangri* ('glass bracelet').

The *banyan* is a remarkable tree. Its branches send out aerial extensions that grow downward. When they reach the soil they form additional trunks. Thus a banyan keeps spreading out in an ever widening circle. One tree can cover a space large enough to shelter a thousand people.

The British gave the *banyan* its name because Hindu merchants, called *banians*, not only took shelter under the tree but also used that area as a market place. They even built a pagoda under the leaves of an immense *banyan* on the southern Iranian coast.

Banian ultimately comes from *vanij*, a Sanskrit word meaning 'merchant'.

A *cheroot* is a cigar with both ends cut square. The source is *churuttu*, a Tamil word meaning 'roll'.

Chit has an interesting history. The Hindu word *citthi* or *cittha* means 'a letter or note'. At first the British translated the noun into *chitty*, but they soon shortened it to *chit* — a memorandum or short note. Then came another example of how the meanings of words expand. Because vouchers for small debts at restaurants or casinos involved the scribbling of a quick note, *chit* came to be synonymous with an I.O.U., a cheque, a bill or even any receipt.

Chit has two other meanings, both from Medieval English and unrelated to each other or to the Hindu-based word:

1. pert young woman (from *chitte*, 'kitten or cub')
2. sprout; shoot (from *chithe*, 'sprout')

In polo a period of play is called a *chukker* or *chukka*. The game did not originate in India, but *chukker* comes from Hindi *chakar* ('wheel'). From the same root we get *chukka*, an ankle-high boot as originally worn by polo players.

Cowrie (sometimes spelt *cowry* or *courie*) is a British alteration of the Hindi word *kauri* — a mollusc of the warm seas or the beautifully polished and often colourful shell of the gastropod. So highly regarded were these shells that the *money cowrie* was once used as currency in parts of Asia and Africa.

If you happen to have a *cushy* job, it must be an easy, comfortable one. British troops picked up the word from the Hindi-Persian *khush* or *khūsh* ('pleasant'). Originally slang, cushy is now considered acceptable by many lexicographers.

144

One would think that *cushion* might have the same root. But it has a long, separate history, and eventually stems from the Latin noun *coxa* ('hip').

Ditty and *ditty bag* are not related. The song can be traced to *dicere*, the Latin verb meaning 'to say', but the sailor's little container for needles, thread, tapes and sundries has an unknown origin. Philologers guess that it comes from an obsolete word, *dutti* ('coarse calico'), and that the loincloth *dhoti* is the ultimate source.

Ghat (or *ghaut*) is a Hindi word meaning 'mountain pass'. It is also the Indian term for a platform or landing place on the bank of a river. We have accepted the spelling and meanings without change.

Some of the platforms are backed by elaborate structures resembling temples, from which the Hindus descend staircases and go bathing. At the head of such a structure is a space where the Hindus cremate their dead. It's called a *burning ghat.*

Howdah is an Anglo-Indian word (from *hauda*). This canopied seat for riding on the back of an elephant has an Arabic source.

Juggernaut is a fascinating word with a startling history. Its parent is *Jagannāth* ('lord of the world'), an incarnation of the Hindu god Vishnu. The story goes that when a large vehicle containing a graven image of the deity moved along through the streets, some devotees got so excited that they threw themselves under the wheels.

Thus *juggernaut* has come to mean

1. any large destructive, overpowering, inexorable force
2. anything requiring blind devotion or cruel self-sacrifice

Mugger is still another instance of the fact that two unrelated English words have exactly the same spelling. The *mugger* from India is a large crocodile (from Hindi *magar*). But now *mugger* has a new meaning — a robber who punches his victim in the *mug*, which is slang for 'face'.

The *purdah* is a kind of curtain used by some Hindus and Moslems to protect their women from the eyes of strangers. It is also the veil used by the females, and the practice itself. The source is *pardah,* the Hindi-Persian word for 'screen or veil'.

Suttee (or *sati*) comes from Hindi-Sanskrit sources meaning 'chaste and virtuous wife'. Historically, a *suttee* was a widow who threw herself on her husband's funeral pyre and was cremated along with him; also, the practice of so doing.

Those linguistic coincidences keep cropping up:

1. *tatty* (from Hindi *tatti*) — a moistened mat or screen placed in a door or window to cool the room
2. *tatty* (presumably from Old English *taetteca*, 'rag') — cheap; inferior.

A *tonga* is a light, two-wheeled carriage used in India. The source is Hindi, *tangā*. The word has absolutely no consanguinity with the name of the Kingdom of Tonga.

A *tulwar* is a curved scimitar or sabre used in Northern India and other Oriental regions. The root of course is Hindi (*talwar*).

Tussore (otherwise *tussah, tussor, tusser*), another word of Hindi-Sanskrit origin, is a kind of silkworm, also the silk that it produces, such as pongee and shantung.

In the previous section *Sanskrit* sources have been cited so often that the language deserves additional attention. Literally, the word means 'well arranged; put together perfectly; refined' — all apt definitions, for Sanskrit is the classical standard language of India. Around 400 B.C. it was the official tongue of the court and the literary vehicle of Hindu culture. It is among the oldest Indo-European subfamilies; hence its importance is immense.

For our purposes a tiny sampling of words from Sanskrit will do:

karma	nirvana	sutra
mahatma	stupa	swastika
mantra		

Karma and *kismet* have become loosely connected in our language as synonyms for fate or destiny. The latter is of Turkish origin and really does mean 'one's lot in life'. *Karma,* on the other hand, means 'deed, act or work'. To a Hindu or Buddhist, *karma* is the force generated by his deeds that will determine his fate in his various future lives.

Mahatma stems from a Sanskrit word meaning 'great soul'. The word is reserved for a revered, wise and selfless person. Naturally, Gandhi earned the epithet.

Mantra was originally a Vedic hymn or prayer. Then it became a mystical incantation or formula for devotion. A person who practises transcendental meditation has a *mantra* as his special word, syllable or sound, and through its use he seeks to release his mind.

Nirvana in Buddhism or Hinduism is a certain state of absolute blessedness. We have adopted the word to mean 'bliss, or freedom from care and pain'.

Stupas are Buddhist shrines that resemble towers.

In Sanskrit, *sutra* means 'string or thread' — hence, 'a string of rules'. The Brahmins of India use the word to signify a precept or aphorism or collection of such maxims as a guide to the conduct of life. In Buddhism, *sutra* is any of Buddha's sermons.

The *Kama Sutra* is a Hindu love manual written in the eighth century. It has recently become popular in the West. *Kama,* as you may have guessed, means 'love'.

Travelling southeast from India, we come to Malaysia. A handful of Malay words, largely connected with commerce, has seeped into our language. In this sampling the ticked words will be briefly discussed.

batik	cootie	sago
√ caddy	kapok	√ sarong
cockatoo	paddy	√ tuan

A *caddy* is a small container for tea. The Malay source is *kati,* a unit of weight that became Anglicized into *catty* (1⅓ pounds avoirdupois). At first the container of one *catty* of tea was spelt the same as the weight, but in time the *t*'s became *d*'s. The word should not be confused with *caddie,* the golfer's helper.

Sarongs became famous when Dorothy Lamour wore them in films of the thirties and forties. To the Malays the wrap-around skirt means 'sheath'.

Tuan is the Malay equivalent of sahib.

Hawaii and other parts of Polynesia have supplied us with their share of interesting words. Here are a few from America's fiftieth state:

Aloha is a Hawaiian's greeting or farewell. It literally means 'love or kindness'.

Lei is a chaplet or garland.

Nene (pronounced 'nay-nay') is a nearly extinct Hawaiian goose, and the state bird. And it's a standby in crossword puzzles.

From Tahiti we have obtained such words as *taro* and *tattoo.*

Taro is a South Pacific staple. This large plant of the Arum genus is cultivated for its underground stems, the source of a food called *poi.*

Tattoo ('make designs on the skin') and *tattoo* ('signal summoning soldiers to their quarters') present us with another etymological double take. The first comes from the Tahitians' *tatau.* The other is a Dutch derivative of *taptoe,* 'shut the tap' — freely translated as 'close the bar-room'.

The Australians are a creative group of word-painters. Their slang alone could be the subject of a treatise or a book. Here are just a few imports from down under.

Boomerang is an aboriginal name for a bent club that can be thrown so as to return to or near its starting point. We have developed several other meanings for that curved stick:

1. a statement or action that backfires on its originator
2. a movable platform for supporting painters of theatre sets
3. a movable stand for supporting stage lights at different heights

Dingo is an aboriginal name for an Australian wild dog.

Kangaroos are leaping marsupial mammals of Australia, New Guinea and adjacent islands. Captain James Cook transmitted the aboriginal word to us after visiting the islands.

Another Australian animal is the *wallaby* (from the aboriginal name *wolabā*). This medium-sized marsupial is a smaller relation of the *kangaroo.*

One of the most interesting Maori words is *kiwi.* The name echoes the call of the bird. In colloquial speech a *Kiwi* is a New Zealander. The edible egg-sized fruit of a subtropical vine is also called a *kiwi.*

Finally, because the *kiwi* is a flightless bird, an Air Force member who stays on the ground is called by that name in military language.

Speaking of birds, let us not forget the *kookaburra,* a large Australian kingfisher having a call that sounds like a raucous guffaw. It is called the 'laughing jackass' by the good-humoured Australians.

The Turks and Persians have endowed us with a fund of words.

Let's examine a sampling from Turkey first. Three of their V.I.P.s are *khan, pasha* and *vizier.*

Khan means 'lord or prince'. A man named Temuchin became a Mongol conqueror in the thirteenth century; he took the name Genghis Khan and swept through northern China, central Asia, Russia and Bulgaria. His grandson, Batu, led the Golden Horde, which broke up into separate *khanates* in the Crimea.

Pasha is another title appended to a Turkish chief's name.

Vizier is the most interesting of the trio because of its derivation. Literally, the title means 'bearer of burdens; porter', because this high officer in Moslem lands performs the tasks that should be the responsibility of the ruler.

In the area of clothing, *caftan, caracal* and *fez* are among the Turkish words familiar to us.

Caftans are coatlike robes with long sleeves and sashes. They are worn throughout the Near East. Some lexicographers claim that the word comes from the Russians rather than the Turks. It can be traced back to the Persians' *qaftan.*

Caracal is the fur for coats obtained from the reddish brown lynx of the same name. Literally, the original Turkish word means 'black ear'. The word was transmitted to us via the French.

Fez also comes to us through the Gallic channel. This red, brimless felt hat was once the headdress of Turkish men.

Two of the Turkish foods we have been introduced to are *baklava* and *yogurt.* The former is a dessert made of paper-thin layers of pastry, chopped nuts and honey. The main accent is on the last syllable.

The popularity of *yogurt* (sometimes spelt *yoghurt*) has increased by leaps and bounds in recent decades because of the growing interest in health foods. This custardlike food, prepared with milk altered by bacteria, is reputed to be the staple of hundreds of people who have attained remarkable longevity.

Have you ever seen a *chibouk*? It's a tobacco pipe with a long stem and a clay bowl. The *hookah* (from Arabia) and *nargileh* or *narghile* (from Persia) are also pipes for smoking. The latter literally means 'coconut', because the bowls were originally made from that fruit of a palm.

Crossword puzzle fans will know *imaret* and *minaret.* The former is a Turkish inn, and the latter is a tall, slender tower on a mosque. The Arabian ancestors meant 'lamp or lighthouse' and eventually 'candlestick'.

149

Turning to the Persians, let us examine a brief selection of our inheritances from that great ancient people. But let me note at this point that Persian, Turkish and Arabic legacies often become mingled, as borrowing among the three groups continued through the ages. Furthermore, we are often indebted to the French, who acted as middlemen in the transition to English.

baksheesh	caravanserai	divan
bazaar	cassock	houri

Baksheesh (or *bakshish*) eventually comes to us from Persia, although a number of other countries got into the act. The word means 'a gratuity, tip or alms'.

Bazaar is derived from the Persians' *bazar* ('market'). In the Orient it still retains that meaning. We have slightly enlarged the connotations. There are church *bazaars* and other sales run by clubs. Also, bazaars have become synonymous with department stores and fairs.

Caravanserais are Eastern inns at which companies of travellers stop at night. The word *caravan* of course is related — and the French are the transmitters.

Cassocks are long outer garments worn by clergymen, altar boys and choristers. The ultimate Persian root is *kazh* ('raw silk'). Again the intermediaries are the French; their word is *casaque*.

Divan in its early Persian form signified 'an account book'. What an amazing metamorphosis in meaning the word has undergone through the centuries! Let's try to trace it via metonymy. First, the office in which the accounts were tabulated became the *divan*. Later the special couch for that agency (or for a council room) was called a *divan*.

Here are some of the meanings for the word:

1. the Turkish privy council that was presided over by the sultan or grand vizier (sometimes spelt *diwan*)
2. any council
3. Moslem court of justice
4. smoking room
5. large, low couch; sofa; davenport
6. collection of Persian or Arabic poems, especially by one author (also spelt *diwan*)

Houri could well be credited to the French or the Arabs. The

150

Persians are in the middle. The original Arabic word (*huriyah*) meant 'black-eyed woman'. The Persians liked the term and developed it into *huri,* which the French altered into *houri.* Two definitions are:

1. a beautiful dark-eyed nymph or virgin of the Moslem Paradise. (Good Moslems will be rewarded by the companionship of *houris* when they die.)
2. a voluptuous, seductive pulchritudinous woman

Our language owes much to the Arabs too. First, let's consider a small selection of people — some good and some evil:

assassin	fellah
Bedouin	ghoul
emir	sultan
fakir	

Assassin comes from an Arabic word meaning 'hashish users'. The original *Assassins* were members of a secret, fanatical Moslem order during the Crusades. While reputedly under the influence of hashish, they terrorized and killed Christians.

Hashish is dried hemp. A drug made from the resin of the plant has an intoxicating effect when chewed or smoked.

Today we generally restrict the meaning of *assassin* to 'a murderer of a politically important person'; but the word can be applied to any ruthless killer, especially one who strikes suddenly.

The *Bedouin* are wandering Arab tribes of Syria, Arabia and North Africa. Hence their name is sometimes used in English as a synonym for *nomads.*

Strangely enough, *nomad* is not of Arabic extraction. Its source is *nomas,* a Greek noun meaning 'wandering about for pasture' — which is exactly what the Bedouin and other nomads do.

Emir and its variations — *emeer, amir* and *ameer* — eventually stem from *amara,* an Arabic word meaning 'to command'. These Moslem rulers are favourites of crossword puzzle constructors. A derivative, *emirate,* also appears often in puzzles.

Fakir comes from *faqir* ('a poor man'). Fakirs are ascetic Moslem or Hindu mendicants, often on the move. The pale orange-yellow colour *peachblow* is also called *fakir.*

A *fellah* is an Arabian peasant or agricultural labourer. The word comes from a verb meaning 'to plough'. The Arabic plural is *fellahin* or *fellaheen.*

Ghoul comes from the Arabic noun *ghūl* ('demon of the mountains'). In Moslem folklore, this evil spirit was reputed to rob graves and feed on corpses. Ugh!

To us *ghoul* is a human grave robber or body snatcher. His purpose is usually to obtain valuables or to remove the corpse for illicit dissection.

Our adjective *ghoulish* is a synonym for revolting.

Sultan means 'ruler' in Arabic. It was once the title of the ruler of Turkey. A *sultanate* is the office of this chief or the region over which he presides.

A *sultana* is the ruler's wife, mother, daughter or sister. Sometimes she is called sultaness.

There is also a *sultana bird* (named for its rich exotic plumage). Finally, a pale yellow seedless grape is called *sultana.* The raisin from the fruit bears the same name.

Here is a miniature miscellany of some other Arab exports to English-speaking nations:

hajj	jihad	sofa
harem	jinn	tamarind
hegira	kebab	tambourine
henna	salaam	wadi

Hajj (sometimes spelt *hadj* or *haj*) is the pilgrimage to Mecca that all Moslems are required to take at least once in their lives. Such a pilgrim becomes a *hajji* — a title of honour in Islam.

Harem comes from the Arabic noun *harim* ('sacred, forbidden place'). It is a house or section of a house in which the Moslem women live. The word can also be applied to the women themselves. For example, a sultan's wives, concubines and maidservants form a *harem.*

An extended meaning is 'a number of female animals that surround and mate with a single male'. Bulls among the fur seals and stallions in a group of mustangs accumulate harems, which they protect jealously from other males.

The original *Hegira* was the flight of Mohammed from Mecca to Medina in 622 A.D. The ultimate Arabic source is *hajara* ('to depart'). In English we use *hegira* to mean 'any flight from danger'.

152

By extension it has even become synonymous with an emigration or mass exodus.

An alternate spelling is *hejira*. The alert reader may have observed that such variants have been cited throughout this chapter. The chief problem is transliteration. When another language uses alphabetic characters different from our own, our scholars estimate by the sounds how a word would be spelt if it were transliterated into English. Often the experts or the original transliterators from different disciplines do not see eye to eye, and four or five different spellings may vie for acceptance. The problem is especially prevalent in our adoption of words from such languages as Greek, Arabic, Hebrew, Russian, Sanskrit, Japanese and Chinese.

Beauticians and the women who frequent their salons are well acquainted with *henna* as a dye or rinse, but it's a good guess that most of them do not know that the word has an Arabic origin. *Henna* is an Old World tropical shrub or little tree. The leaves yield an auburn dye that converts a grey-haired dowager into a kind of redhead.

Jihad has come to mean 'crusade or bitter strife'. The original Arabic word carries the idea of a holy war. Recently I read a magazine article that referred to Ralph Nader's *jihad* against General Motors and other corporations. Thus do the senses of words become enlarged.

Jinn is the plural of *jinni*. What's a *jinni*? In Moslem legend it's a good or evil spirit that can assume the form of an animal or a human and exercise power in one's daily life. Note that the word can be spelt *djin* or *djinn* (transliteration difficulties again!). A corruption of *jinni* is *genie*, influenced by the French *génie* ('spirit'). However, its ultimate source is the Latin word *genius* ('guardian spirit').

Kebab can be *kabob* can be *kebob* can be *cabob*, according to what transliterator is your favourite. The Arabic ancestor is a skewered preparation containing bits of marinated meat. Prefix the word *shish* (Arabic for 'skewer') and you have an entree that is very popular today but was little known in our grandparents' era.

Salaam is a relative of *shalom*, the Hebrew word for 'peace'. Moslems, like the Israelis, use the word as a greeting.

Sofa comes from *suffah*, the Arabic word meaning 'cushion or long bench'. We have gone beyond the divan or settee; now being marketed are *sofa beds* and even *sofa tables*.

153

In the East a *sofa* is a dais fitted with cushions and carpets for reclining above the main floor.

A *tamarind* is a tropical Old World tree yielding an edible fruit. Literally, the Arabic source, *tamr hindi,* means 'date of India'.

Tambourine comes from a French diminutive alteration of the Arabic *tanbūr,* which in turn is borrowed from a Persian word meaning 'drum'. The *tambourine* is a little hand drum with jingling metal discs, and is often used by exotic dancers.

Most interesting of its relations is the *tambour,* because of its many meanings. Among them are:

1. drum or drummer
2. wall of a circular building surrounded by columns
3. embroidery frame or the embroidery made on such a frame
4. kind of lace
5. rolling top of a desk

Wadi has two basic and rather contradictory meanings:

1. a dry riverbed, gully or ravine in North Africa or Southeast Asia
2. the stream that flows through such a valley

The Arabic root, *wādī,* means 'channel'.

In case you're wondering, *wade* is not even distantly related.

Now let's look at a sampling of words imported from Africa:

chigger	marimba	tsetse fly
cola	mumbo jumbo	voodoo
gnu	safari	zombie

Chiggers are bloodsucking larval mites. The original African name, which we also use, was *jigger.*

By coincidence, a pestiferous flea of the West Indies is called *chigoe* (a name with a Carib origin), and people have begun to interchange the names.

The *chigger* is also called 'harvest mite' and 'red bug'.

Cola is a Latinized variant of *kola,* an African tree or the nut that grows on it and is a source of caffeine. Of course the carbonated beverage that is produced from an extract of the nut is known all over the world.

Cola is also the plural of that part of the body called the *colon;*

154

also, the plural of another *colon* — 'rhythmic unit in Latin or Greek verse'.

The *gnu* is one of the relatively few African animals bearing names of local origin. The rhinoceros and hippopotamus are among many with Greek appellations. Giraffes have a French stamp and zebras got their name from the Spanish and Portuguese. And Leo the Lion has a Latin-Greek linguistic history, though the Bantu call him *simba*. Of course the natives have their own names for other animals, but the invading foreigners often preferred Indo-European terms.

Not so with the *gnu*. The Xhosa called it *ngu* — and you can't blame the British for switching the first two letters.

Two smaller antelopes, the *impala* and the *kudu*, were respectively named by the Zulus and the Hottentots, and the *okapi* (cousin of a giraffe) has a native Central African name.

The *marimba* is a percussion instrument resembling a xylophone.

Mumbo jumbo has several meanings:

1. any fetish or idol
2. an object to be dreaded
3. a complicated ritual with many trappings
4. a nonsensical activity intended to confuse
5. senseless language; gibberish

The Mandingo had a tribal god called *mama dyumbo*, which could well be the original ancestor. Ignorance of their language and ceremonies presumably gave rise to the later connotations.

Safari comes to us from the Arabs via Swahili. The Arabic verb *safara* means 'to travel'. Happily, many a *safari* today is enjoyed by tourists with loaded cameras instead of loaded guns.

The *tsetse fly* received its name from the Bantu. The bite of one species causes *nagana* — a Zulu word for a disease of horses and cattle. The pest can also bring on sleeping sickness (trypanosomiasis).

One would think that *voodoo* had a West Indian origin, because the practice is prevalent in that region. Actually, the Creole French borrowed the word from West Africa. The noun *vodu* means 'fetish or demon'. Today *voodoo* is a synonym for black magic.

Hoodoo, too, has African roots. Some lexicographers presume that it's merely a variation of *voodoo;* others suspect that it arose from the Hausa people of the Sudan and meant 'to arouse resentment against another person'. The word is commonly associated with bad luck.

Sometimes a *hoodoo* is called a *Jonah*. That's because the Hebrew prophet disobeyed God's command while sailing on a ship and caused a storm to endanger the lives of his fellow travellers. *Jonah,* you will recall, is the fellow who had a whale of a time.

In West Africa the *zombie* was a python deity worshipped by tribes that practised voodoo. Some Haitians and cults in southern United States have adopted the deity. The believers maintain that a supernatural force can enter a corpse and bring the body back to life in a kind of trance. Like a robot, the person who is reanimated will obey commands automatically.

Thus the name of the deity itself became synonymous with the walking dead. This led to three other connotations:

1. a listless or phlegmatic person, easily manoeuvred
2. a 'weirdo' or 'sap'
3. an ugly or odd person

Afrikaners have also endowed us with some interesting words. Let's start with *Boer* itself. This Dutch noun means 'peasant'. Because a son of the soil was considered to be rude and clumsy and lacking in social graces, our word *boor* cropped up. No pun intended.

The *Boers* are South Africans whose ancestors were Dutch farmers who settled in the area of the Cape of Good Hope in the seventeenth century. Their official language is called Afrikaans — a development of seventeenth-century Dutch. Here is a brief selection of their words that have entered our language.

commandeer	eland	veld
commando	kraal	wildebeest
dorp	trek	

Commandeer stems from *kommandeeren,* a Dutch verb meaning 'to command'. It has three basic meanings:

1. to compel a person to give military service
2. to appropriate, as property, for military purposes
3. to seize arbitrarily for one's own use

156

Commando is a word that the Boers borrowed from the Portuguese and Spanish, but they popularized it so much that we took it over. To Afrikaners a *commando* is a raid or expedition; it is also their word for militia service in the army, or a force of troops.

To us a *commando* is a military unit trained specially for hit-and-run tactics in enemy territory, or a member of such a unit.

Dorp has a Dutch ancestry. In South Africa it's a village or township.

An *eland* is an African antelope. To the Boers it looked like an elk, so they gave it the Dutch name for that animal.

The *eland* has many smaller cousins. Among them are the *dik-dik* (Ethiopian name), *oryx* (from Greek, 'pickaxe') and the *klipspringer*. You can guess that the Boers originated the name for that agile antelope. Their word *klip* means 'rock or cliff'.

Kraal is another Afrikaner borrowing from the Portuguese, whose *curral* means 'pen for cattle'. Our word *corral* is a derivative, of course.

There are several definitions for *kraal*, and the final one is quite shameful:

1. an enclosure for domestic animals, such as cattle and sheep, in South Africa
2. a pen for elephants in Thailand, Sri Lanka and India
3. an enclosure for keeping lobsters, turtles and sponges alive in shallow water
4. a village of South African blacks usually surrounded by a stockade

I am reminded of another word that the Boers have dropped into our language with a horrendous thud — *apartheid*. This is their word for 'apartness', and it stands for strict racial segregation.

Trek in South Africa means 'to travel by ox wagon'. Since this mode is quite different from roaring down the M1 in a Jaguar, the verb also means 'to make a slow, difficult journey'. As a noun it signifies the journey itself. The derivation, naturally, is Dutch: *trekken* means 'to draw along or travel'.

We have not only accepted the Boers' usages of *trek* but have also enlarged the sense to mean 'migrate or migration'.

Veld (or *veldt*) is the South African grassland where the *eland* and the *dik-dik* roam. In Dutch, *veld* means 'field'.

When I first saw *wildebeest* in print I thought that someone in the composing room was three sheets in the wind. I pronounced the word as 'wild beast'; later I discovered that the correct orthoepic sound is 'will-da-beast'.

This variety of the *gnu* actually means 'wild beast' in Dutch. Can you imagine the amazement of those early settlers when they first encountered all those strange, nameless African animals thundering forward in immense herds? And how did they react when they first discovered (and named) the *aardvark* busily burrowing for ants and termites, and the striped, hyena-like, fierce-looking *aardwolf*? For those readers who are devotees of etymology (may your name be legion!), the *aardvark* literally means 'earth pig' in Dutch, and the *aardwolf* means 'earth wolf'.

Since we have been talking so much about the Hollanders, let's move over to Europe and take a quick look at a few of their other contributions to the English language:

burgomaster	polder
howitzer	sloop
monsoon	

A *burgomaster* is the mayor or chief magistrate of a town or city in the Netherlands, Austria, Germany or Flanders. Our word *borough* is a relation.

A *howitzer* is a short cannon for firing shells in a high trajectory. The Dutch borrowed the word from the Germans and Czechs. Originally it meant 'a sling'.

Monsoon is a word that Holland borrowed from Portugal long ago. The Portuguese in turn had taken it from the Arabs. When a *monsoon* blows from the southwest during the period between April and October it brings heavy rains to India and its neighbours. Hence *monsoon* has come to mean 'rainy season'.

Polders are low-lying lands that the Dutch have cleverly reclaimed from the sea, usually through the construction of dykes.

A *sloop* is a fore-and-aft rigged sailing vessel with a mainsail and a jib. It has but one mast. The Dutch source is *sloep*. Possibly a relation is the little French harbour craft called *chaloupe*.

By coincidence, there is another *sloop,* the origin of which is unknown. It's a logger's dray or sled. To *sloop,* in lumberjack's jargon, is to haul logs down a steep slope on one of those sledlike devices. Could it be possible that this *sloop* is a variation of *slope*?

158

In any case, the boss of the operation is a *sloopman*.

Heading northeast, we come to the Scandinavians. Here is a salmagundi* of a few of the words given to us by the Swedes, Norwegians and Danes.

fiord	saga	skoal
narwhal	ski	slalom
ombudsman		

Fiord (or *fjord*) is a narrow inlet between steep cliffs. People who have visited Norway tell me that a boat trip on such an arm of the sea is breathtakingly picturesque. In fact, it's 'gorge-ous'.

Narwhal has a Danish-Norwegian ancestry. In Old Norse, *nahvair* meant 'corpse-whale'. The name came about because of the arctic cetacean's habit of floating upside down, thus displaying its white underside and resembling a floating dead body. Whalers hunt it for ivory and oil.

Ombudsman is delightful and a rather recent import from Sweden where *ombud* means 'deputy or representative'. In Scandinavian lands and in Britain, this official investigates complaints against the government.

In Old Norse a *saga* was a story. It still is today. Usually we think of it as a lengthy adventure tale. Galsworthy's THE FORSYTE SAGA consists of a number of books that relate the ups and downs of several generations in the same family.

Icelandic manuscripts of the twelfth and thirteenth centuries are also called *sagas*. Other Icelandic literary works of approximately the same period are called *Eddas*. An *Edda* is also a collection of Old Norse poetry.

Another Old Norse word, *skith* ('snowshoe'), has given us *ski*. As in many other cases, the noun has also been converted into a verb. And let us not forget the summery derivative, *water-skiing*.

Skoal, too, has an Old Norse ancestry. *Skål* meant 'a drinking cup'. The Danes and Swedes also deserve credit somewhere along the line for transmitting the drinking toast to us. It means 'To your health!'

---

* Salmagundi is a mixture, or potpourri. In its original sense it's a salad of chopped meat, anchovies, eggs and onions. We borrowed the noun from the French *salmigondis*, and they may have taken their word from the Italian phrase *salame conditi* ('salt-flavoured — hence, pickled meat').

In one tale I've heard about *skoal,* the word is allegedly related to *skull,* from the ancient Vikings' practice of drinking mead from their dead enemies' bony toppers. I can't find any proof for that colourful account, but it's true that *scalp* is a linguistic cousin of *skoal.*

Slalom is one of several Norwegian words introduced into English because so many people love to glide down the hills on long, flat runners. To a citizen of Oslo a *slalom* literally means 'a sloping path'. It has come to signify the act of skiing in a zigzag course. *Slalom races* are exciting events in winter Olympics.

In April 1500, Pedro Alvarez Cabral landed in Brazil and claimed the region for Portugal. Colonists and traders soon established a footing there.

But the indigenous Tupi tribes resisted the invasion of their land. As in the case of the North American Indians, the better equipped foreigners finally prevailed. But association with the Tupi, whether hostile or friendly, eventually caused a number of words from their speech to be embraced by the Portuguese, and they in turn disseminated the new vocabulary to other lands and languages. Here are a few examples of Tupi-Portuguese words that we use.

WORD	DEFINITION	ORIGINAL WORD
carioca	1. (capitalized) native or resident of Rio de Janeiro 2. ballroom dance or music for it	*cari* ('white'), *oca* ('house')
cashew	tropical evergreen tree yielding edible, kidney-shaped nuts	*acajú*
macaw	brightly coloured parrot	*macao*
paca	burrowing rodent of South and Central America	*páca*
piranha	vicious, voracious South American fish (also called *caribe,* 'cannibal')	*piranha* ('toothed fish')

The Portuguese borrowed not only from the Tupi people but also from others around the world. In Africa they found the dance called the *samba* and a lemur called *macaco.* In Malaya they discovered the *betel nut,* and in India the *mango* (tree or fruit) and *copra* (dried coconut meat) from which coconut oil is extracted. Persia gave them the *pagoda.*

The Caribs and Tupi taught the foreigners a lethal lesson when they poisoned their arrows with *curare,* a resinous substance obtained from tropical plants. The word is also spelt *curari, curara* or *urari.* In Tupi talk that last spelling means 'he to whom it comes falls'.

Palanquin (or *palankeen*) is our alteration of the Portuguese noun *palanquim.* This covered litter carried on the shoulders of two or more men was once a favourite vehicle for V.I.P.s in eastern Asia. The source is Javanese, and the word is ultimately *palyañka* in Sanskrit.

Another export from Java to Portugal is the Chinese *junk.* The Javanese word is *joń;* the Portuguese altered it to *junco,* and we turned the boat back into a monosyllable noun. Lexicographers disagree on the origin of the other *junk,* meaning 'trash'.

Finally, here is a small taste of words that have come to us from the ancient Romans via Portuguese:

albino	cobra	pintado
auto-da-fé	lingo	sargasso

Albino means 'whitish' in Lisbon. The condition of *albinism* is caused by genetic factors. *Albinos* have white skin and hair and pink eyes. The pigmentation problem also affects animals; for example, there are albino elephants, mice and rabbits. Some plants that lack colouration are also *albinos.*

Auto-da-fé literally means 'act of faith'. The leaders of the Inquisition used this expression to indicate that their devotion to their religion was strong enough to warrant the burning of heretics on pyres. The execution of a non-believer soon came to be called an *auto-da-fé.*

The Latin ancestry combines *actus* ('a doing or act') with *fides* ('faith').

Cobra is a shortening of *cobra de capello,* which means 'snake of the hood' in Portuguese.

Lingo is an alteration of *lingoa* ('tongue' in Portuguese). The Latin grandparent is *lingua.* To us a speech that is regarded as strange or unintelligible is a *lingo.* Synonyms are jargon, cant, argot and even dialect.

Pintado — 'painted' in Portuguese, from Latin *pingere* ('to paint') — has three quite different meanings:

1. a long silvery edible game fish

2. a painted or printed chintz once made in India
3. a Cape pigeon, or black-and-white petrel.

Sargasso is a seaweed. The Portuguese parent is *sargaço*. A related word, via Modern Latin, is *sargassum* — also a variety of seaweed.

The Sargasso Sea is an area northeast of the West Indies, famous as the sea where eels breed. *Sargassum* (also called *gulfweed*) grows there abundantly.

Hebrew, the official tongue of Israel, was spoken by the ancient Israelites and is the language in which most of the Old Testament was written. Like Sanskrit, it has endowed various peoples throughout the world with a wealth of words. Here is a small selection of Hebrew gifts to English:

cherub	hosanna	Pharisee	shekel
Gehenna	kosher	rabbi	shibboleth
hallelujah	Messiah	seraph	Torah

Cherubs have evolved into sweet, innocent, chubby apple-cheeked babies or tots. In the original sense they were *cherubim* — winged angelic beings supporting the throne of God. In art they are often depicted as cupids.

Gehenna comes to us via the Greeks. The original Hebrew expression meant 'valley of Hinnom'. Today the word is a synonym for hell, because the children at Hinnom were once sacrificed to Moloch. Hence the Israelites called the place *Topheth* ('abomination').

Incidentally, *Topheth* or *Tophet* is another synonym for hell. Some other names for that infernal region are *Sheol, Pendemonium, Abaddon* and *Tartarus*.

Hallelujah (or *halleluiah*) stems from a Hebrew phrase meaning 'Praise (ye) the Lord.' The interjection is used as an expression of joy or thanksgiving. It is also a song of praise. Through Greek and Latin, the modification is *alleluia*.

Hosanna is another cry of praise to God. The Hebrew source literally means 'Save, we pray!'

Kosher comes from *kāshēr*, the Hebrew word for 'proper or correct'. Applied to foods, and to restaurants and kitchens, it conveys the idea of being prepared according to Jewish dietary laws.

It's fascinating to observe how enthusiastically Christians have embraced the word as a synonym for genuine or legitimate. Recently my son said to me: 'The guy tried to sell me a diamond ring, but I had a feeling it wasn't *kosher*.'

Messiah comes from the Hebrew word *māshīah* ('anointed'). In Judaism this blessed one is the promised deliverer. To Christians he is Jesus of Nazareth.

The ancient Pharisees, respected observers of traditional rites and ceremonies, have received a bad press. In Matthew 23:23 we read: 'Woe unto you, scribes and Pharisees, hypocrites!' A *pharisee* (note the lowercase first letter) has become a sanctimonious, hypocritical person. We have even developed the adjective *pharisaical.*

Rabbi literally means 'my lord' or 'my master' in Hebrew. This scholar and teacher of Jewish law is usually the head of a *synagogue* (see Chapter 1, p. 13).

A *seraph* is a step higher than a *cherub* in the celestial hierarchy. *Seraphim* have three pairs of wings. Like the little angels just below them, they surround the throne of God. They are represented as fiery beings, full of sacred ardour. Therefore the probable Hebrew origin *saraph* ('to burn') seems appropriate.

Shekel (from *shāqal,* 'to weigh') was an ancient Hebrew unit weighing about half an ounce. It then became a silver coin.

Shibboleth means 'password'. It also connotes a distinctive custom, practice or phrase — hence, a slogan. In Hebrew it meant 'ear of grain, stream or flood' — but that's not important. In ancient days the Gileadites at the Jordan fords used the word to distinguish their own people from their foes, the Ephraimites. The latter group were unable to pronounce the initial *sh* in *shibboleth* when they were challenged. As soon as they said 'sibboleth', they were slain.

Torah means 'law' in Hebrew. It is the entire range of divine knowledge and law in Jewish Scriptures and tradition. The first five books of the Old Testament are called the *Torah.* A synonym from Greek is *Pentateuch.*

Americans, especially New Yorkers, use a good deal of Yiddish ('Judaeo-German') words in their slang, and some of them have become current in Britain.

A *kibitzer* (accent on *kib*) is a fellow who stands behind you while you're playing cards and gives you unwanted advice and criticism. The Yiddish verb *kibitzen* is a variation of the colloquial German *kiebitzen* ('to look on, as at cards'). The eventual source is *Kiebitz* ('lapwing or plover') — a word that probably stemmed from an imitation of the bird's call. Somehow, perhaps from its jerky method of flying or from its habit of hovering around neighbourhoods where food is abundant, the bird became synonymous with a busybody or meddler — and so did any person who kibitzes.

The origin of *kibosh* is disputed. While some philologers think it comes from Yiddish, William Morris relates that the Irish poet Padraic Colum makes a good case for its Gaelic ancestry (*cie bais,* 'cap of death'). When you *put the kibosh* on a project, you squelch it.

Nosh is a Yiddish derivative of *naschen,* a German verb meaning 'to taste or nibble'. *Noshers* probably need to go on a diet, because they are constantly raiding the refrigerator for snacks.

Schmaltz goes back to *Schmalz,* a German word meaning 'melted fat'. *Schmaltzy* paintings, novels or musical offerings are full of sentimentality.

Another meaning for *schmaltz* is 'excessive praise'. Those in the know are hep to the fact that flatterers are laying on the schmaltz. (I use slangy expressions to stress that this word, like many others taken from Yiddish, is still regarded as a vulgar intruder into our vocabulary.)

You will doubtless use some of these Yiddish words even if you are a *goy,* which is the Yiddish word for a Gentile. Actually, it means 'people' in Hebrew, and the plural is *goyim.*

Finally, let us consider the contributions of the Amerinds (Eskimos and American Indians).

Eskimo literally means 'eaters of raw fish or flesh'. The name evolved from the Algonquins, French and Danish.

Here are a few words from the language of these Arctic people:

anorak	Malamute
igloo	parka
kayak	umiak

The *anorak* and the *parka* are heavy hooded jackets originally worn only in the polar regions but now seen almost everywhere in winter time. *Parka* means 'skin', which refers to the pelt of the animal from which it is made. The fleece of sheep is sometimes used as a lining. The fur of dogs or the hides of reindeer are often utilized in making the garment.

The *kayak* and the *umiak* (or *oomiak*) are two Eskimo vessels. The former is a watertight canoe with a skin cover and is often used for hunting; the latter is an open boat having a wooden frame protected by skins. It is used for transportation of people or merchandise and is traditionally propelled by Eskimo women.

Daredevils who love to shoot the rapids have popularized *kayaks.*

The *Alaskan Malamute* is a powerful sled dog that was named for the Eskimo tribe that developed the breed.

From various North American Indian tribes we have received hundreds of interesting words. Some are only current in America, but here is a sampling of words that have crossed the Atlantic.

Bayou comes from the Choctaw noun *bayuk* ('small stream'). The Louisiana French altered the spelling and donated the word to us to describe a sluggish tributary to a lake or river.

A *catalpa* is a tree with large heart-shaped leaves and clusters of whitish flowers. The source is *kutuhlpa*, a Creek word meaning 'head with wings' because of the shape of the flowers.

Chinook was named for an Indian tribe of the West. It's either a hot, dry wind that comes down from the eastern slopes of the Rockies or a warm, moist wind blowing from the Pacific to the northwestern coast in winter or spring.

The king salmon of the Pacific is also called *chinook.*

Moccasin is a word I always have trouble spelling. It has a Narraganset origin. Aside from being a heelless shoe, boot or slipper, it's also a snake. There is also a *moccasin flower,* one of the lady's slippers, aptly enough.

Mugwump is a delightful word with an intriguing sound. The Algonquian root is *mugquomp* ('chief'). Hence *mugwump* came to mean 'an important person'.

Then in 1884, a group of Republicans in the U.S.A. refused to support the party nominee. The others pinned the name *mugwumps* on them, meaning that they were filled with their own self-importance.

Gradually the word took on two new connotations: 1) a political independent and 2) a person who can't make up his mind on an issue. In that last sense a joke has been passed around for many years: 'A *mugwump* has his mug on one side of the fence and his wump on the other.'

The Crees gave us the word *pemmican*. In their language it meant 'fat meat'. They mixed fat and berries with strips of lean, dry meat that had been pounded into a paste. Today adventurers use a similar food for emergency rations. It usually consists of beef, suet and dried fruit.

Those creative Algonquians are responsible for *powwow*. In their language the word signified 'a medicine man or conjurer'. Because the head shaman* was the leader of any formal meeting with the colonists, his name came to be associated with the conferences themselves. Then, as often happens, the noun was also used as a verb.

I should explain that Algonquian embraced more than a score of Indian languages. The tribes included such famous ones as the Arapaho, Cheyenne, Chippewa, Cree, Delaware, Fox, Narraganset, Ottawa and Shawnee.

Tepee has a Siouan origin, for a change. The Dakota Indians' word for dwelling is *tipi,* and that spelling is still an accepted variation along with *tepee.*

Contrary to popular opinion, not all the Indians resided in those cone-shaped tents made of skin and bark. The Plains Indians were the dwellers in *tepees.*

Wampum is one of our many slang words for money. That's because of *wampumpeage* — white shell beads used by Indians in southeastern New England as currency. *Peag* is a less used synonym for *wampum.*

Wigwam in Ojibwa is *wigiwam* ('lodge or dwelling'). This domed shelter of the Algonquians has a framework of arched poles which are covered with leaves, bark, branches, rush mats and hides. A portable form of *wigwam* resembles a *tepee.*

I realize I have short-changed the reader on all the languages I have covered and have omitted some. For example, I have neglected the Tibetans, who gave us such words as *lama, panda, polo* and *yak.* Nor have I been fair to the Hungarians, who have supplied us with such gems as *paprika* and *shako.* And then there are the Caribs

---

* *Shaman* means 'medicine man'. The word is of German-Russian-Sanskrit origin.

and other peoples of the West Indies. Without them we should be missing *papaya, savanna,* a dance called the *limbo* and dozens of other beauties. But this chapter, like all the others in the book, is intended only as a soupçon and — if you will forgive the pun — not a full-course dinner. I do hope it's been digestible!

8 Our Anglo-Saxon Heritage

In Chapter 2 we discovered that the Romans and their descendants or offshoots had contributed the greatest number of words to our dictionaries. But even more important than multiplicity is frequency of use — and that's where our Anglo-Saxon ancestors rise to the top of the heap, at least in our conversational speech.

No one can say with authority whether language started with one group, and then spread out as members of that group went their separate ways, or whether diverse groups were almost simultaneously trying to express their ideas. Most scholars are inclined to believe that the latter phenomenon occurred aeons ago.

At any rate, several prehistoric languages emerged, and each was different from any other. Among them were Hamito-Semitic, Uralic, Bantu and Sino-Tibetan. But the one that we are indebted to is Indo-European, which can be considered as the great-great-grandparent of an amazing family of languages.

Let's picture Indo-European as the roots and trunk of an immense tree with about a dozen limbs, some large and some rather small. One of those limbs is called Italic. Its largest branch is Latin, and the branchlets include Italian, French, Spanish, Portuguese and Rumanian.

Another root is Celtic, which branched off into Irish Gaelic, Scottish Gaelic, Manx, Welsh, Cornish, Breton, Gaulish and others.

Balto-Slavic produced such offshoots as Russian, Bulgarian, Polish, Czech, Slovak, Latvian and Lithuanian.

On another side of the tree, Indo-Iranian gave rise to Sanskrit, and the scions of that language include Hindi, Urdu, Assamese and Bengali.

But one of the sturdiest growths from Indo-European turned out to be Germanic. Its two main branches were North Germanic and West Germanic. The former developed into Old Norse and finally into such languages as Norwegian, Swedish, Danish and Icelandic.

West Germanic is the branch that burgeoned into Dutch, Frisian,

Flemish, Afrikaans, German, Yiddish and — yes! — English.

The original inhabitants of Great Britain were the Britons, or Celtics. They migrated to the islands many centuries before the birth of Christ, and scholars estimate that their original territory embraced southwest Germany, eastern France, northern Italy and Iberia.

Another ancient people, whose continental homeland is in dispute, were the Picts (from Latin *picti,* 'painted people', because they tattooed their skins). Somewhere around 1000 B.C. they settled in parts of Scotland and Ireland. As a separate race they faded out in the eighth and ninth centuries. During the reign of Kenneth I they merged with the Scots.

Caesar's troops invaded Britain in 55 and 54 B.C., but the Romans exercised little influence upon the language of the natives. But the arrival of the Angles, Jutes and Saxons was a different matter. These three tribes crossed the Channel and the North Sea in the fifth century, conquered the inhabitants and settled down in their new surroundings.

The Angles probably came from an area that is modern Angeln, where the borders of northwest Germany and south Denmark meet today. They occupied portions of eastern, central and northern England.

According to disputed tradition, the Jutes (probably Rhine-landers, not Jutlanders) crossed the waters at the invitation of the Britons, who needed help in their battles with the Picts. Under the leadership of Hengist and Horsa, they founded the kingdom of Kent and settled near the present site of London and on the Isle of Wight. As time went by they intermingled with the Saxons and the Angles.

The Saxons were a warlike Teutonic people who originated in the Elbe valley. Charlemagne conquered them and caused them to be Christianized. The Old Saxons remained in Germany, but the group that emigrated to Britain got together with the Angles and held sway until the Norman Conquest.

The above groups brought their different dialects to Britain, and what finally emerged was Old English. It was chiefly a combination of Old High German, Middle Low German, Gothic, Old French, Old Danish, Old Norse and Celtic.

Old English and Anglo-Saxon are synonymous.

Now let me illustrate the point about our debt to the Anglo-Saxons when we use ordinary everyday language. Here is an original story in which *every* word has an Old English background:

At the stroke of five each morning Mother and Father leaped out of bed. Then they began to do many chores about the house. Before the sun rose Mother took water from the well while Father went out into the fields to feed the cows and look after the horses. In summer or in winter, in good weather or bad, everything had to be cared for.

As a small child I often thought how much they must have hated that daily work. Yet they never showed anything but love and hope in our home. They bore hardship without one word of sorrow, and even found time to teach the children how to swim and ride horseback. In the evenings, at dusk, they also taught us the Gospel and little songs about the goodness of God and the wonderful gift of life. They were so thankful that they could give us food to eat and milk to drink as we grew up. They were kind and loving indeed! To my brother and sister and me they were not only kinfolk but true friends.

Isn't it fascinating that not a single Latin derivative appears in those two paragraphs? Not a trace of French, Spanish, Italian — and no Greek word either. Just plain Old English!

Only one word can be questioned. Strangely enough, it is *they*. Some lexicographers give sole credit to Old Norse, but others state that the pronoun comes to us partly from Old English (*thā*) and partly from Old Norse (*thei-r*).

Of course the Anglo-Saxons did not invent all the words in that story, nor was their spelling the same. But their basic vocabulary was passed down to Middle English (ca. 1100—1500), and thence to us. As the centuries elapsed, changes in orthography and nuances of meaning often took place. As an example, here is a sort of flow chart on the progress of the words in the first sentence of our story.

MODERN ENGLISH	MIDDLE ENGLISH	OLD ENGLISH
at	at, atte	aet
the	the	thĕ
stroke	stroke, strake	strican
of	of	of
five	fif	fif
each	ech, elc	aelc, aeghwile
morning	morweninge	morgen
mother	moder	modor

and	and, an	and, ond
father	fader	faeder
leap	lepen	hleapan
out	out	ūt
bed	bed	bedd

As a general rule, most of the following have come down to us from the Anglo-Saxons:

1. basic words such as *bone, hot, man, meat, wife* and *woman* (also some vulgar and scatological 'four-letter' words)
2. irregular verbs
3. pronouns, prepositions and conjunctions
4. names of numbers (but *million, billion*, etc. have a French ancestry)

The West German offshoots have thus provided us with most of the basic words for our modern language. But the Norman Conquest and the Renaissance were instrumental in weaving a linguistic tapestry, with many threads from Greece and Rome. We have inherited a delicious mixture of such reliable, workaday, monosyllabic Old English words as *bad, light, shake, tree, up* and *down,* along with such fanciful polysyllabic beauties as *anfractuous* ('sinuous, winding'), *usufructuary* ('one enjoying the fruits or profits of an estate'), *eudaemonical* ('producing happiness') and *cymotrichous* ('having wavy hair').

Our English language offers something for everybody, far more than any other, whether ancient or modern.

9 Our Animal Kingdom

We humans have made pets of creatures ranging from dogs and cats, gerbils and hamsters, to lions and dolphins. Fauna have interested us to the point of obsession and have taken up lots of space in our dictionaries, not only in straight definitions (from the aardvark to the zebra) but also in phrases and expressions we use every day. We take catnaps, get tips from the horse's mouth, participate in hen parties or stag parties, put on the dog, buy a pig in a poke and often make asses of ourselves.

Our clichés indicate how we associate our own qualities with those that we ascribe to different beasts. One person is as strong as an ox, another as weak as a kitten. Consider the following:

meek (or gentle) as a lamb	sick as a dog
brave (or bold) as a lion	greedy as a hog
fierce as a tiger	busy as a beaver
sly as a fox	mad as a March hare
quiet as a mouse	stubborn as a mule
fat as a pig	poor as a church mouse

Winged creatures also come in for their share of hackneyed similes

busy as a bee	wise as an owl
blind as a bat	free as a bird
bald as a coot	proud as a peacock
happy as a lark	plump as a partridge

The sounds that animals make have also fascinated mankind and have added hundreds upon hundreds of words to various languages. Dogs bark; cats mew; pigeons coo; cocks crow; cows moo; grasshoppers and crickets chirp; owls hoot; nightingales warble; mules and asses bray; sheep and calves bleat and baa; and hyenas laugh.

In all ancient civilizations, great interest was taken in animals.

Aesop comes to mind immediately. That Greek fabulist was a Phrygian slave (ca. 620 — ca. 560 B.C.). His talking beasts depicted human frailties and virtues. A moral was always appended to each tale, and many of those lessons persist in our language today. For instance, 'sour grapes' comes from the story of the fox that could not reach a bunch of grapes. Oh well, he said, they're sour anyway.

No less a personage than Aristophanes, the great Greek dramatist, was an Aesopian devotee. Perhaps that is why he also chose to use creatures in the animal world as vehicles for his satires on the foibles of his era. Witness THE BIRDS, THE FROGS and THE WASPS. In the first of these comedies the birds establish Cloud Cuckoo, or Nephelococcygia, a town existing in midair.

Our feathered friends attracted lots of attention among the ancients. Take the owl, for example. When Athenians ventured out at night, they could hear owls everywhere. Since the goddess Athena bore the same name as the city, the owl became her symbol; and the Romans retained the tradition for Minerva. Wisdom was the special province of both deities, hence today we say that a shrewd person is 'as wise as an owl'.

The *phoenix* is a legendary, beautiful bird of Egyptian-Arabian origin. It was reputed to live to a ripe old age (five hundred or six hundred years) in the desert, then burn itself on a pyre and rise from the ashes as fresh as a daisy. Consequently it has become a symbol of immortality or resurrection, and the word is applied to one that recovers miraculously after ruin or near destruction.

The *roc* is another fabulous bird from the same regions. In The Arabian Nights it was described as so huge that it could carry off elephants as food for its nestlings.

When a person destroys something that has brought him good fortune or success, we say that he has 'killed the goose that laid the golden eggs'. This expression dates back to an old Greek fable in which a farmer owned such a goose. Greedy for more gold, he slaughtered the goose and opened it up to seek additional precious eggs.

Chanticleer comes from two French words, *chanter* ('to sing or crow') and *cler* ('clear'). As in the Middle Ages, it still is a synonym for rooster. *Reynard* continues to be an appellation for a fox. Like *chanticleer,* it has come down to us from the Medieval 'bestiary' (or 'beast epic') ROMAN DE RENART, in which the fox tries to outwit the cock.

Let us now turn to the ancients' obsession with four-legged creatures. Several of these beasts are still over our heads. *Canis Major* and *Canis Minor* (named for their shapes) are constellations near Orion. One is 'the larger dog', the other is 'the lesser dog'. Also high in the sky are *Ursa Major* and *Ursa Minor. Ursa* is the Latin name for a female bear. Both constellations were originally named by the Greeks. *Arktos* is the Athenian word for bear. It still remains active for astronomers. Arcturus (literally, 'bear keeper') is a first magnitude star in the constellation Boötes.

The *horse,* if one believes classical mythology, was created by Poseidon, who was later named Neptune by the Romans. *Hippo* was the Greek word, *equus* the Latin, for this wonderful animal. From both roots we have mined a bonanza.

hippic	relating to horses or horse racing
hippocampus	legendary sea horse having the tail of a dolphin or a fish
hippocentaur	centaur (man having a horse's body)
Hippocrene	poetic inspiration
hippocrepiform	shaped like a horseshoe
hippodrome	1. stadium for chariot races
	2. arena for horsemen to perform in
	3. sports contest with a predetermined winner
	4. to fix a sports contest
hippogriff } hippogriffin }	mythical monster, part horse, part eagle, part lion
hippology	study of the horse
hippopotamus	aquatic animal
hippus	spasmodic contraction of the pupil of the eye
equerry	officer of a royal household responsible for the care of horses
eques	Roman knight
equestrian } equestrienne }	horseman; horsewoman
equestrianism	horsemanship
equid	ungulate animal (horse, zebra or ass)

The derivation of the word Hippocrene merits attention. It was originally an ancient Greek fountain that supposedly spouted when Pegasus struck the ground with his hoof. In his 'Ode to a Nightingale' Keats wrote: 'O for a beaker full of the warm South,/Full of the true, the blushful Hippocrene.'

Monsters such as the *hippogriff,* the *griffin,* the *Harpies* and the

Minotaur thrilled the Athenians. Lest we sneer at their penchant for unnatural creatures, let us rememer that civilized men today are enthralled by Bigfoot in the Northwest, the Abominable Snowman (Yeti) in the Himalayas, the Loch Ness Monster and the strange beings that reputedly land here in UFOs.

One of the terrifying animals in Greek mythology is the *Chimaera.* Homer described it as having a lion's head, a goat's body and a dragon's tail. Well, a Corinthian hero named Bellerophon mounted the winged Pegasus and slew the awful thing. However, like the *phoenix,* the *Chimaera* has been resurrected. In its original spelling it lives today in the form of an ugly fish, related to the shark. Ichthyologists call it an elasmobranch.

But in modern usage, as in many other cases involving ancient diphthongs, the *Chimaera* has become a *chimera.* Here are some current definitions for that Attic atrocity:

1. any monster, in painting or sculpture, having disparate parts
2. a horrible or unreal creature of the imagination; a fantastic fabrication or illusion
3. a utopian dream or aim
4. an organism that is partly male and partly female, or an artificially produced individual (perhaps a clone?)

A related adjective, *chimerical,* carries the sense of the third definition above. Get-rich-quick projects are usually *chimerical.*

In PARADISE LOST, Milton spoke of 'Gorgons and Hydras and Chimaeras dire'. The *Gorgons* were three witchy sisters led by Medusa. Instead of hair, serpents crowned their heads. A certain mean-looking jellyfish is called a *medusa.* And one of the edible mushrooms bears the name medusa's head, as does a weedy rye grass.

Gorgon today is a synonym for a hag. In O. Henry we find '*gorgonizing* him with her opaque yellow eyes' — a reference to the Greeks' belief that Medusa's stare could turn a person to stone.

(In case you're wondering, Gorgonzola cheese has no connection with Medusa or with the French writer. It's named for the source, an Italian town near Milan.)

Hydra was another of those frightful creatures dreamed up by the imaginative Greeks. The serpent had nine heads. Every time one was cut off, two shot up in its place. 'Twas a *herculean* task to put the thing out of its misery.

In this age of big business it is interesting to observe Ralph Nader's crusaders doing battle with the '*hydra-headed* conglomerates'.

The ancients named eight of the twelve signs of the zodiac for members of the animal kingdom. Let us take a look at three of them.

Taurus is the Latin noun for 'bull'. It has sired a delightful stock of English words:

taurine	bovine
taurocephalous	bullheaded
tauroesque	in the style of a bull
taurolatry	worship of bulls
tauromachy	bullfighting or bullfight
tauromorphic	resembling a bull

Modern toreadors would be interested in *taurokathapsia*, an ancient Cretan sport in which the performer grasped the horns of a bull and somersaulted over him.

Pisces is the plural of *piscis,* the Latin noun for fish. It has netted us a nice collection of words:

Pisaster	genus of starfishes
piscan	relating to fishes
piscary	fishing rights; place to fish
piscation	fishing
piscatorial } *piscatory*	relating to fishermen
pisciculture	the art of breeding, developing and improving fish
pisciculturist	superintendent of a fish hatchery
piscifauna	the fishes of a given region
piscina	basin for certain ablutions, usually in a sacristy
piscine	having fishlike qualities

Capricorn translates literally into 'goat horn'. It is tempting to surmise that the isle of Capri was named for a goat. Research yields the information that the original name was Capreae, but that's as far as it goes.

Goat itself comes to us from an Old English word, *gāt.* The *goatee* is so named because it resembles the beard sported by a male goat.

Scapegoat ('a person bearing the blame for others') has a

fascinating Hebraic history. It is really an *escape goat*. During Yom Kippur the high priest would bring two goats forward. Lots were cast to see which of the two would be sacrificed. The priest then symbolically laid the sins of the people on the head of the goat that had been spared. Weighed down with the burden of all those misdeeds, it was taken outside and allowed to escape.

To get one's goat is a well known Americanism meaning 'to vex or anger'. But did you know that the *goatsucker* is a nocturnal bird? The name stems from an ancient belief that it steals the milk from a she goat. The *nightjar* is a goatsucker. Why is it called a *nightjar*? Because it makes a harsh, jarring nocturnal noise.

Like the *goatsucker,* there is also a *cowsucker*. It's not a bird but a harmless snake. Again the appellation arose because of a widespread belief: the word got around that the snake slithered up at night and milked cows.

The *cowslip* is a primrose that grows in the British Isles. (In America it is a synonym for the marsh marigold.) Does it mean a flower that makes a cow take a header? Well, not exactly. *Slyppe* or *slype* ('paste, slime or dung') is the derivation. Apparently the blossom thrives on natural fertilizers in the pastures.

A word I like is *cowcatcher.* Originally it meant a triangular frame in front of the old 'iron horses', designed to clear the track of obstructions. In the modern vernacular it is a brief TV or radio commercial placed just before a programme.

Cow, as a verb meaning to intimidate, is simple to assimilate when one considers how docile beef-on-the-hoof are driven into stockyards. But don't be fooled by *coward.* That word can be traced back to *cauda* (a Latin noun for 'tail'). Literally, a *coward* is a person who turns tail.

The Hindus revere steer and are forbidden to eat their flesh. Hence we have coined the term *sacred cow,* meaning a person, group or organization that is immune to all criticism.

The cow's mate, of course, is the bull, the *taurus* we were looking at before we were led astray. He is also the consort of a female alligator, elephant, elk, moose, seal, terrapin or whale. And what a wealth of words we derive from this virile fellow! The *bulldog,* for instance, named not only for his fierce, muscular appearance but also for his early role as a bull baiter.

Bulldoze was originally *bulldose,* or a 'dose for a bull'. Thus it meant a severe thrashing. Later it came to mean 'intimidate' or, if you will, 'cow'. Today a *bulldozer* is a bully, a type of revolver, a machine for clearing land or the operator of that vehicle.

The origin of *bully* will come as a surprise to most readers. It has nothing to do with the animal. Instead it dates back to Dutch and German words for 'sweetheart', 'lover' or even 'baby talk'. Years ago it meant 'a fine fellow'. Another meaning was 'pimp'.

In such a chiefly British expression as '*Bully* for you!' the interjection denotes congratulations. That idea certainly seems close to the sources of the word.

Finally, there is *bully beef*, which has a strictly French background. It's derived from *boeuf bouilli*, and can be traced back to the Gallic verb *bouillir* ('to boil'). Some lexicographers state that *bullion* comes from that same French verb, while others maintain that it is related to *billion* (a small French coin) and dates back to *bille* ('a stick or bar'). At any rate, *bullion* is now used in two principal senses: gold and silver regarded as raw material, or a heavy fringe or lace of twisted gold or silver thread.

To add to the confusion, there is the papal *bull* — a formal, sealed document. It's a shortening of the Latin word *bulla* ('seal'). The Italian offshoot is *bullettino*, from which we get our word *bulletin*.

But *bullet* comes from the French *boulle* ('ball') and is a cousin of the verb *bowl*. When you bowl someone over, you literally knock him down with a ball. Bowling, needless to say, comes from the same source.

Philologists either disagree or have doubts about the origin of the *bulls and bears* in the stock markets. But there is no quarrel about such expressions as *bull in a china shop* or *take the bull by the horns*.

That handsome bird, the *bullfinch*, was so named because of its thick neck. And the term *bullfrog* was coined because of the amphibian's size and bull-like croak.

Another sign of the zodiac, an exemplar of strength and ferocity, is the *lion*. It is the symbol of Great Britain and of Venice. Ethiopia's Haile Selassie was called the 'Lion of Judah', and the epithet for Richard I of England was 'Lion-Hearted'.

Celebrities are called *lions* because they dominate the social scene. When we make a fuss over such people, we *lionize* them.

The animal is responsible for several common phrases, too. Anyone who gets *the lion's share* receives the largest part — or all. And *the lion's mouth* is a place of great peril, while *a lion in the path* indicates a dangerous obstacle. We also speak of *bearding the lion in his den* — confronting some fearsome person in his own surroundings.

It's also dangerous to *have a tiger by the tail*. Like the lion, that jungle beast has been adopted by a number of groups. Clemenceau, the French statesman, was nicknamed *'Le Tigre'* because of the bold programme he launched in an effort to defeat the Germans in World War I. A *paper tiger,* in contrast, is a person or a nation that appears to be strong or powerful but is actually weak.

But most interesting are the many appendages given to the word to form other nouns. *Tigereye* (the gem) and *tiger lily* (the flower) are prime examples. *Tiger* also precedes bass, beetle, bittern, fish, frog, mosquito, moth, pear, python, rattlesnake, salamander, shark, weasel, wolf and quite a number of other words.

The *wolf* has gained a reputation for savagery and cruelty that starts in the nursery, where we are taught to fear this cousin of the dog, villain of 'The Three Little Pigs' and 'Little Red Riding Hood'. Poverty-stricken people try to *keep the wolf from the door,* and all of us beware of that diabolical deceiver, the *wolf in sheep's clothing.** When we alarm others unnecessarily we *cry wolf,* and when people are summarily evicted they are *thrown to the wolves.*

A masher who comes on too strong or who makes advances to many women is a *wolf*. When we eat ravenously, we *wolf* our food. And certain jarring sounds on string instruments or old organs are *wolves* to musicians.

'Who's afraid of the big, bad wolf?' Well, Mr. Disney, we are!

In our symbolism, the direct opposites of the *wolf* are the *sheep* and the *lamb*. To one we attribute such adjectives as silly, timid and defenceless. The other is considered to be a dear person or a dupe.

Most lexicographers agree that *lamb* and *elk* have the same origin, probably in the Greek word *elaphos* ('deer'). If you find that hard to believe, so do I. We do not have many common phrases that are derived from *lamb,* but there is one notable religious reference. In John 1:29, Jesus is called 'the Lamb of God, which taketh away the sins of the world'. The male of the species has given us the verb *ram* ('to strike against with a heavy object') and such a noun as *battering ram.*

---

* *Wolf in sheep's clothing* is a phrase derived from Matthew 7:15: 'Beware of false prophets, which come to you in sheep's clothing, but inwardly they are ravening wolves.' Perhaps Aesop should get some credit for the phrase, too.

In Old English and other tongues of yore the *buck* was a 'male goat'. As the years progressed, this animal became a male deer or antelope. However, the term is still applied by some to sires of other animals, such as the hare, rabbit, guinea pig, rat, and — yes — the goat. It is even descriptive of the male salmon, shad and other game fish.

We do get some interesting words and phrases from this animal. *Buckskin* is obvious. The slang word for a dollar also applies; it is a shortened form of *buckskin,* which was an item of trade with the Indians. *Buckshot* fits too. But people with buck teeth will not be happy to learn that the term refers to the denticulation of the same beast.

But we mustn't be fooled by *buckaroo, buckboard, bucket, buckle, buckthorn* and *buckwheat.* Those words have far different origins, which the reader is invited to look up if he cares to.

We all know the phrase '*pass the buck*'. It comes from an old type of knife called a *buckhorn* because of the shape of its handle. This object was often used as a counter in early poker games to indicate the next dealer. When you *passed the buckhorn* — soon abridged to *buck* — you were no longer responsible for the first move in the card game.

Did you ever wonder if a *reindeer* was so called because Santa controlled it with *reins*? Forget it! *Reins* stem back to the Latin *retinere* ('to hold back'). But *reindeer* comes from a Scandinavian combination (*hreinn* plus *dyr*). The first part meant *reindeer* and the second part meant *deer* — a good example of tautology.*

In boxing it's illegal to hit one's opponent with a *rabbit punch,* or chopping blow to the back of the head. The expression is derived from the manner in which a rabbit is stunned before being killed and butchered.

Welsh rabbit is probably of jocular origin, because it has no connection with a bunny. It's a seasoned dish made of melted cheese on toast. Sometimes beer is added. Sober chefs who don't want to confuse people call the dish *Welsh rarebit.*

Because the animal is weak and timid, players who are poor at such games as tennis, golf, cricket or even poker are called *rabbits.*

Speaking of games, *hare and hounds* is a popular children's sport in which the 'hounds' chase the 'hares', who are given a start.

* *Tautology* — needless repetition of an idea; from two Greek roots, *taut* ('same') and *logos* ('word'). A highfalutin synonym is *pleonasm.*

From *hare* we also get *harebrained* ('giddy or flighty') and the blue flower called the *harebell*. In Middle English the spelling was *harebelle,* and lexicographers assume that the plant got its name because it grew in places frequented by those little leporids.

Another animal hunted by the hounds is the *fox.* Because of its cunning this animal has generated the verb *to fox* and the adjective *foxy.*

The horse's gait called the fox-trot was probably so named because it requires short, broken steps, the kind taken by the comparatively short-legged fox. The theory also applies to the dance of the same name.

Fox terriers were once used to drive Reynard from his *foxhole.* With their tails wagging gaily, *foxhounds* still perform that task.

Finally, there is *foxfire* — an eerie phosphorescent light caused by fungi on decaying wood. It's possible that the name originated because of the resemblance of this glow to the silvery quality of certain fox fur.

Mention of the hounds reminds me that those persistent canines also gave us a common verb. When a person is *hounded,* he is pursued relentlessly.

Because swift steamers and ocean liners could travel so fast, they were soon called *greyhounds.* An American bus company latched on to the term with great success.

A *buckhound* is not a pursuer of the almighty dollar but a variety of deerhound. Both are Scottish hunting dogs.

It's easy to see why a private eye or detective who never gives up in his pursuit of a missing person or criminal is called a *bloodhound.* But if you were a poor speller, you might misinterpret the *horehound.* It's an aromatic Eurasian plant from which a cough remedy or candy is extracted. It has absolutely no connection with those deep-voiced canines. *Hore* is a variation of *hoar* ('grey'), and the second syllable comes from *hune,* an Anglo-Saxon term for 'plant'. The *horehound* has many hoary, downy leaves, hence the name.

Dogs in general have received a bad press even though they are reputed to be 'man's best friends' and are probably the most popular pets. We incorporate them into such demeaning phrases as *go to the dogs, dog in the manger, dog-tired, dog-cheap* and *lead a dog's life.* When we damage books we *dog-ear* them. We define ruthless self-interest as *dog-eat-dog.* Furthermore, a fellow who has fallen out of favour is said to be *in the doghouse.*

181

Even worse, a mean and despicable person is defined as a *dog* or *cur.* Mongrels are any animals of mixed breeding, but we usually attach canine significance to them. When we're disgusted we say 'Doggone!' Sailors are not happy to be assigned to the mealtime *dogwatch,* although it lasts only two hours.

Do cute little dogs fare any better? Well, consider the way we sneer at *puppy love* and the fact that one meaning for *pup* is 'an inexperienced or objectionably brash person'. And of course the female dog gets the same slap in the face. Think of the uses of the word *bitch.*

Even the poets, prophets and prosaists have joined the parade and have refused to *let sleeping dogs lie.* In the following quotations *man bites dog:*

'You called me a dog.'
  (Shylock to Antonio, in THE MERCHANT OF VENICE)

'Am I a dog, that thou comest to me with staves?'
  (I Samuel 17:43)

' "Who touches a hair of yon grey head
Dies like a dog! March on!" he said.'
(Whittier, 'Barbara Frietchie')

'I'd beat him like a dog.'
  (Sir Andrew, in TWELFTH NIGHT)

'Doth the moon care for the barking of a dog?'
  (Burton, ANATOMY OF MELANCHOLY)

However, as the saying goes, *every dog has his day.* We do have some expressions that favour our canine companions. 'Hot dog!' is an expression of delight — a term, by the way, derived from the imagined resemblance of a frankfurter to a dachshund. The cartoonist T. A. Dorgan ('TAD') coined the name.

Dogged can mean 'obstinate', but it also has acquired a more gratifying connotation to us lovers of the genus Canis. It carries the idea of 'unshakable' or 'unremitting'.

Does *dogma* stem from the same source? Not at all! Its origin is not Old English but Greek. This synonym for doctrine comes from *dokein* ('to seem good'). Its cousin, via Latin, is *decent.*

182

In English phraseology our feline companions fare somewhat better than the canines. Something we enjoy might be called *the cat's pyjamas* or *the cat's whiskers*. We pay grudging admiration to agile *cat burglars,* and we state that 'a cat has nine lives' because it always seems to land on its feet. We also repeat an old saying when we declare that 'a cat may look at a king', meaning 'Who's afraid of the V.I.P.?'

Games like *puss in the corner* enhance the image of *Felis catus.* And the fun attached to making a *cat's cradle* from looped strings is also relevant.

Moreover, pleasant associations spring up from such children's stories and rhymes as PUSS IN BOOTS and 'The Cat and the Fiddle'. As tots we hated Johnny Green for putting poor pussy in the well and liked Johnny Stout for pulling her out. Nor can we forget the grinning Cheshire cat immortalized by Lewis Carroll.

But the cat comes in for some subtle and outright disparagement too. Consider *scaredy cat, catty* remarks, *catcalls* and such expressions as *no room to swing a cat* or *as nervous as a cat on a hot tin roof.* Even *kittenish* has come to mean 'affectedly coy'.

Another derogatory word, *cat's-paw* ('dupe, tool or puppet') has a fascinating origin. It can be traced to an old fable in which a monkey who wanted to get some roasted chestnuts out of a fire used the paw of his feline friend.

When we *bell the cat* we take a dare. In this instance, too, a fable is the source. In a conversation among mice, one suggested that they hang a bell on the cat's neck to warn them of their foe's approach. But a wise mouse retorted, in essence, 'Fine! But who will bell the cat?'

Letting the cat out of the bag is revealing a secret. This phrase comes from a piece of rural trickery in days gone by. Con men of that time would place a cat in a sack and pretend it was a pig fit for roasting. If they were careless, their deceit was disclosed. A related phrase is 'to buy a pig in a poke'. The *poke* in this sense is a sack. In 'The Shooting of Dan McGrew', Robert W. Service refers to *a poke of dust,* meaning 'a bag of gold dust'.

Pussyfoot was the name given to W. E. Johnson, a law-enforcement officer and prohibitionist. To *pussyfoot* is to act cautiously or timidly or to be noncommittal on an issue. The derivation is obvious.

A cougar or lynx is sometimes called a *catamount.* This is a delightful abridgement of cat-a-mountain ('leopard'). The original phrase in Medieval English was 'cat of the mountain'.

A *catkin* is an inflorescence on a *pussy willow*. (Naturally!) Catkin is an alteration of an old Dutch word for 'kitten' and is so named because it looks like a cat's tail. And, incidentally, for the same reason a certain marsh plant is called a cattail.

Puss (the slang word for 'face') does not have any relation to cats. It comes from a Gaelic alteration of 'buss'. The word *pus* meant 'lip'. So when a thug threatens to smack someone in the *puss*, he means that he'll give the fellow a 'fat lip'. *Sourpuss* ('grouch') is an extension from the same root.

Catnip, catmint, catnap, catboat and *catwalk* are all related to grown-up kittens, but *catsup* is not. The alternative spelling, *ketchup*, gives it away. It comes from *kĕchap*, a spiced fish sauce in Malay.

You may ask, 'What about *caterwaul* ("to howl") and that creeping larva called the *caterpillar?*' The answer is that both have a feline origin. The latter is very intriguing. It literally means 'hairy female cat'.

While checking up on the above I came across *Catorama*. 'Ah,' methought, 'It's an exhibition or display of Maltese, Siamese and other breeds!' But, no! Here's the definition given by WEBSTER'S THIRD NEW INTERNATIONAL DICTIONARY: 'A genus of deathwatch beetles (family Anobiidae) including some that are pests of stored grain.'

'Deathwatch?' That adjective made me do a double take. Hastily I flipped the pages forward and discovered: 'Any of various small beetles . . . that are common in old houses where they bore in the woodwork and furniture making a clicking noise probably by knocking the head against the wood.' Visions of haunted houses popped into my head. I was satisfied, but I had goose pimples.

Underneath the above entry, WEBSTER'S THIRD referred me to *book louse*. Well, I'd heard of *bookworms*, but never *book lice!* Consumed with curiosity, I flipped forward and read: 'An insect of the family Antropidae . . . that is injurious to books and papers.' Okay so far. But what about that family? 'Antropidae' had a strangely familiar ring to it.

Once more my fingers did the walking, with great expectations that were instantly rewarded. The Antropidae were named for *Antropos,* one of the three Fates in Grecian mythology. She was the meanest one, because she finally cut the thread of life. Her sister Clotho did the spinning, and Lachesis determined the length of one's years, but inflexible Antropos scissored you into oblivion.

Now let me quote WEBSTER'S THIRD again concerning the Antropidae: 'A widely distributed family of wingless insects . . . that include most book lice and that feed on organic debris and often damage processed foods, book bindings, herbarium specimens and similar stored products.'

But the note relating to the derivation is even more interesting: 'From the belief that the ticking sound made by some species of book lice forebodes a death.'

And so we come full circle, having started with *Catorama*. I cite the above as only one of the many adventures that one can have if one really peruses an unabridged lexicon. As someone has said before me, 'The more I learn the more ignorant I realize I am.'

Well, that's just about enough coverage for *cats and dogs*. Now let's get to our other four-legged associates, the equines.

The word *horse* probably has a Germanic and Old Norse background; lexicographers aren't sure. In medieval times it was spelt *hors*. Let's look at some varieties.

The *mustang* has a Hispanic origin, from mesten(g)o. Literally, it's a stray animal. Some experts state that the name actually dates back to *mixtus*, the Latin past participle of *miscere* ('to mix'). Indeed, the mustangs are a mixed breed. The story goes that long ago they mingled with domesticated herds on the prairies and produced hybrids.

The *bronco* is also of Spanish descent. Appropriately enough, the word means 'rough'. The *pinto* is a calico horse or pony. Any Mexican can tell you that the word means 'spotted'. It's assumed that the Spanish American adjective was derived from the Vulgar Latin. *Pinctus* meant 'painted'. In the western United States a mottled horse is often called *paint* by cowboys.

But *horse* itself has given rise to an abundance of phrases and expressions. We say, 'That's a horse of a different colour' when we refer to something entirely different. Shakespeare mentioned metaphorically *a horse of the same colour* in TWELFTH NIGHT, so the saying probably goes back at least to the Elizabethan era.

Not long before the reign of Elizabeth I, Thomas Heywood wrote: 'A man may well bring a horse to the water, but he cannot make him drink . . .'

James Polk, the eleventh President of the United States, was the first *dark horse* to be elected. His name was not even mentioned at the Democrats' convention in 1844 until the eighth ballot. He came out of nowhere to win the race for candidacy. The term obviously arises from racecourse jargon. An unknown contender is 'dark' because the form books shed no light on him.

To the sport of kings we also owe such phrases as *back the wrong horse* ('support a loser') and *from the horse's mouth* (meaning that the jockey's mount in the race had actually talked and promised to win).

Locking the stable door after the horse has been stolen is simple to translate into 'taking precautionary actions too late'. Heywood wrote in 1546, 'No man ought to looke a gift horse in the mouth.' The proverb dates back to Saint Jerome in 400 A.D. It refers to the fact that a horse's worth can be assessed by its age, and the condition of its teeth is an excellent criterion.

There are those, however, who advise us: 'Always look a gift horse in the mouth.' This reversal may have some connection with the *wooden horse* or *Trojan horse,* terms now synonymous with people or things designed to destroy from within.

My Irish mother used to say: 'If wishes were horses, beggars would ride.' Not until years later did I appreciate the aptness of that saying. Recently I've discovered that it appears in John Ray's ENGLISH PROVERBS (1670).

In contrast, *Hold your horses!* and *Don't get on your high horse!* present no great difficulty in interpreting their intended messages.

Whoever came up with *horse feathers* as a syonym for bunk or nonsense had the touch of a poet. Maybe he was referring obliquely to Pegasus, that winged horse of Greek mythology. In any case, he made a good point.

Medieval households had horseshoes nailed to their doors to drive away witches. Was it because the object would kick them away? I don't know, but it's certain that today a *horseshoe* is one of the many symbols of good luck.

One-horse is another picturesque word. It means 'second-rate, inferior, petty'. Though the adjective is most commonly used with *town,* it is sometimes affixed to such other nouns as *theory, lawyer, farm* and *exhibition.*

Sometimes plants, insects or fish that are relatively large and coarse have the word *horse* prefixed to their names. Examples are *horse chestnut, horse mushroom, horse nettle* and *horse radish.* Among the insects there are the *horse fly* and *horse ant.* At sea we find the *horse mackerel* and *horse mussel.*

Sea horse has many meanings. Among them are:

1. walrus
2. fabulous creature, half horse and half fish
3. genus of teleostean fish of genus Hippocampus
4. large whitecap on a wave

I find it fascinating that we still measure the might of an automobile engine in terms of *horsepower*.

One of the many meanings of *pony* relates to drinks. It's half a jigger, or three-quarters of a fluid ounce. But a *pony* is also a *crib*, a word-for-word translation of a foreign-language text used illicitly by students.

If a gambler puts a *pony* on a horse in a race, he's betting £25 on it. Incidentally, if he wagers a *monkey* he's betting £500.

As an adjective, *coltish* means 'playful or frisky'. The noun *colt-pixie* is next of kin. It means 'a mischievous hobgoblin supposed to appear as a colt and mislead men or horses into bogs'.

The counterpart of a *colt*, of course, is a *filly*, a word related philologically to *foal*. Male chauvinists refer to high-spirited young girls as *fillies*. It intrigues me to notice that Frenchmen designate a young, unmarried girl as a *jeune fille*. Actually, fille comes from the Latin word *filia* ('daughter').

Why do we call an inferior or aged or unsound horse a *nag*? This word is related to the Dutch noun *negge* ('small horse') and is eventually derived from 'neigh'. Incidentally, it has no alliance with the verb meaning 'to engage in petty faultfinding'. That word is probably of Scandinavian origin and once meant 'to gnaw'. How appropriate!

Betters at Ascot and Newmarket often describe a 'nag' as a *gee-gee* — originally a nursery name for a horse. When a horse is told to 'gee up', that is a command to go faster. In America, *gee* tells the animal to turn right, *haw* to turn left.

Finally, here is a potpourri of expressions in which a whole variety of animals' names are taken in vain.

The opossum (shortened to possum) is reputed to feign death when frightened or threatened. Thus people who *play possum* are dissembling or pretending ignorance.

White elephant has a fascinating history. Long ago the king of Siam was the only person allowed to own an albino elephant, because they were so rare. But, like other pachyderms, they had enormous appetites and were expensive to keep. And so, whenever the king felt dislike for a courtier, he would present the poor fellow with a white elephant and wait for him to be financially ruined.

Kangaroo courts disregard or pervert the law or justice. Sometimes they are set up by prisoners or vagabonds or lynch mobs. They are so named because decisions are reached by leaps and bounds.

The expression *ride piggyback* is an alteration of 'pick-a-back' or 'pick-a-pack'. Today piggyback is also used as a verb; when loaded truck trailers are placed on freight cars, they *piggyback*.

Because the bee is regarded as a busy little creature, its name has been attached to all kinds of activities, such as *sewing bees* and *spelling bees*.

The *crowbar* is so named apparently because the tool originally had a forked end that looked like a crow's foot. Incidentally, wrinkles around the outer corners of the eyes are called *crow's feet* because of their resemblance to the bird's footprints.

When poker players *feed the kitty*, they ante up. Actually the phrase means to put money into a jug. Kitty dates back to a Medieval Dutch word *kitte* or *kit*, meaning 'jug or vessel'.

Monkey jacket or *monkey suit* is a slang term for a uniform, because organ grinders used to dress their simian companions in little coats. The term is now sometimes used for a dinner jacket.

Obviously, in a single chapter it's impossible to cover all the phrases that involve the multitude of creatures on land and sea. Readers may like to track down the meanings and derivations of some of the following:

red herring	a bee in one's bonnet	count sheep
rat race	squirrel away	the goose hangs high
skunk cabbage	stool pigeon	loan shark
duck soup	pig Latin	mosquito boat
for the birds	cub reporter	eager beaver
as the crow flies	weasel words	dovetail

10　Literary Largess

Just as myths and legends have contributed to our language, so have the great writers — and some who are not so great. Most of them have been novelists and playwrights; strangely enough, the pickings from poetry are comparatively meagre. Novelists and playwrights tend more to emphasize and exaggerate a single trait or feature of a character, thus inadvertently paving the way for that individual's entry into our dictionaries. Most of the time the characters retain their initial capitals when they become part of our vocabulary.

In this connection, let's look at some of Charles Dickens' creations.

Even though old Ebenezer reformed at the end of A CHRISTMAS CAROL, a mean and miserly person is a *Scrooge*.

A *Micawber* is a thriftless person who constantly looks forward to an improvement in his fortunes, just like the lovable character in DAVID COPPERFIELD. Micawberish means 'habitually hopeful'.

In MARTIN CHUZZLEWIT, Seth *Pecksniff* is a hypocrite who talks in pious terms and simultaneously employs every means to enrich himself. *Pecksniffery* therefore is religious hypocrisy.

From the same novel the British have obtained a lowercase noun. Sarah *Gamp* was a nurse who carried a big cotton umbrella. Hence a *gamp* has become a large umbrella.

The hero of THE PICKWICK PAPERS is a generous fool. Hence *Pickwickian* people are benevolent simpletons. The adjective also applies to expressions that a speaker or writer uses in a special or recondite sense; the reason is that members of the Pickwick Club often employed words and phrases in a non-literal way.

Jonathan Swift in GULLIVER'S TRAVELS conceived the land of Lilliput, where the inhabitants were only six inches tall. Consequently *Lilliputian* means 'very small'.

Gulliver also visited Brobdingnag, a land in which the giants were sixty feet tall. Thus *Brobdingnagian* has become a synonym for colossal or huge.

In the same book the Yahoos are described as beastly creatures.

Today a *yahoo* is an uncouth person and *yahooism* is rowdyism.

Another satirist, François Rabelais, has contributed a different synonym for huge. In GARGANTUA AND PANTAGRUEL his hero is a gigantic king. From that source our adjective *gargantuan* was coined. By the way, Rabelais didn't actually invent the word 'Gargantua'; in medieval folk literature the character was a mammoth hero.

Pantagruel, which literally means 'all-thirsty', was the equally colossal son of Gargantua. Because of the prince's penchant for coarse wit with derisive undertones, we have been given *Pantagruelism* — a synonym for cynical humour.

In the same work, Panurge is a friend of Pantagruel. This high-spirited rascal is ready to do anything. Rabelais borrowed the name from the Greek *pan* ('all') *ergon* ('work'). In English *panurgic* means 'prepared for all kinds of work'.

Those first three letters, *p-a-n,* have been especially prolific in the production of literary words in our language.

Panjandrum now signifies a pretentious official or pompous personage. In some nonsense lines the playwright Samuel Foote coined the word back in the eighteenth century.

Pangloss is an optimistic tutor in Voltaire's CANDIDE. The adjective *Panglossian* now means 'all is for the best in this best of all possible worlds'. By the way, CANDIDE is not the mother of *candid.* Quite the opposite is true. Both have their origins in the Latin adjective *candidus* ('white, bright').

Finally, let's consider *Pandemonium,* a word that John Milton created in PARADISE LOST as a synonym for Hell. Literally, it means 'all demons'. The evolution of various senses of the noun is fascinating. From the internal regions ruled by Satan, it developed into any centre of evil; then it became a wild, disorderly place, and that idea led to our present connotation: an uproarious condition or a state in which noise and tumult prevail.

Shakespeare has popularized *Shylock* as a relentless creditor and *Romeo* as a lover. Interestingly enough, a *romeo* is also a man's slipper, and a *juliet* is a woman's slipper.

Robert Burns and W. S. Gilbert have also contributed. The Scottish cap called a *tam-o'-shanter* (often shortened to *tam* or *tammy*) is named for Tam O'Shanter, hero of a Burns poem. And in THE MIKADO Gilbert created a character called *Pooh-Bah* whose title was Lord High Everything Else. Hence the name is applied to any official who holds a variety of public and private positions. It also designates a person who gives the impression of being a V.I.P.

An Italian physician, astronomer and poet named Girolamo Fracostoro has, I regret to report, given us *syphilis*. In his poem 'Syphilis sive Morbus Gallicus' the hero suffers from venereal disease.

But probably the most amazing endowment from poetry is our word *pamphlet*. In the twelfth century a Latin poem called 'Pamphilus, seu de Amore' became very popular. This small, thin book served to create a new word in our vocabulary.* *Pamphleteer* is a derivative.

But the writers of prose dominate in this field, largely for reasons previously mentioned. For example, Harriet Beecher Stowe created *Uncle Tom* and *Simon Legree*. Today the former is used as a term of contempt, signifying a black person who toadies to whites. A *Simon Legree* is a cruel taskmaster.

In ROBINSON CRUSOE, by Daniel Defoe, the hero first met his devoted servant on a Friday and named him after that day. In modern usage a *man Friday* (or nowadays, a *girl Friday*) is a faithful and efficient factotum.

Robert Louis Stevenson created Dr. Jekyll, a virtuous physician who drinks a potion by which he is transformed into a vicious brute. Calling himself Mr. Hyde, he commits various crimes. Thus a *Jekyll-and-Hyde* personality in our modern vocabulary is similar to one suffering from schizophrenia.

A. Conan Doyle has given us a master of deduction who constantly humiliates Scotland Yard. *Sherlock Holmes,* or simply *Sherlock,* is a synonym for detective, and *Sherlockian* is an adjectival outgrowth.

Miguel de Cervantes Saavedra created the chivalrous hero, Don Quixote. He had an excessively romantic imagination and even tilted at windmills, taking them for giants. Today a *Quixote* is a rash, idealistic person, and *quixotic* means 'over-chivalrous, impractically imaginative'.

Mary Shelley, second wife of the great poet, wrote a Gothic romance called FRANKENSTEIN OR THE MODERN PROMETHEUS. In the book a young scientist named Baron Frankenstein brings to life a monster out of soulless corpses and is ruined by his own creation. Folks often confuse the inventor and the invention, and today a *Frankenstein* may be a man-made monster with a human

---

* *Pamphilus* was originally a disciple of Plato's.

shape, or any agency that troubles or destroys its creator. For example, the H-bomb may be the *Frankenstein* that puts an end to us earthlings.

John Lyly, an English author of the sixteenth century, wrote two prose romances in which the chief character was Euphues. The author's artificial, affected style gave rise to *euphuism* — a synonym for high-flown diction. This should not be confused with *euphemism,* the substitution of an inoffensive word for an objectionable one. The Greek ancestry for that noun can be roughly translated as 'good speech'.

It's interesting to see how *John Bull* emerged as a personification of the English nation or of the average Englishman. Early in the eighteenth century a writer named John Arbuthnot dreamed up the nickname. This Scottish-born author depicted his British kin as affable people who could also be crusty; Arbuthnot's personification of England was a bull-headed farmer. The French were represented by Lewis Baboon and the Dutch by Nicholas Frog.

In 1697 a Frenchman named Charles Perrault was the first to put down on paper an old folktale about a man named Bluebeard who has murdered six wives and hidden them away in his castle. His seventh wife, Fatima, discovers his crime and he tries to kill her too. But in the nick of time her brothers rush in and slay the villain. A bluebeard is now a man who slays a succession of women, whether they are wives or not.

Hans Christian Andersen published THE UGLY DUCKLING around 1835. Today an *ugly duckling* is any person or thing that looks unpromising but develops marvellously and gains admiration and respect.

In an early beast epic, REYNARD THE FOX, *Bruin* was the name of a bear. That epithet for the animal exists in our language; and a fox is still called *reynard.*

In THE ARABIAN NIGHTS, a prince named Barmecide invited a beggar to dine with him. Then he pretended to serve a variety of viands, but the plates were empty. When the beggar good-naturedly went along with the joke, Barmecide relented and gave him a hearty meal.

Despite the happy ending, a *Barmecide feast* now retains the idea of fakery. Here are some definitions for the phrase:

1. illusion of plenty

192

2. make-believe feast
3. pretended hospitality or generosity

THE THREE PRINCES OF SERENDIP is a Persian fairy tale in which the itinerant heroes constantly discover valuable or pleasant things that they are not seeking. Around 1754, Horace Walpole coined the word *serendipity* in allusion to the Persian story. It carries the idea of having an aptitude for making fortunate discoveries.

When Sir Alexander Fleming and his colleagues accidentally left some culture plates exposed, a mould developed and prevented the spread of bacteria on the specimens. Fleming was about to throw the plates away when he suddenly realized that some unknown substance on the mould had the power to kill bacteria. That was indeed a *serendipitous* series of events. Incidentally, he called the substance Penicillium, which is the genus name of the mould. The antibiotic compound from it is penicillin.

In THROUGH THE LOOKING GLASS, Lewis Carroll coined the word *chortle* — possibly as a combination of 'chuckle' and 'snort'. To *chortle* is to sing or chant gleefully or to chuckle laughingly.

Chortle is a portmanteau* word — that is, an arbitrary combination of two words. *Smog* is a good example, combining 'smoke' with 'fog'. Lewis Carroll loved such words. Take, for instance, "Twas brillig and the slithy toves . . .' My guesses as to the combinations are as follows:

brillig	=	brilliant	+	lighted
slithy	=	slimy	+	lithe
toves	=	turtle	+	doves

The gifts of playwrights to our vocabulary are numerous and interesting. What follows is a sampling.

A *lothario* is a gay blade who seduces women. The noun comes from the name of a young rake in THE FAIR PENITENT (1703), a play by Nicholas Rowe.

If you have ever wondered why we use *simon-pure* as a synonym for genuine or authentic, rather than peter-pure or paul-pure or tom-dick-and-harry-pure, the answer is that Simon Pure is a Quaker in A BOLD STROKE FOR A WIFE (1718), a play by Susanna

---

* *Portmanteau* is a French-English word for a type of travelling bag. Literally, it means 'carry a cloak'. *Portmanteau words* carry a double load.

Centlivre. An imposter claims that he, and not Simon, is Pure, but in the end our hero proves that he's the real McCoy — I mean the authentic Pure.

Not so pure is Tartufe, in a Molière play (1664) of the same name. The imposter dupes his host into giving him title to all the property owned by his victim. Meanwhile, like Dickens' Mr. Pecksniff, he pretends to be a very pious man. He is finally undone and hauled off to gaol. Today a *tartufe* (or *tartuffe*) is a religious hypocrite.

Mrs. Grundy is religious, but she's no hypocrite. In Tom Morton's play SPEED THE PLOUGH (1798) she is a prudish neighbour of the main characters. Although she never appears on stage, her role is important because the characters keep asking one another, 'What will Mrs. Grundy say?' Hence any person with a narrowly conventional or intolerant attitude is a *Mrs. Grundy* or simply a *Grundy*.

Another married woman who has made quite a name for herself in our language is Mrs. Malaprop, a character in Sheridan's THE RIVALS (1775). Words are her chief problem; she mixes them up. For instance, she talks about being 'as headstrong as an *allegory* on the banks of the Nile'. She *reprehends* when she should be apprehending, and so on, and so on.

Malapropism, therefore, is gross or ludicrous misuse of words, especially through confusion of those that sound alike. Some of my favourites are:

'That young violinist is certainly a child *progeny!*'
When we visited Athens, we saw the *Apocalypse.*'
'Send the package by *partial* post.'

Then there is the little Catholic girl in New York City who said she was taught her *cataclysm* at school.

It should be noted that Sheridan took the name for his blundering character from *malapropos,* which means 'inappropriate'.

As a boy, I was reading Washington Irving's story about Rip Van Winkle. The author referred to Rip's wife as a *termagant,* and the context must have helped me, because I immediately knew that the word meant 'a quarrelsome woman'. But many years elapsed before I discovered the original source of the shrew. Originally she was an imaginary Eastern deity, probably invented by the Crusaders. In medieval plays Termagant was a boisterous, overbearing character. He caused lots of tumult on stage. Note how his sex changed when he entered our dictionaries.

Such devilish statements provide me with a nice transition to *Mephistophelean,* which means 'fiendish, sardonic, crafty or malevolent'.

Mephistopheles, a devil in medieval legends, was made into a real character by Goethe when he wrote FAUST (1808). In that play the fiend tempts the old scholar into a pact by which Faust will sell his soul in return for comprehending all experience. Variations of the legend appear in Christopher Marlowe's DR. FAUSTUS and Thomas Mann's DOKTOR FAUSTUS. Gounod's Faust is probably the most famous musical offshoot.

The play TRILBY (1894) was based on George du Maurier's novel with the same name. A soft felt hat with an indented crown was worn by one of the characters in the drama. The British milliners seized on the popularity of the play and produced a hat called a *trilby.*

The *trilby* is a relative of the *fedora.* Whence comes that hat? Well, in 1882 (thirteen years before the du Maurier novel became a play) a Frenchman, Victorien Sardou, wrote a drama called FEDORA, which starred Sarah Bernhardt. The hat she wore created a sensation, and the milliners again responded to opportunity's knock.

Dropping down from the top of the head to the neck, we find the *Peter Pan collar,* named for the traditional close-fitting article worn by J. M. Barrie's little boy who ran away to Never Land to escape growing up. Frances Hodgson Burnett's hero in the novel LITTLE LORD FAUNTLEROY is also remembered by a collar. A *fauntleroy collar* is a wide collar on a frilly shirt.

Finally, on the subject of clothes made notable by literature of all sorts, we come upon a *Mother Hubbard.* It's a full, loose gown worn by women. Why? Well, artists who depicted the woman in futile search for a bone for her hungry canine always showed her in that kind of garb.

Now let's look at a few additions to the English language from the literature of our own century. *Babbitt* is the prime example, stemming from the novel of that name by Sinclair Lewis (1922). George Babbitt is portrayed as a smug businessman, living a conventional and comfortable life and having no cultural values whatsoever. Hence a *Babbitt* has become a synonym for a self-satisfied, unthinking, middle-class conformist striving for material success and little else.

195

Sportswriters have given us some new words too. One example is *Tom and Jerry,* which is not so modern. In 1821, Pierce Egan — an English expert on outdoor games — wrote Life in London. In that book he described Tom and Jerry Hawthorne, who liked *la dolce vita.* Today their first names are a hot, eggy, spicy but sweet rum drink.

An up-to-date contribution is from Jack Conway, a baseball player and sportswriter who is reported to have coined the word *palooka,* which now hovers between acceptance and rejection by lexicographers. The word originally applied to an inept boxer or other athlete. More recently it has evolved into a synonym for any clumsy person or oaf. Cartoonist Ham Fisher gave the noun lots of publicity when he created a boxer named Joe Palooka.

Cartoons and comic strips are not exactly literature, but those media have also been adding words to our language — from David Low's Colonel Blimp to H. T. Webster's Caspar Milquetoast. Thomas Nast invented the Democratic donkey, the Republican elephant and the Tammany tiger.

You won't find Mutt and Jeff, Bud Fisher's characters, in your dictionary, but I've heard their names all my life. Because I'm six feet five, whenever I stand next to a small person someone is sure to remark, 'Mutt and Jeff!'

Superman is one of our words, but not because of the comic strip. He's a superior human being considered by Friedrich Nietszche as the idealized goal of our evolutionary struggle for survival.

Walt Disney's Mickey Mouse has become a slangy adjective with several meanings:

1. corny, as dance bands or music
2. childish; unrelated to reality
3. commercially slick

Finally, W. Heath Robinson must not be left out. The ingenious creations of that artist have become famous. Any complicated diagram or contraption designed to achieve a simple result is now called a *Heath Robinson gadget.*

I must point out that this chapter, like so many others in this book, is not meant to be comprehensive or encyclopaedic. Various readers may be disappointed to see that their own favourites from literature have been omitted. All I can say is that I have tried to offer a representative sampling of our literary largess.

196

11 Eyebrow Raisers

If you're squeamish about sex you may wish to skip this chapter. But our dictionaries are filled with terms pertaining to biology, physiology, scatology, lovemaking and the sexual drive. Only a comstocker would decide to omit any reference to them in a book on vocabulary.

It is also true that many words appear on the surface to have no relation to any of these areas, but actually do, either through usage or their etymological background.

For example, *meretricious* looks innocent enough. Most people think of it as a synonym for tawdry, showy, gaudy, specious or deceitful. All those connotations are correct, but the first meaning of the word is 'pertaining to a prostitute'. Since women of the earliest profession often bedeck themselves with cheap ornaments and are not known for straightforwardness and honesty, it's easy to see how *meretricious* became synonymous with cheap ostentation and deception. The Latin root is *meretrix*, meaning 'whore'.

Most fascinating is the ultimate root — *merere* (or *mereri*), *meritus*. The verb means 'to earn'. And so it's ironic that *merit, meritorious, emeritus* and other such derivations are all linguistic kin of prostitutes.

Roger is a word we all know. A pirate's flag is called a *Jolly Roger*. And in recent usage *roger* has become a code word for the letter *r* and stands for 'received'. When a radio operator says 'Roger!' he is telling his communicator that he's got the message.

But *roger* is also a vulgarish verb meaning 'to copulate with or have sexual intercourse'. No less a poet than Ezra Pound wrote '. . . occasionally rogered the lady.' The word is believed to have arisen because of the use of *roger* as a name for the penis.

Rut is another word with more than one meaning. Actually, there are two basic ancestors of *rut,* both from Old French: *rote* or *route* ('way') and *rut* or *ruit* ('roar'). As an English noun it means a male deer's annual state of sexual excitement. When a stag is *in rut* he bells.

The word has been broadened to mean sexual excitement in any mammal. A related word is *oestrus* (from Latin *oestrus,* 'gadfly or

197

frenzy'). When a bitch is in heat, it is said to be *oestrous* or *oestruating*. Some lexicographers say that *oestrus* and *ire* are etymologically related.

Incidentally, the period of sexual quiescence after the cycle is over is called *anoestrus*. And it should be noted that *oestrogen*, from the same frenzied root, is a female hormone.

Pumpernickel is such a tasty bread that I hesitate to reveal its scatological source. In an early form of German, *pumpern* meant 'to break wind'. *Nickel* meant 'a goblin or demon', specifically the Devil. Since the sourdough bread caused gas and was as hard as the devil to digest, its high-sounding (or low-sounding) name evolved.

My first contact with *defecate* came when I was a nine-year-old boy who owned a dog named Prince. Unfortunately the mongrel was too clever for me. He found several ways to get out of the house clandestinely. An angry neighbour screamed at me: 'Stop your dog from *defecating* on my lawn!'

Now you can imagine my bewilderment. What had Prince done? Finally I looked the word up, and it wasn't easy. At that age my knowledge of orthography was shaky. Then I discovered the definition — or I should say definitions. Number Two seemed to be the most applicable.

1. to clear from impurities; to clarify; purify or refine. (Certainly Prince wasn't refined!)
2. to void excrement. (What the heck was excrement?)
3. in sugar manufacturing, to clarify juice

I zeroed in on 'excrement' and discovered it was 'faecal matter'. Faecal? The dictionary referred me to 'faeces'. There I learned that faeces meant 'ordure'. Okay, what's ordure? The answer was dung. Now I was getting close. Dung, the dictionary said, was manure. For some reason I knew the meaning of that word. In those days horses outnumbered automobiles and often spoiled our games of Skelly and hopscotch in the middle of a street.

I looked up from the dictionary and exclaimed, 'So that's what Prince did! Oh, s--t!'

Sometime in my salad days I learned the expression *hoist with one's own petard*, meaning 'hurt by one's own schemes'. I always assumed that a *petard* was some kind of shaft. If someone had told me it was a firecracker, I might have demurred. But that's exactly what a petard is. Originally the word referred to a case containing an explosive for breaking down bridges, barricades and gates.

Like that of *pumpernickel,* the derivation is a bit offensive. The word comes from the French verb *péter* ('to break wind') and ultimately from the Latin infinitive *pedere* (which has the same meaning).

Of course our most common word for the emission of gas from the intestines is *fart.* The word has a long history, dating back to the original Indo-European great-great-grandparent. In Middle English the verb was *ferten* or *farten.*

Can you imagine the howl that would arise if a crossword puzzle editor ever defined *avocado* as 'fruit from the testicle tree'? The word can be traced to a Spanish alteration of a Nahuatl term. That ancient Mexican tribe believed that the fruit had power as an aphrodisiac.

Testicles presents a different linguistic problem. Would you believe that they are related to such words as *testament, testify* and *attest*? The Latin root is *testis* ('witness'). *Testicle* is a diminutive derivation. The experts guess at the connexion. those male sex glands, they say, might be 'witnesses to virility'.

In that connection, *anorchous* is a high-sounding word that means 'having no testes'. Some equestrian owners castrate certain male horses, which then become *anorchous* and are called geldings. Castration is the removal of testes or ovaries. When applied to females it is called spaying. Both words have a Latin background: castrate literally means 'to prune with a knife'; the Romans inherited the word from Sanskrit. *Spay* comes from *spatha* ('broadsword').

Eunuchs are castrated men who protect a sultan's harem. Their name has a Greco-Roman ancestry and literally means 'guardian of the bed'.

Mankind's almost obsessive interest in sex is remarkably revealed in synonyms for *prostitute* (from *prostituere* — a Latin verb meaning 'to expose in public'). Aside from meretrix, we have the following samples: *harridan, strumpet, drab, harlot, trull, doxy, chippy, whore,* * *trollop, hooker, floozy, slut* and *hustler.* The

---

* *Whore* has an interesting history. It can be traced to Old High German (*huara*), Old Norse (*hora*), Gothic (*hors*). But lexicographers say that it is also related to the Latin adjective *carus* ('dear') via *kama,* the Sanskrit word for 'love or desire'.

  Caress and *cherish* are members of the family. So is *charity* — and that's a laugh!

Parisian version, *cocotte,* has also been added to our dictionaries; literally, it means 'hen'. A related noun is *cocodette* — a French call girl.

Houses of ill repute have also intrigued the slangsters. There are at least fifty vulgar words or phrases for such places, including *cat-house, notcherie, service station* and *shooting gallery. Brothel* is the 'refined' term for all these. It comes from a Middle English verb meaning 'to waste away'. The word was originally applied to lewd men or women; then it became associated with the scene of their activities. The Italian synonym, which we sometimes employ, is *bordello.*

Putage is fornication by women, and *putanism* is habitual prostitution. *Pornocracy* is government by harlots. But who would vote for such *pornerastic* women? *Philopornists,* of course!

Courtesans are high-class harlots. Usually the mistresses of noblemen are given that euphemistic name. *Concubine* can also be defined as 'mistress'. But in more common usage such a woman is one who cohabits with a man although not married to him. The name is derived from *concubare,* 'to go to bed together'. The sleeping compartment called a *cubicle* has the same ancestry.

Libido has been popularized by the psychoanalysts of the Freudian school. In recent decades it has been equated with desire for sex. The ultimate Latin ancestor is *libere* ('to please or gratify'). Love has come to us via the same root or route.

Speaking of routes, we note that the *libido* can take many different courses. Most humans are *heterosexual*; the object of their desire is a person of the *other* sex. But some are *homosexual*: the Greek root *homo** means 'same'.

The most common designation for a female who prefers sex with others of her own gender is *lesbian.* The source for the word the island of Lesbos, in the Aegean. There the poet Sappho and her feminine followers were reputed to have had sexual relations with one another. *Sapphist* therefore is a synonym for *lesbian.*

Furthermore, a *tribade* is a woman who attempts to simulate heterosexual practices with another woman. Their activities are called *tribadism* or *tribady,* from the Greek verb *tribein* ('to rub').

Such females may use a *dildo,* which is an object shaped like an erect penis. The origin is uncertain, but it is possible that the word

---

* *Homo* is also a Latin noun meaning 'man', as in the familiar phrase *Homo sapiens* (literally, 'wise man').

may be a corruption of *dill,* the pickle. Some experts guess that *diletto* (Italian for 'delight') is the source.

In slanguage, male homosexuals have been given such derogatory names as *queers, fairies, pansies, fruits, fags* and *queens.* The last of that list often appear in *drag,* meaning that they dress up in women's clothes. Nobody seems to know how *drag* acquired that connotation.

All of the above people are *paraphiliacs;* they go in for sexual practices that the majority of people consider abnormal. Such deviations are called *perversions* (from a Latin verb meaning 'to turn the wrong way'), and a pervert is construed to be anyone from a misdirected person to a morally corrupt individual.

A euphemistic term that has gained popularity in recent years is *gay.* That word stems from the Old High German *gāhi* ('hasty or rash'). Its first meaning today is 'excited and merry'.

The general term for the practices of male homosexuals is *sodomy,* after the people of Sodom. A synonym is *buggery,* which has an ecclesiastical background. The word can be traced to a Middle English corruption of Bulgarian. It seems that Bulgarians preferred the Eastern Church, which the majority of religious Europeans regarded as heretical. Hence *bugger* arose as a term for a worthless fellow and then was extended to signify a *sodomite.*

Some homosexuals are *pedophiliacs;* their sexual desires are directed towards children. A pederast is a lover of boys, and *pederasty* is sexual relations with a boy. In this case the boy is called a *catamite* — from an Etruscan alteration of Ganymede, cupbearer of the gods and beloved of Zeus.

In one sense *sodomy* is not restricted to homosexuals. It is used as a synonym for *fellatio,* oral stimulation of the male organ, whether by another male or by a female. Other spellings are *fellation* and *fellata.*

Oral stimulation of the female organ is called *cunnilingus,* a word that comes straight to us from Latin; it means 'one who licks the vulva'.

Vulva is also from Latin. In that language it means 'integument, wrapper, covering or womb'; the parent verb is *volvere* ('to roll or turn'). In English *vulva* has come to mean 'the external female genital organs'.

The Romans' noun for those genitalia was *cunnus.* It's interesting to note that the word *kunte* sprang up in Middle Low German, and later, in Middle English, the spelling was *cunte.* Both nouns, as well as our own shortened form, designate the female pudendum.

Pudendum is the gerundive of *pudēre*, 'to be ashamed'. Related words are *pudency* ('modesty, prudishness') and *pudibund* ('prudish').

The most sensitive part of the *pudendum* is the *clitoris* (pronounced with the accent on the first syllable). It's an erectile organ that corresponds to the male's penis. The source is *kleitoris*, a Greek word meaning 'small hill'. An interesting relative is *matroclinous* — 'having predominantly maternal hereditary traits'. *Clitoridectomy* is female circumcision.

You may be surprised to learn that *penis* is a Latin word for tail. The Romans called it *membrum virile* ('male limb'). *Membrum* comes from a Sanskrit word meaning 'a decaying thing' or 'a thing grinding in the socket'.

The Romans are also responsible for our word *pubes* — the hair appearing on the lower abddomen during adolescence. The eventual root of those hairs is *puer* ('boy'). Some related words are:

puberty	stage of life at which the individual becomes capable of reproduction; hence, youth
puberulent	
puberulose	minutely downy
pubescent	adolescent; having a fuzzy surface; downy

Phallus is a word that the Romans borrowed from the Greek *phallos* ('penis'). The Indo-European source is said to be *bhel* ('to swell'). In modern English the noun refers to the penis or clitoris, but the latter word gets short shrift in actual usage. This is probably because an image of the penis as the organ of reproduction was worshipped in Grecian festivals honouring Dionysus. This practice is called *phallicism.* One of the ancestors of *phallus* is the Latin verb *flare* ('to blow').

But the most startling member (no pun intended) of the family is *ithyphallic.* It means 'having an erect penis'. Consequently other definitions have evolved — 'obscene' and 'lustful', for example.

As is often the case in other areas of our language, our more refined vocabulary has a Greco-Roman background, while our vulgar 'four-letter words' usually have a lusty Anglo-Saxon or Teutonic heritage. For instance, sometime between the twelfth and fifteenth century our ancestors developed the word *fucken* from a Germanic word meaning 'to strike or penetrate'. In the same

202

period the Dutch came up with *fokken* ('to strike or copulate with'). The lower classes held on to such words through the centuries, while the literati preferred classical terms.

Copulate is a good example. Its source is *copulare* ('to unite or couple'). We have also perpetuated *copula*, the Romans' term for a bond or link. It has different significance to grammarians and logicians, which the reader may wish to pursue, but it can also mean 'sexual union' today.

Another polite substitution for our four-letter shocker is *coitus*, which means 'meeting' in Latin. When the male withdraws purposely prior to his orgasm,* the procedure is called *coitus interruptus*.

Somewhat less refined is *fornication*, because the copulatory activity is not sanctioned by marriage. The derivation is fascinating. In ancient Rome a *fornix* was an arch, and in the late republican period a vaulted underground dwelling with that name was frequented by prostitutes. Hence a *fornix* became a symbol for a brothel, and the other derivatives emerged.

When a wife fornicates, her husband becomes a *cuckold*. Lexicographers guess that *cuckold* is related to an Old French word *cucu* ('cuckoo'). That bird is notorious for leaving its eggs in other birds' nests, and the female habitually changes mates. A *cucking stool* is a chair to which such persons as shrews, prostitutes and cheats were fastened and exposed to public mockery. Its Middle English ancestor, *coking-stole* or *cucking stol*, was literally a toilet seat.

Among the women who are not necessarily fornicators we must consider *flirts* and *hussies*. The ancestor of the former is an Old French verb, *fleurter* ('to touch lightly; to move from flower to flower').

Hussy comes from a Middle English word for housewife. Today it has acquired other meanings:

1. pert, impudent girl; minx
2. lewd or brazen woman; strumpet

Broad is another slang word for a woman, especially one with loose morals. Some philologers claim that the word is an alteration

---

* *Orgasm* can be traced to *orgasmos*, a Greek noun derived from the verb *organ* ('to grow ripe, to swell with moisture or lust'). *Orgy* is not a relative. Its Greek root is akin to *ergon* ('work')!

of *bawd* ('a woman who keeps a brothel'), but others state that it is a shortening of *broad-minded*.

In a punny sense, *lechers* are broad-minded. Such lewd men owe their name to an Old French verb that literally means 'to lick'. They lead a life of *debauchery*, a word that we looked at in Chapter 5.

Two other men of the lecherous ilk are *reprobates* and *profligates*. Both have Latin roots. The former comes from *reprobare* ('to disapprove of or condemn'); the ancestor of the latter is *profligare* ('to strike down to the ground; to ruin'). *Rakehells, rakes and roués*, by the way, are kin to the above lechers.

All the foregoing men can be described as lustful and lascivious. They are also *salacious* — a word that can be traced to the Latin verb *salire* ('to leap or to cover sexually'). *Salacious* does double duty; it's also a synonym for pornographic.

In its literal sense, from its Greek roots, *pornography* means 'writing of harlots'. In one modern use it still is a description of prostitutes. But chiefly it's a synonym for *curiosa* or *erotica*.

Eros has provided us with another word, coined by Havelock Ellis — *autoerotism*, which means 'sexual arousal or satisfaction obtained without a partner'. It can be contrasted with *alloerotism* ('sexual feeling or activity finding its object in another person').

A common *autoerotic* practice is *masturbation*. Lexicographers assume that the word eventually comes from the Latin *manus* ('hand') and *stuprare* ('to defile').

In Genesis 38:9, Onan is described as practising *coitus interruptus*. Such withdrawal before ejaculation is now called *onanism*, but Judah's son's act has also come to be equated with masturbation. In old wives' tales, addiction to *autoerotism* is supposed to cause *cecity* ('blindness') but it's more likely to lead to *oligospermia* ('scantiness of semen').

Autocopulation has nothing to do with back seats. It's defined as 'self-copulation that infrequently occurs in some hermaphroditic worms'. That's carrying autoerotism to an extreme! Those worms are certainly *ambisextrous*. They are also *androgynous* (simultaneously male and female).

In connection with the lower animals, here are four other eyebrow raisers:

amplexus	the mating embrace of a frog or toad
clicket	to be in heat or copulate, as foxes and hares

| go to buck | copulate, as female hares with male hares |
| *pizzle* | the penis of a bull |

The *incubus* was a demon believed to lie upon sleeping women for the purpose of sexual intercourse. His female counterpart was the *succubus*, who somehow found a way to lie beneath soporose men in order to engage in coitus. Their names were well chosen: in Latin *incubare* means 'to lie upon' and *succubare* means 'to lie under'.

Both words live in modern English in different ways. An *incubus* is a nightmare, literally or figuratively. A *succubus* is a fiend or another of the many synonyms for a prostitute.

Buxom is another word with an incredible history. In Middle English it meant 'humble, obedient'. Then it evolved into 'physically flexible, pliant' and 'blithe or lively'. But today it carries only two chief senses: 'vigorously plump' and 'having a full bosom'.

The Greeks' *pygos* ('buttocks') has endowed us with several interesting descendants. Two of them are *macropygia* and *steatopygia*. The former is a genus of long-tailed pigeons. Literally, they have large rumps. *Steatopygous* people have too much fat on their buttocks.

The Romans, via the Athenians, have also contributed to our rear views. *Gluteus maximus* and *gluteus medius* and *gluteus minimus* are all muscles in the buttocks. *Gluteal* means 'pertaining to the buttocks'.

To a Scotsman the same area is the *curpin*. As an aside, the Scots have also come up with a word for the familiar rumbling in our stomachs. Their word for that flatulent* state is *curmurring*.

We have a plethora of synonyms for our posteriors. Among them are fundament, haunches, stern, dorsal region, lumbar region, hindquarters, bottom and rump. Slangsters have come up with *fanny* (in honour of some anonymous female of that name), arse, backside, can, prat and many other words. *Bum*, a mainly British word, has given rise to *bumf* — short for *bum fodder* — meaning toilet paper, and by extension official documents or any excessive paperwork; also to the short Eton jacket called a *bumfreezer*.

---

* *Flatulent* means 'full of air or other gas, especially in the intestines or stomach'. The Latin ancestor *flatus* means 'act of blowing or breaking wind'. Some synonyms for *flatulent* are turgid, inflated, pompous, pretentious and bombastic. The adjective can appropriately apply to orators who are 'full of hot air'.

By metonymy *can* has also become a toilet. *Prat* has led to *pratfall*, a favourite laugh-getter of low comics who tumble backwards. In recent years that refugee from burlesque has developed into a synonym for any humiliating mishap or blunder.

And here is a list of other words relevant to this chapter — a completely disjointed list:

coprolalia	excessive use of obscene language
aischrolatreia	worship of filth; cult of the obscene
parthenic	relating to virginity
colposcopy	visual inspection of the vagina
anaphrodisiac	absence or impairment of sexual desire
aproctous	having no anal orifice
anacreontic	amatory
atocia	female sterility
algolagnia	sexual pleasure derived from inflicting or suffering pain
cyesis	pregnancy

12 Test Yourself

Here are fifty spelling demons. In each case you have a choice between a correctly spelt word and a misspelling. Tick the one that is correct. The answers appear on p. 221, in the Appendix.

A score of 90 per cent or better is *excellent*; 80-89 per cent is *good*; 70-79 per cent is *fair*. If you fall below 70 per cent, you should brush up on your orthography.

1. asinine	assinine	26. persistent	persistant
2. existance	existence	27. auxilliary	auxiliary
3. develop	develope	28. paraphernalia	paraphenalia
4. occurrence	occurence	29. impresario	impressariao
5. indispensible	indispensable	30. deleterious	deliterious
6. accommodate	accomodate	31. picnicked	picniced
7. silouette	silhouette	32. weird	wierd
8. harrass	harass	33. permissible	permissable
9. procede	proceed	34. momento	memento
10. vermillion	vermilion	35. innocuous	inocuous
11. personell	personnel	36. ecstasy	ecstacy
12. seize	sieze	37. liaison	liason
13. stupify	stupefy	38. cacchinate	cachinnate
14. embarassed	embarrassed	39. rococo	roccoco
15. supercede	supersede	40. battalion	battallion
16. innoculate	inoculate	41. nickel	nickle
17. resistance	resistence	42. concensus	consensus
18. mocassin	moccasin	43. committment	commitment
19. reconnoitre	recconnoitre	44. separate	seperate
20. resuscitate	resusitate	45. geneology	genealogy
21. asphixiate	asphyxiate	46. sacreligious	sacrilegious
22. renascence	renasence	47. inadvertent	inadvertant
23. irrelevant	irrevelant	48. iridescent	irridescent
24. sacharine	saccharine	49. dichotomy	dicotomy
25. privilege	privelege	50. Pharaoh	Pharoah

THE MORE THE EERIER

Here are ten singular nouns. You are asked to spell the presently accepted plural for each. The answers are on p. 222, in the Appendix.

1. knight-errant   4. hypothesis   7. jackanapes
2. talisman   5. pelvis   8. cinerarium
3. manservant   6. embryo   9. auspex
                                    10. monsieur

HATES AND FEARS

The Greek root *mis-miso* means 'hate'.
Match the following 'hate' words with the definitions. The answers appear on p. 222, in the Appendix.

1. misoxene   a. one who hates marriage
2. misocapnist   b. one who hates strangers
3. misopedist   c. one who hates children
4. misogynist   d. one who hates tobacco smoke
5. misogamist   e. one who hates women

The Greek root *phobia* means 'fear'.
What kind of fears are the following?
See p. 222, in the Appendix.

1. agoraphobia   6. toxiphobia
2. acrophobia   7. herpetophobia
3. heliophobia   8. triskaidekaphobia
4. gynephobia   9. nosophobia
5. thanatophobia   10. ochlophobia

IRRELIGIOUS

Here are ten people associated with churchly activities. Surprisingly, all of them can be defined in secular terms. Can you match the two columns? The answers appear on p. 222, in the Appendix.

1. bishop   a. rose-coloured starling or man-of-war fish
2. cardinal   b. calf too young for veal
3. nun   c. card game
4. deacon   d. kind of buoy
5. priest   e. bird, colour or woman's cloak in the eighteenth century
6. Pope Joan   f. kind of beetle
7. sexton   g. strong purple

8. acolyte	h. African weaver bird
9. pastor	i. follower
10. monsignor	j. short club to stun or kill a captured fish

BUILDING VOCABULARY

Three vocabulary tests are given below. In each case choose the word or phrase that most closely defines the word in italics.

55—60	You should compile your own dictionary.
50—54	You qualify as an editor.
45—49	You qualify as an English teacher.
40—44	You ought to write a book.
35—39	You ought to read a book.
25—34	You ought to read lots of books.
Below 25	You may wish to tear up this book.

The answers are on p. 222, in the Appendix.

VOCABULARY TEST — 1

1. *scarify*   a. frighten b. reduce to dross c. hunt insects d. scratch

2. *sobriquet*   a. card game b. bunch of flowers c. nickname d. serious essay

3. *syncope*   a. harmony b. elision of letters c. union of parties d. simile

4. *thrasonical*   a. euphonious b. rational c. short-tempered d. boastful

5. *benedict*   a. bachelor b. hermit c. newly married man d. anything well said

6. *factotum*   a. adding machine b. clique c. general handyman d. copy

7. *veridical*   a. green b. lofty c. truthful d. manly

8. *factitious*   a. artificial b. quarrelsome c. divisive d. fragile

9. *farrago*   a. shrew b. mixture c. veterinary d. a sort of grain

10. *termagant*   a. scolding woman b. final session c. monster d. deserter

11. *vitiate*   a. adhere b. corrupt c. enliven d. convert into glass

12. *perfunctory*   a. indifferent b. useful c. precise d. prompt

13. *pariah*   a. sycophant b. outcast c. upstart d. rampart

14. *meretricious*   a. tawdry b. well deserving c. southerly d. fruity

15. *proem*   a. preface b. verse c. offspring d. preemption

16. *sententious*   a. sagacious b. terse c. aged d. full of feeling

209

17. *flatulent*   a. level b. noisome c. pretentious d. verbose
18. *traduce*   a. lead across b. vituperate c. lead astray d. slander
19. *enervate*   a. weaken b. make strong c. mollify d. repair
20. *majuscule*   a. steward b. precept c. capital letter d. staff of office

VOCABULARY TEST — 2

1. *prawn*   a. light carriage b. tool c. shrimp d. baby food
2. *magma*   a. monkey b. molten rock c. Greek letter d. largeness
3. *gibus*   a. jest b. small mast c. rodent d. opera hat
4. *biggin*   a. tea cup b. grafted fruit c. enlargement d. nightcap
5. *pharos*   a. Egyptian crown b. lighthouse c. chariot d. bird's nest
6. *meuble*   a. penetrable b. laughable c. tillable d. traceable
7. *giglet*   a. ship's boat b. frivolous girl c. dance hall d. strangulation
8. *firkin*   a. cask for butter b. sweet pickle c. high shoe d. waistcoat
9. *moiety*   a. hardness b. softness c. plethora d. half
10. *abigail*   a. headdress b. aunt c. lady's maid d. type of skirt
11. *purlieu*   a. French soldier b. street c. outskirts d. stew
12. *marplot*   a. thrust b. interferer c. damaged property d. agate
13. *agnomen*   a. surname b. patronymic c. shepherd d. epithet
14. *cabal*   a. horseman b. occult doctrine c. intrigue d. phaeton
15. *widgeon*   a. hybrid pigeon b. duck c. fence rail d. dam
16. *precent*   a. lead in singing b. go before c. counterfeit d. ninety-nine
17. *goliard*   a. minstrel b. javelin c. magician's wand d. grey whale
18. *gibbous*   a. apelike b. deathly c. jocular d. protuberant
19. *aeneous*   a. heroic b. white with rage c. having a brassy colour d. pastoral
20. *acescent*   a. steely b. becoming sour c. perfumed d. growing strong

VOCABULARY TEST — 3

1. *peculate*   a. embezzle b. congeal c. sin d. trade cattle
2. *levigate*   a. stutter b. lighten a burden c. grind into powder d. strengthen
3. *boniface*   a. innkeeper b. newly married man c. pretty girl d. holy person
4. *enchorial*   a. musical b. hooklike c. native d. repetitive
5. *plangent*   a. royal b. beating noisily c. schematic d. easily understood

6. *dotation*   a. endowment b. excessive love c. fixed point d. tax
7. *abecedary*   a. imported raisin b. primer c. simpleton d. nursery rhyme
8. *acclinate*   a. accustom b. recline c. slope upward d. come to a point
9. *fimbriate*   a. scale b. fringed c. grind d. rave
10. *ampulliform*   a. electric b. obese c. dilated d. attractive
11. *precative*   a. sinning b. beseeching c. rubbing d. dangerous
12. *adminicle*   a. growing on b. group c. auxiliary d. warning
13. *tramontane*   a. foreigner b. farmer c. rugged d. wavering
14. *acuminate*   a. united b. cloudy c. high d. pointed
15. *festination*   a. window dressing b. happiness c. haste d. gluttony
16. *adscititious* a. fortunate b. wise c. supplemental d. founded on truth
17. *lexiphanicism* a. pretentious phraseology b. legally sound practices c. legibility d. over-use of dictionary
18. *tralatitious* a. on the side b. singsong c. figurative d. migratory
19. *adiaphorous*   a. expanding when heated b. transparent c. widespread d. indifferent
20. *impignorate*   a. pawn b. strike against c. make insinuations d. involve

WORD ORIGINS

Choose the word in each group which does not come from the same root as the others. The answers appear on p. 222, in the Appendix.

1. sediment   sedition   sedentary   session
2. volatile   volume   voluble   involute
3. voice   invoice   vowel   advocate   invoke
4. vaunt   vain   advantage   vanity   evanescent
5. magnate   major   mayor   mastodon   majesty
6. cockade   peacock   coquette   cockatrice
7. vestige   vestigial   investigate   invest
8. money   mint   monetary   minatory   admonition   monitor
9. minute   minuend   menu   miniature   diminish   minuet
10. ligature   ally   liable   league   beleaguer

ETYMOLOGY TEST

Choose the word in each group which does not come from the same root as the others. The answers appear on p. 223, in the Appendix.

1. annoy, nuisance, noisome, ennui, odious

2. spiral, spirit, conspire, sprite, sprightly
3. trite, attrition, nutrition, terse, try, triturate
4. desolate, sole, console, solitaire, sullen
5. effigy, finger, fingent, fiction, faint, feign
6. infant, infantry, fate, fairy, nefandous, profane
7. popular, poplar, people, pueblo, populous
8. poetaster, disaster, astral, asterisk
9. sally, exile, consult, insult, resilient
10. censure, incense, candid, candidate, incendiary

OUT AND DOWN

Here is a new anagrams puzzle with an interlocking feature. To the right of each word, fill in an anagram using all the letters. To start you off, the answer to the first word is ORACLE.

When you finish, look at the first letters of the words you have filled in. They should form an anagram for roasting.

The answers appear on p. 223, in the Appendix.

coaler _____ heeding _____

antler _____ gobelin _____

rugged _____ hornets _____

lamina _____ rotates _____

A MAD, MAD WORLD

Can you match the manias in Column 1 with the definitions in Column 2? A score of 80 per cent or better qualifies you as a maniac.

The answers are on p. 223, in the Appendix.

1. dipsomania	a. inordinate passion for music
2. melomania	b. abnormal desire for food
3. phaneromania	c. fad involving imitation of painted porcelain
4. sitomania	d. delusions of grandeur
5. eleutheromania	e. madness for postage stamps
6. potichomania	f. excessive sexual desire
7. erotomania	g. alcoholism
8. theomania	h. zealous pursuit of freedom

9.	megalomania	i.	morbid habit of picking at a superficial body growth, as biting fingernails
10.	timbromania	j.	delusion that one is God

LOVERS

Match the words in Column 1 with the definitions in Column 2. The answers appear on p. 223, in the Appendix.

1.	philosopher	a.	lover of the beautiful
2.	philodespot	b.	lover of God
3.	philodox	c.	lover of tyranny
4.	philogynist	d.	lover of learning
5.	philocalist	e.	one who loves his own opinion
6.	philiater	f.	one devoted to the practical arts
7.	philozoist	g.	lover of wisdom
8.	philomath	h.	lover of women
9.	philotheist	i.	lover of animals
10.	philotechnist	j.	one interested in medical science

ALTERNATES FOR DEMOCRACY

Here are ten forms of government. From the list below choose the correct word for each type of rule. The answers appear on p. 223, in the Appendix.

1. rule by riffraff or gangsters
2. government by the worst people
3. rule of the majority
4. government by the military
5. government by workers
6. rule by harlots
7. government by aged persons
8. government by the wealthy
9. rule of gold
10. government by upstarts

aristocracy	ergatocracy	kakistocracy	oligocracy
arithmocracy	gerontocracy	monocracy	plutocracy
autocracy	hagiocracy	neocracy	pornocracy
chrysocracy	hierocracy	ochlocracy	stratocracy

WHO'S IN CHARGE?

Here are ten different leaders. From the list below, choose the correct word for each V.I.P. The answers appear on p. 223, in the Appendix.

1. chief of a clan
2. ruler of a church
3. head of an unorthodox sect
4. chief magistrate of a modern Greek province
5. toastmaster
6. leader of a revolt
7. one of the few who have the power
8. chief of a sacred order
9. commander of a thousand men
10. governor, viceroy

anarch	heresiarch	nomarch	polemarch
chiliarch	hierarch	oligarch	scholarch
ecclesiarch	matriarch	patriarch	symposiarch
exarch	monarch	phylarch	tetrarch

SPECIALITIES

Here are ten fields in which people specialize. From the list below choose the correct word for each of the studies, arts or sciences. The answers appear on p. 224, in the Appendix.

1. science of kissing
2. study of birds' nests
3. art of engraving on precious stones
4. study of molluscs
5. scientific study of ants
6. obstetrician's field
7. study of mosses
8. catalogue of saints
9. art of treating fractures
10. bellringer's art

agmatology	cytology	glyptology	myrmecology
areology	dendrology	hagiology	oenology
caliology	enigmatology	malacology	philematology
campanology	gerontology	muscology	tocology

A PENNY FOR YOUR THOUGHTS

Complete the word in Column 2 according to the clue given in Column 1. The correct answers appear on p. 224, in the Appendix.

1. a reddish cent   ru _____
2. a bright, shining cent   lu _____
3. a cent causing evil   ma _____
4. a cent just appearing   na _____
5. a cent at rest   qu _____
6. a rather old cent   se _____
7. a vanishing cent   ev _____
8. a greenish cent   vi _____
9. a cent that changes colour   ir _____
10. a cent going out of use   ob _____
11. a flowering cent   fl _____
12. a cent breaking out afresh   re _____
13. a frothy cent   ep _____
14. a soothing cent   de _____
15. a cent tinged with red   ruf _____
16. a slightly swollen cent   tum _____
17. a cent approaching whiteness   can _____
18. a rather smooth cent   gla _____
19. a concealed cent   del _____
20. a cent becoming obscure   la _____

A LEAGUE OF NATIONS

Complete the word in Column 2 according to the clue given in Column 1. The correct answers on p. 224, in the Appendix.

1. a nation of violent outbursts   de _____
2. a nation of thinkers   ra _____
3. a nation of fortune-tellers   di _____
4. a meditative nation   ru _____
5. a nation of travellers   pe _____
6. a dilatory nation   pr _____
7. a nation of thunderous
   denunciations   fu _____

8. a nation of interdependent links co _____
9. a nation capable of
        metapsychosis   re _____
10. a forgiving nation   co _____

THE ANT COLONY

Here is a list of 'ant' words designed to build and strengthen your vocabulary. The answers appear on p. 224, in the Appendix.

1. a sinful ant   pe _____
2. a green ant   ve _____
3. a nonchalant ant   ins _____
4. a biting ant   mo _____
5. a howling ant   ul _____
6. a penetrating ant   po _____
7. a disagreeing ant   discr _____
8. a swimming ant   na _____
9. a voracious ant   cor _____
10. a bellowing ant   bl _____
11. a helping ant   adj _____
12. a second-sighted ant   cl _____
13. a nonconforming ant   rec _____
14. a powerful ant   pu _____
15. a rustling ant   su _____
16. a glittering ant   cor _____
17. a scourging ant   fla _____
18. a crying ant   cl _____
19. a feigning ant   si _____
20. a blunt ant   he _____
21. a yawning ant   osc _____
22. a gaudy ant   cli _____
23. a night-walking ant   no _____
24. a creepy ant   hor _____
25. a drooping ant   nu _____
26. a nest-building ant   ni _____
27. a shiftless ant   fai _____
28. a priestlike ant   hi _____
29. a ghostly ant   rev _____
30. a wildly dancing ant   Cor _____

216

FIND THE STRANGER

In the following groups, choose the one word that does not belong with the others. The correct answers appear on p. 224, in the Appendix.

1. salamander, triton, gerrymander, newt, eft
2. perjurer, taradiddler, pseudologist, cicerone, ananias
3. garand, gibus, gatling, bowie, derringer
4. Nesselrode, tartuffe, napoleon, flan, frangipane
5. depone, depose, testify, certify, execrate
6. meritorious, tawdry, brummagem, meretricious, specious
7. salmagundi, olio, gallimaufry, pilpul, potpourri
8. endemic, exiguous, indigenous, autochthonous, natal
9. miscreant, poltroon, caitiff, dastard, recreant
10. jargon, lingo, jingo, dialect, cant

THE BLOCKBUSTER

Caution! Do not take this test if you have a weak heart. It's fiendishly calculated to drive the most placid of people up the wall. If you score 50 per cent, consider yourself a pansophical savant.

The answers, if you dare or care to look, appear on p. 224, in the Appendix.

1. *pandiculation*
    a. ability to speak several languages
    b. a stretching of the body, as after a long sleep
    c. a confusion of noises
    d. a complete code of the laws of a country
2. *ponticello*
    a. change in the register of a boy's voice
    b. bridge of traverse nerve fibres
    c. musical instrument used in the Middle Ages
    d. member of an Italian council of priests
3. *gallinipper*
    a. French barfly
    b. fowl related to the Bantams
    c. sail used only in a fierce storm
    d. large mosquito or bedbug
4. *lentiginous*
    a. freckled
    b. fasting
    c. having leafy stalks
    d. living in still waters

5. *auscultation*
   a. the act of vaulting, as with a pole
   b. the effect of turbulence in the air
   c. the act of listening, as with a stethoscope
   d. a breaking away from orthodox practices
6. *chrematistics*
   a. garbled data, as from a computer
   b. the study of wealth
   c. the art of producing liqueurs
   d. selective study of passages from various authors
7. *peristeronic*
   a. pertaining to spiral shells
   b. relating to pigeons
   c. having a beautiful back
   d. of Vitamin D
8. *omphaloskepsis*
   a. meditation while staring at one's navel
   b. treatise on the verses of troubadours
   c. cynic's view of life
   d. sexual impotence
9. *usufructuary*
   a. one enjoying the profits of another's property
   b. person who eats only fruits
   c. arsonist
   d. jack-of-all-trades; factotum
10. *philematology*
    a. the study of the works of Saint Paul
    b. discourse on love
    c. branch of numerology dealing with words
    d. the art of kissing
11. *leiotrichous*
    a. wearing a chaplet
    b. creeping up slowly on prey
    c. having straight smooth hair
    d. muscular
12. *hermeneutic*
    a. mystical
    b. interpretive
    c. solitary
    d. pertaining to saints
13. *cameralistics*
    a. candid photography
    b. art of secret arbitration
    c. study of mechanical gears
    d. science of public finances

14. *sillographer*
    a. parodist
    b. draftsman
    c. writer of satires
    d. person with erratic handwriting
15. *malversation*
    a. hubbub
    b. lisping
    c. corrupt administration
    d. incorrect rhyming
16. *nemoricole*
    a. cabbagelike
    b. pertaining to the stone flies
    c. living underground, as a worm
    d. inhabiting groves
17. *oblivescence*
    a. the act of forgetting
    b. gradual shading
    c. dimness
    d. approach to death
18. *gerontogeous*
    a. crippled
    b. relating to the eastern hemisphere
    c. senile
    d. having a sexual attraction towards older people
19. *hypocorism*
    a. pet name
    b. arterial dysfunction
    c. abnormal sensitivity of the skin
    d. satanic doctrine
20. *eudaemonical*
    a. pertaining to exorcism
    b. hellish; infernal
    c. living in a haunted house
    d. producing happiness

Appendix

CHAPTER 2

SOLUTION TO 'LATIN MOTTOES' QUIZ

1—e, 2—c, 3—a, 4—h, 5—f,
6—b, 7—d, 8—g

CHAPTER 4

ROOTS AND THEIR DERIVATIVES

ag, act (ig)—act, agendum, agent,
agile, agitate, ambiguous,
coagulate, cogent, exact,
exigent, fumigate, fustigate,
interaction, intransigent, levigate, litigate, navigate,
objurgate, prodigal, purge,
retroaction, transact
cad, cas—accident, cadaver,
cadence, cadent, cascade, case,
chance, chute, decay, decidu-
ous, incident, occasion,
recidivism
cap, capt, cept, cip—cable,
capable, capacious, capstan,
caption, captious, captive,
captor, capture, catch, chase,
accept, anticipate, conceive,
concept, except, inception,
incipient, receive, receptive,
recipient, susceptible
clud, clus—clause, cloister, close,
conclude, exclude, exclusive,
include, inclusive, occlude, pre-
clude, recluse, seclusion
cur, curr, curs—concourse, concur,
corridor, courier, course,
currency, current, curriculum,
cursive, cursory, discourse,
excursion, incur, intercourse,
occur, precursor, recourse,
recur, succour
fac, fact, fect, fic—affect, affection,
artifact, beatific, benefactor,
benefit, comfit, confection,
counterfeit, defect, deficient,
deficit, discomfit, edifice, effect,
efficacious, efficient, facile, fac-
simile, fact, faction, factitious,
factor, factory, factotum,
factual, faculty, fiction,
fictitious, imperfection, infect,
malefactor, manufacture,
officiate, perfect, proficient,
profit, refectory, rubefacient,
sacrifice, satisfaction, suffice,
sufficient
frag, fract—fracas, fraction,
fractious, fracture, fragile,
fragment, fragmentation,
frangible, infraction, refract,
saxifrage, suffrage
leg, lect, lig—collection, diligent,
election, elegant, eligible,
intelligence, lectern, lecture,
legend, legible, legion, neglect,
negligent, sacrilege, select
mit, miss—admittance, commis-
sion, commit, commitment,
committee, compromise, demit,
dismissal, emissary, emit,
intermission, intermittent,
manumit, mass, mess,
message, missal, missile,
mission, missionary, non-
committal, omit, permission,

premise, promise, remiss,
remit, submit, surmise,
transmission
pend, pens—append, appendix,
compendium, compensate,
depend, dispense, expend,
expenditure, expensive,
impend, pendant, pendulous,
pensive, peso, penthouse, perpendicular, propensity, sus-
pend, suspense
plic, pli—application, complaint,
complicate, duplicate, explicate,
implicate, imply, plait, pliant,
replicate, supplication
sed, sid, sess—assess, assiduous,
dissident, obsess, preside,
president, possess, reside,
residence, residual, seance,
sedentary, sediment, session,
siege, subside, subsidy,
supersede
sent, sens—assent, consensus,
consent, dissension, insensate,

presentiment, resent, scent,
sense, sensibility, sentence,
sententious, sentient,
sentimental, sentinel
solv, solu, solut—absolute,
absolution, absolve, dissolve,
dissolute, insoluble, insolvable,
resolve, solve, solvent, soluble
ten, tin, tent—abstain, abstention,
contain, content, continence,
continent, continue, detain,
detention, entertain, lieutenant,
maintain, obtain, pertain,
pertinacious, pertinent, retain,
retention, sustain, sustenance,
tenable, tenacious, tenant,
tenement, tenet, tennis, tenon,
tenor, tenure
volv, volu—convoluted, convolu-
tion, devolve, evolution, evolve,
involute, involve, involvement,
revolution, revolve, vault, volt,
voluble, volume

CHAPTER 12

1. asinine
2. existence
3. develop
4. occurrence
5. indispensable
6. accommodate
7. silhouette
8. harass
9. proceed
10. vermilion
11. personnel
12. seize
13. stupefy
14. embarrassed
15. supersede
16. inoculate
17. resistance
18. moccasin
19. reconnoitre
20. resuscitate
21. asphyxiate
22. renascence
23. irrelevant
24. saccharine
25. privilege
26. persistent
27. auxiliary
28. paraphernalia
29. impresario
30. deleterious
31. picnicked
32. weird
33. permissible
34. memento
35. innocuous
36. ecstasy
37. liaison
38. cachinnate
39. rococo
40. battalion
41. nickel
42. consensus
43. commitment
44. separate
45. genealogy
46. sacrilegious
47. inadvertent
48. iridescent
49. dichotomy
50. Pharaoh

ANSWERS TO 'THE MORE THE EERIER'

1. knights-errant
2. talismans
3. menservants
4. hypotheses
5. pelvises or pelves
6. embryos
7. jackanapeses
8. cineraria
9. auspices
10. messieurs

ANSWERS TO 'HATES AND FEARS'

1—b, 2—d, 3—c, 4—e, 5—a

PHOBIAS

1. of open spaces
2. of heights
3. of sunlight
4. of women
5. of death
6. of being poisoned
7. of reptiles
8. of the number thirteen
9. of catching a disease
10. of crowds

ANSWERS TO 'IRRELIGIOUS' QUIZ

1—h, 2—e, 3—d, 4—b, 5—j,
6—c, 7—f, 8—i, 9—a, 10—g

ANSWERS TO VOCABULARY TESTS

1. 1—d, 2—c, 3—b, 4—d, 5—c,
   6—c, 7—c, 8—a, 9—b, 10—a,
   11—b, 12—a, 13—b, 14—a,
   15—a, 16—b, 17—c, 18—d,
   19—a, 20—c
2. 1—c, 2—b, 3—d, 4—d, 5—b,
   6—a, 7—b, 8—a, 9—d, 10—c,
   11—c, 12—b, 13—d, 14—c,
   15—b, 16—a, 17—a, 18—d,
   19—c, 20—b
3. 1—a, 2—c, 3—a, 4—c, 5—b,
   6—a, 7—b, 8—c, 9—b, 10—c,
   11—b, 12—c, 13—a, 14—d,
   15—c, 16—c, 17—a, 18—c,
   19—d, 20—a

ANSWERS TO 'WORD ORIGINS'

(The root(s) common to the related words in a group is enclosed in parentheses.)

1. sedition: from *se*, aside, and *ire*, to go (*sedere, sessus*, to sit)
2. volatile: from *volare*, to fly (*volvo, volutus*, to roll)
3. invoice: from Fr. *envoyer*, to send, or *envois*, things sent (*voc, vok*, to call)
4. advantage: from Fr. *avant*, before (*vanus*, empty)
5. mastodon: from Gr. *mastos*, breast, and *dont*, tooth (*magnus*, great; comparative of *magnus* is *major*)
6. cockatrice: from Lat. *caucatrix*, crocodile (*coccus*, seed)
7. invest: from *vestire*, to clothe (*vestigare*, to trace)
8. minatory: from *minae*, projections or threats (*monere, monitus*, to warn) N.B. The Romans coined money in the temple of Juno Moneta!
9. miniature: from *minium*, a brilliant red (*minuere*, to lessen)
10. beleaguer: from A.-S. *leger*, bed (*ligare*, to bind)

(The root(s) common to the related words in a group is enclosed in parentheses.)

1. nuisance: from *nocere,* to hurt or harm (*odium,* hatred)
2. spiral: from *spira,* a coil or twist (*spirare,* to breathe)
3. nutrition: from *nutrire,* to nourish or nurse (*terere, tritus,* to rub or wear out)
4. console: from con-*solari,* to comfort (*solus,* lonely or alone)
5. finger: from A.-S. *finger* — same meaning (*fingere, fictus,* to form or invent). *Fingent* means 'moulding' or 'fashioning' (pronounced 'finjcnt').
6. profane: from pro-*fanus,* a temple (*fari, fatus,* to speak). *Nefandous* means 'unfit to speak of'.
7. poplar: from *populus,* a poplar tree (*populus,* people)
8. poetaster: from Gr. *poies,* a maker, and *aster,* a suffix meaning 'inferior' (Gr. *aster,* a star)
9. consult: from *consulere,* to consider (*salire,* to leap)
10. censure: from *censére,* to value or tax (*candére,* to be glowing white)

N.B. candidates for office in Rome were clothed in glittering white robes.

ANSWERS TO 'OUT AND DOWN'

ORACLE
RENTAL
GRUDGE
ANIMAL
NEIGHED
IGNOBLE
SHORTEN
TOASTER

NOTE: The first letters of the above words form ORGANIST, which is an anagram of ROASTING.

ANSWERS TO 'A MAD, MAD WORLD'

1—g, 2—a, 3—i, 4—b, 5—h,
6—c, 7—f, 8—j, 9—d, 10—e

ANSWERS TO 'LOVERS'

1—g, 2—c, 3—e, 4—h, 5—a,
6—j, 7—i, 8—d, 9—b, 10—f

ANSWERS TO 'ALTERNATES TO DEMOCRACY'

1. ochlocracy
2. kakistocracy
3. arithmocracy
4. stratocracy
5. ergatocracy
6. pornocracy
7. gerontocracy
8. plutocracy
9. chrysocracy
10. neocracy

ANSWERS TO 'WHO'S IN CHARGE?'

1. phylarch
2. ecclesiarch
3. heresiarch
4. nomarch
5. symposiarch
6. anarch
7. oligarch
8. hierarch
9. chiliarch
10. exarch

ANSWERS TO 'SPECIALITIES'

1. philematology
2. caliology
3. glyptology
4. malacology
5. murmecology
6. tocology
7. muscology
8. hagiology
9. agmatology
10. campanology

ANSWERS TO 'A PENNY FOR YOUR THOUGHTS'

1. rubescent
2. lucent
3. maleficent
4. nascent
5. quiescent
6. senescent
7. evanescent
8. virescent
9. iridescent
10. obsolescent
11. florescent
12. recrudescent
13. spumescent
14. demulcent
15. rufescent
16. tumescent
17. canescent
18. glabrescent
19. delitescent
20. latescent

ANSWERS TO 'A LEAGUE OF NATIONS'

1. detonation
2. rationation
3. divination
4. rumination
5. peregrination
6. procrastination
7. fulmination
8. concatenation
9. reincarnation
10. condonation

ANSWERS TO 'THE ANT COLONY'

1. peccant
2. verdant
3. insouciant
4. mordant
5. ululant

6. poignant
7. discrepant
8. natant
9. cormorant
10. blatant
11. adjutant
12. clairvoyant
13. recusant
14. puissant
15. susurrant
16. coruscant
17. flagellant
18. clamant
19. simulant
20. hebetant
21. oscitant
22. clinquant
23. noctambulant
24. horripilant
25. nutant
26. nidificant
27. faineant
28. hierophant
29. revenant
30. Corybant

ANSWERS TO 'FIND THE STRANGER'

1. gerrymander
2. cicerone
3. gibus
4. tartuffe
5. execrate
6. meritorious
7. pilpul
8. exiguous
9. miscreant
10. jingo

ANSWERS TO 'THE BLOCKBUSTER'

1—b, 2—a, 3—d, 4—a, 5—c,
6—b, 7—b, 8—a, 9—a, 10—d,
11—c, 12—b, 13—d, 14—c,
15—c, 16—d, 17—a, 18—b,
19—a, 20—d